CW01095202

C.G. Jung Foundation Zürich Edition

Painting Therapy on the Basis of C.G. Jung's Analytical Psychology

by

Ingrid Riedel & Christa Henzler

Ingrid Riedel
Christa Henzler

Painting Therapy

On the Basis of C.G. Jung's Analytical Psychology

DAIMON
Verlag

Translated from the original German title "Maltherapie auf Basis der Analy-tischen Psychologie C.G. Jungs" © 2016 Patmos Verlag. Verlagsgruppe Patmos im Schwabenverlag AG, Ostfildern

English language translation © 2022 by Daimon Verlag and Father Otto Betler

The publisher and the authors wish to thank the C.G. Jung Foundation Zürich for their generous support of the publication of this book; Father Otto Betler for his painstaking translation of the German text and Steve Arthers for his meticulous editing of the text and references for this edition.

Cover illustration: Painting Nr. 3. The Plants vs Destruction (see p. 43).

ISBN 978-3-85630-788-2

Copyright © 2022 Daimon Verlag, Einsiedeln

All rights reserved.

Contents

Part I:
Painting as Self-Creation

Part II:
The Painting Series and its Interpretation

Part III:
Painting in a Group

Part IV:
Painting in the Therapeutic Practice

Foreword to the English Edition

Maltherapie by Ingrid Riedel and Christa Henzler is an admired German language text in the field of picture interpretation, and The C.G. Jung Foundation Zürich is delighted to sponsor its English publication. With its insightful and practical case studies brought to life, its many full-color plates and its strong theoretical grounding, *Painting Therapy, on the Basis of C.G. Jung's Analytical Psychology*, the English translation of the original German-language manuscript, adds to the vibrant work in dream and other imagistic forms of the Jungian analytical therapy process. The work leads us through theoretical concepts of painting therapy according to Jung, to illustrated case studies highlighting the importance of painting series, to painting in groups and a section with summarized practical advice for the therapist. It also includes a rich bibliography and reference list for further investigation and personal study.

My own attraction to Dr. Riedel's work began many years ago with a memorable lecture unfolding a German fairy tale. This was early in my training and was far too complex for me to grasp at that time. Dr. Riedel went through every image and element, asked questions of us, invited our insights, and allowed our stumbles. Father Otto was standing at the front translating back and forth from English to German and back to English. Dr. Riedel made the lecture so important by walking around and around each image, teaching us that there is not just one way, that working with images and understanding symbolic language is dynamic, unique and will always depend upon the particular situation of the client. This book reflects a similar compelling style and is accessible to a broad public who may be interested in "painting from the unconscious" including, but not limited to students in art therapy, Jungian analysts in training as well as practicing therapists.

Both Ingrid Riedel and Christa Henzler are training analysts and supervisors at the C.G. Jung Institute in Zürich, and their close collaboration on this work reflects their expertise and experience in working with pictures and in the practical application Jung's analytical psychology. In *Memories, Dreams, Reflections*[1], in *The Red Book*[2], and more recently with the publication of the *Black Books 1913 – 1932*[3], we can read first-hand and see more clearly the importance of Jung's personal work with images and symbols, in dreams, active imaginations and paintings, as well in his daily life. It is no surprise that working with images and symbols is a core element of Jungian Analysis and is an essential component of every training program in Analytical Psychology.

While there are several books and many articles in German on Jungian picture interpretation, there are fewer in-depth publications available in English. The Board of the C.G. Jung Foundation Zürich recognizes the value to international training candidates and analysts worldwide of publishing this work in English to support their work with images.

We give special thanks to Father Otto Betler for his tireless work and skill in the translation itself, to Robert Hinshaw for Daimon Verlag's interest and expertise in publication, and to Steve Arthers as translation editor and for leadership of the translation project. We thank the Foundation donors who believed in this project with particular thanks to the late Kimberly D. Ritter Arndt and Family for their generosity. We especially thank Ingrid Riedel and Christa Henzler for their welcome contribution to the field!

1 Jaffé, Aniela: *Memories, Dreams, Reflections by C.G. Jung*, Pantheon, New York, 1962.
2 Jung, Carl Gustav: *The Red Book: Liber Novus*. Edited and introduced by Sonu Shamdasani. Preface by Ulrich Hoerni. Translated by Mark Kyburz, John Peck, Sonu Shamdasani. W.W. Norton & Company, Philemon Series, 1st Edition 2009.
3 Jung, Carl Gustav: *The Black Books 1913-1932: Notebooks of Transformation*. Edited by Sonu Shamdasani. Translated by Martin Liebscher, John Peck, Sonu Shamdasani. New York & London. W.W. Norton & Company, Philemon Series, 2020.

The C.G. Jung Foundation Zürich is a non-profit organization based in the US. It was founded in 2015 by accredited Jungian analysts to support programs that expand the reach of Jungian psychology in association with the C.G. Jung Institute, Zürich. It is the hope of the Foundation that this book will be the first of a series to make German-language texts more accessible to our international students on key subjects in the institute's diploma curriculum.

Carol Walnum, Jungian analyst
President C.G. Jung Foundation Zürich
Portland, Oregon, 2022.

Translator's Note

Translating this book into English was a labor of love, and simultaneously a very thorough review of all I learned about painting interpretation and sand play in my education at the C.G. Jung Institute of Zürich. Having the good fortune to analyze under Ingrid Riedel, I know first-hand what she can read out of a painting and how she uses that information to explain and to heal.

Both Ingrid Riedel and Christa Henzler delight in the colors, shapes and situations which the psyche produces in dreams and reproduces on paper. This delight sharpens their attention to the details which can guide analysands to wholeness, and it encourages their analysands to draw and dream even more. Their wonderful book is both a how-to for the therapist and an explanation for amateur artists seeking to understand their own drawings.

When I offered to translate one of Ingrid's books as a birthday present, I did not expect that it would be this one. Being a Benedictine monk, I thought she would ask me to translate *St. Hildegard of Bingen: Prophet of Cosmic Wisdom*, or that delightful work *Mysticism of the Heart: Masters of Inner Freedom* in which she describes the interior freedom achieved by the great women mystics Hildegard of Bingen, Teresa of Avila, Marguerite Porète, Edith Stein, and Dorothee Sölle. But Ingrid's priority was to her students. She therefore asked me to translate this standard work of Jungian painting therapy. When I fretted that the book was 352 pages long, Ingrid smilingly assuaged my dismay with, "Now, now Otto, you must acknowledge that a third of the book is pictures."

Now the translation is finished. Steve Arthers has done his best to correct my English. Elisabeth Strobl has tried to eliminate the typos. And to make the book really helpful to an English-speaking audience, Steve Arthers and his daughter Emily have tracked down English translations of as many references and footnotes as can be found. We can all be grateful for this concerted effort to make this standard work on Jungian painting therapy accessible to the English-speaking world. My greatest thanks goes to Ingrid and Christa for writing the book.

Father Otto Betler

Part I:

Painting as Self-Creation

In a way a patient could say, "by painting myself,
I create myself."

C.G. Jung

Introduction

When we take palette and brush in hand and spontaneously paint something for our own enjoyment – whether practiced painters or not, whether alone or in a group – the resulting pictures contain a wide variety of motifs, contents, colors, and forms. And later when we look at them and discuss them together, sometimes we want to say, "Now, that really says something about you!" We often recognize that our apparently random pictures, which seem to have arisen out of the moment, have very much to do with us.

We paint each thing precisely thus and not otherwise, lavender and not yellow, autumn and not spring. Therefore, every tree or flower that we choose to paint is simultaneously an impression of what we observe in nature and an expression of our self. Every landscape that we paint, whether mellow or vibrant, wide or narrow, is an expression of our mood at that moment. Our very essence is sometimes revealed in such a landscape. The range of colors we prefer – the blue-violet-green tones or the red-orange-yellow tones – betrays much about our personality type, i.e. whether we are more introverted or extroverted[1]. When carefully analyzed in this way, each picture confirms what we know about our mood and our desire either for contact or for privacy. But more than

---

1   The differentiation between extroverted and introverted personality types comes from Carl Gustav Jung. Ascribing "cool" colors to one type and "warm" to the other can already be found in: Goethe, Johann Wolfgang von: Goethe's *Theory of Colours*, translated by Charles Lock Eastlake. Cambridge, Massachusetts 1970, § 764, 777.

that, pictures manifest our search for our self: our quest and longing for identity.

The famous Mexican painter Frida Kahlo (1907-1953) painted dozens of self-portraits in the course of her decades-long career. These paintings express the artist's essence and mood through her facial expressions and clothes, but also through the landscapes in the background with their colors and hues, and the animals and plants that appear in them. From portrait to portrait, new colors, new forms, and new stylistic elements emerge that she could not have allowed in the beginning. Her radiant expression surrounded by flaming red in a late self-portrait from the year 1949[2] is a great example.

It is the same in our own paintings; and they don't have to be self-portraits at all. New colors, new forms, new symbols appear from picture to picture revealing our expanding self-understanding. By painting things, we allow them to happen, and they transform us: painting is self-creation.

Such joy, such expansion, such rapprochement to the greater self! This is what painting a poppy in full bloom meant for a young man who had long avoided the color red because of the negative associations it carried for him. As a hemophiliac he had always avoided the color of blood, which was so dangerous for him. But red is at the same time the color of vitality. By being hyper-careful to avoid wounds, from which he really could bleed to death, he had simultaneously avoided the whole area of vitality. In coming to tolerate red, he was finally able to allow his first love of a woman, and also to go dancing and hiking without excessive fear of wounding himself – something that could, of course, happen at any time.

For those who find the color yellow too flamboyant and loud, the same kind of breakthrough may happen when they finally dare to use it in their painting. Yellow is the color of radiance, of resplendence. These are essential elements of life. But to paint with yellow requires the courage to reveal more of oneself.

---

2   Herrera, Hayden: *Frida: A Biography of Frida Kahlo*, New York, 1983. Copy of the painting from 1949 "The Love Embrace of the Universe, the Earth (Mexico), Myself and Señor Xolotl", where the painter portrays her deepest reason for being in the interconnection of all things.

Even with green, the color of vegetation, some people have their difficulties. Especially with yellow-green and poison-green they fear being overgrown by nature (perhaps the nature in themselves). Our attitude toward green and its use in pictures can often indicate how much natural energy we possess or lack.

Many have difficulty with dark colors and the shadow side of life that they symbolize, a side that may even be evil. They don't allow anything to escape that might be mean or lowly and reflective of the other side of their personality. This dark side has been banned from consciousness even though the shadowy side possesses undiscovered strengths that are often associated with the color black. People with an idealized self-image can sometimes have great difficulty integrating black into their paintings. In connection with this, I was impressed by the way one young woman put it after she had discovered black: "I now begin my painting with black. Then all the other colors can pick something up from it and unfold themselves with more strength."

Some find angular and sharp forms uncomfortable – Marc Chagall, for example. Almost his entire opus is full of curves and harmonious forms. A little more contrast and opposition might have given his work a stronger accent. On the other hand, some actually avoid the round and the harmonious in their pictures, because they fear being pigeonholed or robbed of their defined contours. They fear the power of the positive mother archetype that underlies curved forms.

Self-creation through painting occurs as our creations become ever freer and richer from picture to picture. Little by little we allow the full spectrum and the whole color wheel to be included, even though our personal preference for certain colors is likely to remain unchanged.

In therapy, stabilizing the ego into a coherent complex can be a giant step forward, yet self-creation through painting means far more than the structuring of our ego. The Self-creation that C.G. Jung is talking about is a creative work that allows the Self – the center of our person to which the ego is subordinate – to emerge and to reveal itself ever more intensely. This Self condenses into visible forms that gradually become more distinct from picture to picture.

Self-becoming, which Jung describes as "the individuation process", is the royal road to healing: the emerging personality simply outgrows individual problems and shortcomings. This is just as true for self-actualizers as it is for therapy patients.

I am writing this book not only for working psychotherapists and painting therapists, but for anyone who enjoys painting. We have much to gain from setting our unconscious creative processes in motion, objectifying them on paper, and sharing them with others.

Building a Painting Therapy upon Jung's Foundations

Jung based his concept of therapy upon the observation that every life form unfolds naturally, a tendency which Aristotle called entelechy. Entelechy is a being's inner plan or pattern that determines who or what it is to become and how it is to develop. It enables us to outgrow problems through an ever more differentiated unfolding of this human pattern – according to which each of us is continually formed.

One of the greatest symbols of this process is the tree, and Jung used it often. When a tree loses its branches to storms or to the saw, it grows bark to cover its wounds. So too, the human psyche strives to develop according to its inner pattern, no matter what happens to it. When I think of perfect self-development, the image comes to mind of a freestanding linden tree near the village of Hofgeismar. The tree grows alone in an open pasture near a brook. It was able to develop freely because everything needed as nourishment was there in abundance, and no neighboring trees or boulders interfered with its growth.

One could argue that a completely different example would better illustrate Jung's point about the growth tendency of trees, namely a gnarled pine tree clinging to a cliff. It wraps its roots around the very boulders that obstruct its growth, and even uses their solidity for its own stability. By entwining itself, it slowly pushes up through the boulders into the light, the many scars on its trunk illustrating the history of this struggle. More impressive than the unobstructed linden tree, this pine demonstrates what the unfolding tendency of a tree really is: what it means for its pine-ness to be realized even under the hardest conditions. Thus has this pine tree achieved its individual, unique and essential form.

In his introduction to the classic Chinese book of life, *The Secret of the Golden Flower*, Jung describes the process by which psychological problems are outgrown – problems that appeared insoluble on the conscious level. "I had always worked with the temperamental conviction that at the bottom there are no insoluble problems, and experience justified me insofar as I have often seen patients simply outgrow a problem that had destroyed others. This "outgrowing," as I formerly called it, proved on further investigation to be a new level of consciousness. Some higher or wider interest appeared on the patient's horizon, and through this broadening of his outlook the insoluble problem lost its urgency. It was not solved logically in its own terms but faded out when confronted with a new and stronger life urge. It was not repressed and made unconscious, but merely appeared in a different light, and so really did become different. What, on a lower level, had led to the wildest conflicts and panicky outbursts of emotion, from the higher level of personality now looked like a storm in the valley seen from the mountain top".[3]

Jung's understanding of human nature and his concept of therapy that goes with it, can be likened to the growth process of a tree. Healing the damage suffered during growth means nothing more than engaging, supporting, and strengthening the tree's own growth potential. In humans we call this the individuation process – the taking on of our true form, regardless of how good or bad the growing conditions.

But how do we figure out the pattern according to which each and every one of us develops?

According to Jung, our inner images, symbols, and dreams inform us of these deeper developmental patterns. The images reveal what lies beyond our waking consciousness and our conscious planning. These inner images reveal themselves either in spontaneous thoughts that

3   Jung, Carl Gustav: *The Collected Works of C.G. Jung (hereafter CW)*, vol. 13, *Alchemical Studies*, translated by R.F.C. Hull. Princeton: Bollingen series XX, 2nd Edition 1970. Commentary on "The Secret of the Golden Flower" § 17.

compel us to action, or in daydreams and night dreams that motivate us to paint or sculpt them into images. Often the tree itself is the motif.

The black tree in autumn of a 60-year-old nurse (Image 1) looks really disheveled, and yet five red apples from the summer are still hanging on. They look especially sweet and worth picking. The apples remind the painter of a gift that a particularly salty patient once gave her. The patient wished to express her gratitude for the good care she had received. In the colored original, soft blue stripes fill the left edge of the painting. These hint at further possibilities for personal development and self-creation beyond the heavy, black tree that must be reckoned with at first glance.

Image 1. Tree with Apples

The key is to get our conscious mind to connect with the images arising from the unconscious. Often these emerging motifs and tendencies contradict and oppose the conscious intentions of the ego. That was the case with the nurse. She tried to mask her potential for hope in a dark picture. She tried to deny it, and did not want to see it.

A picture can only really serve the process of self-creation when it comes into contact with the ego. But the ego will only allow this contact when in itself it is able to function in an intact and coherent way. This was the case with the painter of the black tree. However, those with an incoherent ego are at risk of being flooded by the images welling up from the unconscious. Both the pre-painted inner image and the act of painting that image can unleash this flood. In such cases the ego will try to ban both the conscious act of creating the picture as well as acceptance of the original inner image.

Carl Gustav Jung himself suggested using art in the context of analytical psychology and therapy. In the years after his separation from Freud, between 1912 and 1918, Jung experienced a storm surge of inner images. He referred to it as his "descent into the unconscious". Artistic activity was essential to his regaining inner orientation. As is well known, Freud and Jung parted ways over Jung's discovery of a "collective unconscious," a realm of the unconscious beyond the personal sphere. If the personal unconscious is the cellar of the soul, where suppressed elements of our individual life history are stored, much, much deeper down is the collective unconscious where the mines of the soul house the treasures of humanity itself. Among these natural treasures are the symbols – the great agents of healing. Jung records this discovery in his book, *Symbols of Transformation*.[4]

In *Memories, Dreams, Reflections*[5], Jung describes how as a ten to twelve-year-old, he loved to lose himself in play, building villages and castles out of pebbles. Later, during the crisis brought on by the separation from Freud, he rediscovered his connection with playing that had meant so much to him as a child. He began to play again despite a strong interior resistance and constraint. Jung credits this as a turning point in his development, and since that time, he attempted to consciously fantasize his emotions and find images for them. He developed the habit of regularly writing down his emotions, then painting them or sometimes even carving them in stone. He also painted images from his dreams. He was

4 Jung, Carl Gustav: *CW*, vol. 5, *Symbols of Transformation*.
5 Jaffé, Aniela, *Memories, Dreams, Reflections by C.G. Jung*, Pantheon, New York, 1962.

able to make his interior images more deeply understandable by painting them. "At any time in my later life when I came up against a blank wall I painted a picture or hewed stone. Each such experience proved to be a *rite d'entrée for the ideas and works that followed hard upon it.*"[6] An especially important discovery that grew out of this active imagination, and which he carefully depicted many times, was Jung's inner guide whom he named "Philemon".

Jung first describes this method of portraying images in his 1929 essay, "The Goals of Psychotherapy".[7] He goes further a few years later in an essay called "The Archetypes and the Collective Unconscious".[8] Here he requests his patients to "paint in reality what they have seen in dream or fantasy".[9] How artistically the work turns out should not matter, "but something more and other than mere art, namely the living effect upon the patient himself".[10] The very act of producing the images, Jung observed, is itself a form of imagination. This is active imagination, because in drawing, the active conscious is working alongside the unconscious to set its symbols free by making them conscious. The painting process steers, tests, and takes responsibility. Jung continues: "Because his fantasy does not strike him as entirely senseless, his busying himself with it only increases its effect upon him. Moreover, the concrete shaping of the image enforces a continuous study of it in all its parts, so that it can develop its effects to the full. This invests the bare fantasy with an element of reality, which lends it greater weight and greater driving power."[11]

Jung included several activities in his description of active imagination: the painting of images arising from the unconscious, wrestling in our fantasy with figures from the unconscious, playing, dancing, and movement. What matters most is establishing a connection with the configurations and images originating in the unconscious to the point of engaging in dialogue with them. Thus can we dialogue with paintings

6   Ibid, p. 210.
7   Jung, Carl Gustav: *CW*, vol. 16, *The Practice of Psychotherapy*, § 66-113.
8   Jung, Carl Gustav: *CW*, Vol. 9.1, *The Archetypes and the Collective Unconscious*, §525-626.
9   Jung, Carl Gustav: *CW*, vol. 16, *The Practice of Psychotherapy*, §102.
10 Ibid, §104.
11 Ibid, §106.

and with the figures that appear in them. Such dialogue can result in long series of paintings where, from picture to picture, figures (including problem figures) can be discovered and grasped.

Here is one such series in which the woman in analysis learned through her painting to work through a deep-seated mother-daughter problem. The problem had so constellated in her, that over and over again in life, ambivalence would flame up against certain attachment figures, including against the therapist. She finally learned to develop trust and to use it against this ambivalence. In this long series of many individual paintings, symbolic images of the daughter and of the mother keep appearing together, and they are constantly rearranged into new constellations of relationship to one another.[12]

If it is true, as Jung believed, that the creation of pictures from the unconscious is an act of active imagination, then it makes sense to combine Jung's teaching on active imagination methodologically with painting, as I will now attempt to do. The combination can take place either as a way of activating active imagination before painting, or of further developing the symbols that have already been painted through guided imagination.

What painting therapy offers beyond mere active imagination is the concrete picture itself. It becomes something we can set before us and gaze at, and in this way, draw even more from the unconscious. It could be a picture of a fear, a bodily pain, or an image out of the unconscious such as a dream scene.

Of course some degree of the freedom that is inherent in natural imagination is sacrificed by such concretization. Painting therapy stays nearer to consciousness than does active imagination. The creative act does not lead to relaxation and a subsequent increase in imagination, but rather to a fully awake condition in which the image is taken from the imagination and consciously fashioned.

There is also a type of painting that does not begin with a preconceived inner image, but rather lets itself be led by the emerging colors and shapes appearing on the page and be captivated by the spontaneously developing forms. Another type of painting begins very consciously

12 Compare with the section "Relationship and Dependence" on page 123 in this book.

perhaps even with a sketch of an image out of a dream or from the imagination. But then during the painting process, both conscious and unconscious powers conjoin, so that the activity is carried out partially like a conscious process, partially like an unconscious one. The results prove over and over again to be especially creative and therapeutically effective.

However, Jung emphasized "that the mere execution of the pictures is not enough. Over and above that, an intellectual and emotional understanding is needed; they require to be not only rationally integrated with the conscious mind, but morally assimilated. They still have to be subjected to a work of synthetic interpretation."[13] This belief, so characteristic of Jung, distinguishes his method from those in which conscious interpretation is rejected, for example in the method of Arno Stern[14]. Jung's method of interpretation involves centering processes that lie outside of consciousness, but to which he attributed a major influence upon the conscious personality. These express themselves for the most part at a symbolic level, for example in the form of mandala pictures. Jung illustrated and interpreted one such centering process complete with a series of pictures in his essay, "A Study in the Process of Individuation".[15] The series begins with a picture of a woman sitting contemplatively on a cliff overlooking the coast. Later in the series, lightening will strike the cliff, breaking off a stone, and still later this broken-off stone will become her Self-image in mandala form. In the first picture the stone is already there, but still clumped together with other stones, which symbolize her problems.

In his essay, "The Practice of Psychotherapy," Jung describes the goal of his therapy: "my aim is to bring about a psychic state in which my patient begins to experiment with his own nature, a state of fluidity, change and growth where nothing is externally fixed and hopelessly petrified."[16]

13 Jung, Carl Gustav: *CW*, vol. 16, *The Practice of Psychotherapy*, § 111.
14 Stern, Arno: *L'Expression*. Neuchâtel 1973.
15 Jung, Carl Gustav: *CW*, Vol. 9.1, *The Archetypes and the Collective Unconscious*, § 525-626, Picture Series: Pictures 1-24.
16 Jung, Carl Gustav: *CW*, vol. 16, *The Practice of Psychotherapy*, § 99.

Specifically concerning painting, he wrote in "Psychological Problems of the Present": "In the same way that we say a patient paints himself, we could say that he creates himself."[17] Jung considers every picture to be a self-portrait, and because the painter creates it, he simultaneously works on himself and the image of his own essence. Describing the effect of pictures, he states in the same essay: "these pictures do produce effects which I must admit, are rather difficult to describe. When the patient has seen once or twice how he is freed from a wretched state of mind by working at a symbolic picture, he will thenceforward turn to this means of release whenever things go badly for him. In this way something invaluable is won, namely a growth of independence, a step towards psychological maturity. The patient can make himself creatively independent by this method".[18]

We can say that this method of constructive creativity, and its interpretation, is in no way exclusive to the realm of psychotherapy. An example of such creative independence is illustrated by the picture series "Under the Sign of Sophia" in the second part of this book.

Jung's suggestion to paint and use pictures in the therapeutic process was taken up and further developed both by his students and his friends. Jolande Jacobi should be the first to be mentioned. She furnished one of the first methodical guides to the interpretation of images from the unconscious in her book, *Vom Bilderreich der Seele, (Out of the Soul's Realm of Images)*.[19] Moreover, she maintained that painting can be encouraged in a variety of therapeutic situations, even during psychotic episodes. Thus she introduced one of the first models of Jungian painting therapy in a psychiatric clinic. Although every patient must gradually discover his/her own means of depiction, she suggested to begin with an archetypal symbol. Jacobi worked with groups. None of Jung's other students had attempted this. She prophetically noted: "Trying it with a group was for me an experiment which might possibly develop into a new instrument

---

17 Jung, Carl Gustav: *Modern Man in Search of a Soul*. Martino Fine Books, Eastford 2017, reprint of 1933 US edition, p. 80.

18 Ibid.

19 Jacobi, Jolande: *Vom Bilderreich der Seele: Wege und Umwege zu sich selbst*. Olten/ Freiburg im Breisgau 1969. (Not available in English. Available as Italian translation: *Dal regno delle immagini dell'anima percorsi diretti e vie traverse per giungere a se stessi*, translated by Murrau, Marina Pia .Editioni Magi: Roma 2003).

in the analyst's hand."[20] Painting in groups has indeed become a wide-spread method, although it is undeniable that the Jacobi-Jung method of painting in groups has its origins in individual therapy. Later on I will spell out more precisely the implications of painting in a group setting.

In Germany, stimulated by Jung's ideas about painting therapy, Gustav Richard Heyer developed his own method using artistic creativity. He gathered his experiences into an article entitled "Artistic Practices in Psychotherapy".[21]

Today therapeutic work with pictures and the interpretation of images from the unconscious hold pride of place in the institutions where Jungian analytical psychology is taught. These are considered fundamental to the creative work with material from the unconscious. Many studies have been carried out in conjunction with Jung Institutes in places like Zürich, Stuttgart, Berlin, and Bremen, which add to our understanding of painting and pictures. Ursula Eschenbach included work with pictures in many of her studies of youth and adult psychotherapy. A fine example is her beautiful contribution "Symbols of a Maturation Process in Feminine Identity".[22] In 1993 Rosmarie Daniel's exciting book, *Archetypal Signatures in the Unconscious Painting Process*,[23] became available.

Susan Bach, who lived in London, worked primarily with critically ill children. She encouraged them to paint, and through the resulting picture series she could accompany them on their way to getting better or worse, whichever was the case. Those paintings document and explain what is going on inside the patient. Bach's book, *Life Paints its Own Span: On the Significance of Spontaneous Paintings by Severely Ill Children*,[24]

20 Ibid., p. 245.
21 Heyer, Gustav Richard: "Künstlerische Verfahren" in Frankl, Victor Emil; Gebsattel, Victor E von; Schultz, Johannes Heinrich (Editors): *Handbuch der Neurosenlehre und Psychotherapie* Vol IV. Munich 1959. (An English language review of the book is found in the *Journal of American Psychology*, Volume 118, issue 4, October 1961.)
22 Eschenbach, Ursula: "Sinn-Bilder eines Reifungsprozesses weiblicher Identität" in Pflüger, Peter Michael (Editor): *Die Suche nach Sinn heute*. Olten / Freiburg im Breisgau 1989, pp. 177-183.
23 Daniel, Rosmarie: *Archetypische Signaturen im unbewußten Malprozeß*. Fellbach 1993.
24 Bach, Susan: "Spontanes Malen schwerkranker Patienten: Ein Beitrag zur psychosomatischen Medizin" (*Acta Psychosomatica* 8, 1966); and further in Bach, Susan: *Life Paints Its Own Span: On the Significance of Spontaneous Paintings by Severely Ill Children*. Einsiedeln 1991.

appeared also in German. I call it simply "Spontaneous Painting of Severely Ill Patients." From working with Susan Bach and later with Elisabeth Kübler-Ross, Gregg M. Furth came to write *Healing Through Painting*,[25] which surveys mainly quickly-sketched, spontaneous drawings of a sickness or of a family background situation and illustrates some possible interpretations of them for diagnostic or therapeutic purposes.

Already in his 1975 diploma thesis at the C.G. Jung Institute of Zürich, Paul Brutsche was considering the appearance of psychiatric coherence and incoherence in drawings. The thesis, entitled "The Psychological Meaning of Perspective in the Drawings of Analysands,"[26] demonstrates that conclusions can be drawn about the stability of the ego complex based on how the patient portrays perspective in drawings. One can often distinguish an ego that holds together and is stable (coherence), or an ego that is falling apart and is unstable (incoherence), as is the case with psychosis or schizophrenia.

Also available is a graphic book of children's drawings from Ursula Baumgardt[27]. My own books on color, form and most recently on pictures, lay the foundation for her interpretations of these drawings out of the unconscious.[28]

I can't fail to mention Christa Henzler's 1985 diploma thesis at the University of Kassel: "Aspects of Painting Therapy with Particular Attention to its Usefulness for Interpretation in Depth Psychology"[29]. Several of her findings are included in this present book. *Painting to Survive*

25 Furth, Gregg, M: *The Secret World of Drawings: Healing through Art*. Boston 1988.
26 Brutsche, Paul: *Die psychologische Bedeutung der Perspektive in Analysanden-Zeichnungen*. (Diploma thesis for the C.G. Jung Institute Zürich) 1975.
27 Baumgardt, Ursula: *Kinderzeichnungen – Spiegel der Seele*, Zürich 1985.
28 Riedel, Ingrid: *Farben in Religion, Gesellschaft, Kunst und Psychotherapie*. Stuttgart 1983 (Eighteenth printing completely reworked, expanded, and reformatted in 2008); further Riedel, Ingrid: *Formen: Kreis, Kreuz, Dreieck, Quadrat, Spirale*. Stuttgart 1985 (Fifth printing completely reworked, expanded and reformatted under the title Formen: *Tiefenpsychologische Deutung von Kreis, Kreuz, Dreieck, Quadrat, Spirale und Mandala*. Stuttgart 2006); and further Riedel, Ingrid: *Bilder in Religion, Kunst, und Psychotherapie: Wege zur Interpretation*. Stuttgart 1989 (Reworked and newly formatted under the title *Bilder in Psychotherapie, Kunst und Religion: Ein Schlüssel zur Interpretation*. Stuttgart 2005).
29 Henzler, Christa: *Aspekte der Mal-Therapie unter besonderer Berücksichtigung des tiefenpsychologischen Interpretationsansatzes*. (Diploma thesis for the Department of Social Sciences Universität-Gesamthochschule Kassel) 1985.

(2003) arose from Henzler's diploma thesis at the C.G. Jung Institute of Zürich. I was honored to contribute a few passages about working through grief by painting[30].

G. Clauser[31] introduced the term *"Gestaltungstherapie"* in 1960 (which could be translated as design therapy, art therapy, creation therapy, creativity therapy or formative therapy), and he considered it a "psycho-therapeutic treatment based on depth psychology" with the specialization *"Maltherapie"* (painting therapy) falling under the umbrella term *"Gestaltungstherapie"*. The term became accepted, but can become too narrow, when for instance it is understood in the sense of E. Biniek, who criticizes Clauser's definition of *Gestaltungstherapie*: "G. Clauser's definition lacks not only the broad notion of encounter, which facilitates creativity; it also lacks the integrative aspect, which is so important for treatment, especially of those with psychosis. Personal expression is not the only thing that counts; just as important are encounter and healing. This makes it necessary to expand his definition."[32]

In recent years *Gestaltungstherapie* has been incorporated more and more into the treatment of psychological and psychosomatic in-patients. It can be of help in a broad array of psychosomatic afflictions including neuroses, depressions, anxieties, and compulsions. However, the diploma thesis of Manfred Krapp, *"Gestaltungstherapie* as Part of the Psychotherapy of the Psychoses",[33] warns with convincing arguments against using painting therapy during acute psychoses. Manfred Krapp bases his position on the groundbreaking work of Gaetano Benedetti[34] and the diploma thesis of Margitta Giera-Krapp[35] to emphasize that

---

30 Henzler, Christa; Riedel, Ingrid: *Malen um zu überleben: Ein kreativer Weg durch die Trauer.* Stuttgart 2003.

31 Clauser, Günter: "Gestaltungstherapie" in *Praxis der Psychotherapie 5,* 1960, pp. 268-275.

32 Biniek, Eberhard: *Psychotherapie mit gestalterischen Mitteln.* Darmstadt 1982.

33 Krapp, Manfred: *Die Gestaltungstherapie als Beitrag zur Psychotherapie der Psychosen.* (Diploma thesis for the C.G. Jung Institute Zürich) 1986.

34 Benedetti, Gaetano: "Die Symbolik des schizophrenen Patienten und das Verstehen des Therapeuten" in Hartwig, Helmut; Menzen, Karl-Heinz (Editors): *Kunst-Therapie.* Berlin 1984.

35 Giera-Krapp, Margitta: *Ein Beitrag zur Therapie der frühen Störungen.* (Diploma thesis for the C.G. Jung Institute Zürich) 1985.

painting therapy is not helpful for patients during the restitution phase of the ego after psychotic episodes of a schizophrenic or manic nature.

Painting therapy has proven successful in out-patient treatment of both individuals and groups too, especially in the treatment and follow-up of addictions, anxieties, depressions, and not least in cases of narcissism. It used to be questioned whether or not people suffering from any of the broad range of psychosomatic disorders (including narcissism) are capable of symbolizing and thereby creating images. This has now been answered positively in light of successful experiences with painting therapy in this population. Such people are basically capable of symbolizing, but admittedly that capability must first be awakened and fostered.

Shortly before I finished the manuscript for this book, Gertraud Schottenloher's dissertation landed in my lap. She was able to demonstrate and prove the effectiveness of painting therapy for the disorders formed early in life.[36] The basic foundation for painting therapy is, according to her, the "mother field," especially for narcissistically wounded people. By constellating the so-called mother field, one creates an analogy to the constellation of the positive mother complex.

Active imagination and painting therapy have also proven themselves helpful in the psychological and psychotherapeutic accompaniment of the terminally ill even in the final phases, and also with suicidal patients. In that borderland between life and death, painting therapy can keep the path to the self and to the unconscious clear and accessible. Later in this book I will present some case studies to illustrate this.

Moreover, for those who are interested in their own development and in stimulating their natural individuation process, artistic creativity such as painting is the method of choice. We may paint for prophylactic reasons to head off developmental repression and keep disorders in check, or simply out of the joy of being creative persons who are further creating ourselves. Either way, I love to work with painting groups where

---

36 Schottenloher, Gertraud: *Das therapeutische Potential spontanen bilderischen Gestaltens unter besonderer Berücksichtigung körpertherapeutischer Methoden.* (Dissertation for the University of Zürich, 1989); also Gabriel, Holgrid: "Die Behandlung früher Störungen mit kunsttherapeutischen Mitteln aus der Sicht von C.G. Jung" in *Integrative Therapie 2-3,* 1987 (Bibliography by Furth, see Note 25, painting by children and youth is emphasized here. Not available in English).

the participants are interested in the unfolding and development of their creative potential without seeking direct therapy. And I really do see this as carrying on the Jungian tradition: Jung always considered the individuation process, and its expression in symbolic-creative activity, to be a natural process. It just happens that this process can also be encouraged and supported with therapy.

To conclude this chapter, I would like to reiterate that I have focused on the Jungian literature that has further developed the concept of painting therapy. Two more works appeared in 2003 that are worthy of mention, one by Linda Briendl[37] and one by Christa Henzler[38]. Beyond that, various new therapies using creativity have been developed in recent decades, and they are based on a wide variety of psychotherapeutic theories. It would exceed the intention of this book to discuss all these positions, as much as I would like to do so. The same goes for the wonderful developments in so-called "Art Therapy" coming out of the Anglo-American world.

37 Briendl, Linda: "Die Wiederbeheimatung in der Welt der Gefühle" in Emrich, Hinderk; Riedel, Ingrid (Editors): *Im Farbenkreis der Emotionen.* (Festschrift in honor of Verena Kast's 60th Birthday). Würzburg 2003.

38 Henzler, Christa: "Malen gegen den Tod: Die Funktion des Malens bei der Durchschreitung von Trauerphasen" in Emrich, Hinderk; Riedel, Ingrid. (Editors): *Im Farbenkreis der Emotionen.* (Festschrift in honor of Verena Kast's 60th Birthday). Würzburg 2003.

The Mechanisms of Therapeutic Painting

How exactly does painting therapy work and what are the therapeutic mechanisms? Several elements seem to be at work:

1. the *creative process* itself,
2. the *symbolizing process* of the imagination that creativity requires,
3. the *discussion and interpretation processes*, and
4. the encounter and *relationship process* between therapist and client (or group) while painting and in later discussions.

In other words, four separate processes are at play in painting therapy, all of which can be more or less therapeutically effective: *creation, symbolization, discussion, and relationship.*

What is specifically Jungian about painting therapy? Jung emphasizes imagination and the symbolizing process. But then he insists on discussion and deriving meaning from the material that has been drawn from the unconscious into the painter's consciousness. A Jungian approach uses painting as one element of a wider psychotherapy that works with unconscious material. This material includes the basic complexes, projections, symbolization in dreaming and waking states, as well as the transference and countertransference. Contextualizing painting in this way is particularly fruitful but is not absolutely necessary, since painting after all is a natural process that also sets free the powers of self-creation and fosters the individuation process outside the therapeutic context.

Now I want to examine each of the four processes one-at-a-time. Although in painting they are constantly mixing into and influencing each other, each one alone can be therapeutically effective.

1. The Creative Process

The creative process as such is an innovative process of change that produces something new. The psychological effects of creativity have been researched and published by many psychologists, including Verena Kast and Erika Landau[39]. Creative processes occur in phases. As the phases unfold, they produce an integrating and renewing effect on the psyche. This effect is especially significant for the ego-complex, enhancing its feeling of self-worth.

The process starts with an *incubation phase* in which we are, as it were, pregnant with germinating ideas. A *search and retrieval phase* follows that tries to come up with just the right inner image. As that inner image begins to form, the tension of the search is relieved in an *ah-ha experience*, signaling the advent of the *resolution phase*. Here an ever-clearer picture comes into the imagination, which we attempt to realize through creative activity. The incubation and search phases can begin before we have started to paint, or they can happen during the painting itself, whereby we experiment with colors and forms until an idea arises for us to compose.

In a final phase, the *verification phase*, the painting is self-critically reviewed. We compare the concrete image against the inner image to see whether the two are in sync with each other, and whether the picture can withstand the scrutiny of others (the Group, the therapist) to whom it will be shown. It is typical in this verification phase for the artist to get up in the middle of the night and change something, because it is not yet quite right. A famous example is that of Marc Chagall, who deeply trusted his own intuition, and would get up to continue painting because the drying colors "were ready to arrange themselves". Like a pregnancy, the creative process can – after enduring the pressure of the incubation phase – gush forth in an emotional release so that a picture

39 Landau, Erika: *Psychologie der Kreativität*. München 1969, pp. 61-73.

is born in the resolution phase. Then a distinct lifting of the mood becomes noticeable in contrast to the generally depressive mood during the incubation period. As the affected person, I experience myself again as an active, creative agent and not a passive sufferer. This is even the case when I have taken on the painting of my fear and depression, because now I have given it a face that I can behold, confront, and grapple with. Already in his 1916 essay "The Transcendent Function", Jung describes what we would today call the "Creative Process". Jung's notion of symbol generation corresponds to the incubation phase, when energy from the unconscious wells up to enliven consciousness. Creative people can sense very well that something is happening within them at such a time, although their conscious experience still cannot bring the pieces together. But then comes the next step, the ah-ha moment, where the juggling in the depths of the unconscious takes on a recognizable shape. It becomes a creative idea, a symbol. When this happened, Jung would call it "a living birth"[40].

In the painting process artists have produced something that satisfies and maybe even makes them proud. In any case a feeling of self-worth is imparted, even in those with a depressive structure who have trouble trusting and owning such feelings. Their problem is, as Fritz Riemann states in *Anxiety: Using Depth Psychology to Find a Balance in Your Life* (German: Grundformen der Angst"[41]), whether and how they can succeed in bringing forth something new of their own. The product of painting can build up the self: I have produced something! I can show it off and discuss it with others. The creative child in me has again stirred.

The Creative Child in the "Mother Field"

Often this creative child is painted simultaneously as a symbol of regression and of development. If we have experienced ourselves as artists, then we know what it is to experiment with our character. The process brings us very near to Jung's goal in therapy. As we earlier noted, Jung

40 Jung, Carl Gustav: *CW*, vol. 8, *The Structure and Dynamics of the Psyche*, translated by R.F.C. Hull. Princeton: Bollingen series XX, 2nd Edition 1969, §189.
41 Riemann, Fritz: *Grundformen der Angst*. 41st printing, Munich 2013.

wished to make his patient able "to experiment with his own nature, a state of fluidity, change, and growth where nothing is eternally fixed and hopelessly petrified." [42] Whoever begins to paint, has already started to become creative – first of all in the playing field of the painted picture, but also in the field of real life.

Painting requires a lot of problem solving. The solutions that we must come up with in order to execute our pictures correspond to solutions concerning the real picture of our own life: our life story, our actual problems, and ultimately our own self-creation. We are sometimes plagued by a feeling of powerlessness against the problems and pains of life. But insofar as we create, we are lifting ourselves out of paralysis and above this feeling of powerlessness. The moment we start painting, we cease to be merely a victim of overwhelming events. The creative child in us stirs. Often childlike feelings come up and we could playfully just lie on the floor and paint. Childhood was for many of us the last time that we freely, spontaneously, and joyfully let painting flow from ourselves.

If we can again paint like a child, the positive mother archetype is simultaneously constellated – the "Mother Field". Paul Haerlin [43] captures the gist of this constellation in a lovely expression, namely: a space to be, an unquestioning self-forgetting participation in life like we first experienced, if we were lucky, early on when we were part of our Mother – a belonging which existed before expectations were ever placed on us, and which enables the healing life energies to arise out of the unconscious and lets them flow into creativity. It is the primal feeling of *being carried*: the first and earliest matrix of consciousness. This kind of *being carried* gives rise to an interior disposition enabling "the fingers to flow with colors while the arms forget themselves, becoming mere extensions of interior sensitivity, which pours itself out onto the paper. Then can the inner reality express itself unhampered and takes over the reins: the painter participates in the "intelligence of the psychic", which is at

---

42 Jung, Carl Gustav: *CW*, vol. 16, *The Practice of Psychotherapy*, §99.
43 Haerlin, Peter: *Wie von selbst: Vom Leistungszwang zur Mühelosigkeit*. Weinheim, Berlin 1986. (Not available in English). See also a saying of Jung's: "The living mystery of life is always hidden between Two, and it is the true mystery which cannot be betrayed by words or depleted by arguments." in Jung, Carl Gustav: *Letters of C.G. Jung*, Volume II, Edited by Gerhard Adler and Aniela Jaffé. Routledge 1976, p. 581.

this level indistinguishable from the "intelligence of the cosmic". The pictures generated out of this participatory mindset nourish the feelings of significance and appreciation."[44]

Children would never claim they have the competence to express themselves in painting. They simply know they can paint – they don't question it. They naturally jump at the chance to create just like fish in water. Their ability to create and to symbolize develops just as early as their ability to ensoul a "transitional object"[45] such as a doll or a teddy bear. Children can bestow a sort of life on this object in order to experience part of the mother in it. This enables them to bridge those periods of separation from the mother by playing with the object. They imagine (play) the relationship between mother and child.

When this interior child stirs, it constellates a further fundamental symbol, the "child archetype" which can unleash tremendous healing powers. The archetype of the child is a symbol of becoming and of the future. Ernst Bloch once referred to this as "archetypal hope encapsulated".[46] He meant by it, that facet of the archetype pointing to the future. Children can also constellate themselves as motifs in their artwork. This is graphically illustrated by the fourth picture (47) in the chapter about "Relationship and Dependence".

According to Jung, to encounter our own art, or any symbol for that matter, is far more than an intellectual deliberation. Such encounters can ultimately unleash the helpful powers of the self, the powers underlying the complexes and archetypes. As creative artists we work directly on our self-creation by painting. We stimulate our individuation and thereby our own self-healing.

As already mentioned, this creative work has the potential to turn a painter's mood around from self-destructive rage or crippling depression to a healthy self-forgetfulness. Spontaneous, unexpected joy might then germinate – joy in the creative activity, joy in the success of creating, and

---

44 Schottenloher, Gertraud: *Das therapeutische Potential spontanen bildnerischen Gestaltens*, p. 109.
45 Winnicott, Donald, Woods: *Playing and Reality*. London 1971.
46 Bloch, Ernst: "Die Befreiung der archetypisch eingekapselten Hoffnung" in *Das Prinzip Hoffnung*, Gesamtausgabe. Frankfurt am Main 1959, p. 187. English translation: *The Principle of Hope*, Volume 1 (Studies in Contemporary German Social Thought), MIT press Cambridge Massachusetts, revised 1959, translated 1986.

joy from the product – the picture itself. In some cases, this joyful pride can work retroactively on the painter's feeling of self-worth. Therefore, very often the artist will hang the resulting picture on a wall at home in order to relive over and over again the heightened feeling of self-worth that is bound with the picture. Further, the picture can be shared with the therapist or the painting group and then talked about. This can elicit a positive echo that further strengthens the already good feeling the painter has in relation to the picture.

Such work can diminish fragmentation. (Fragmentation – also known as dissociation, or a breakdown – is the breaking up of the personality into fragments of itself that can happen, for example, after a separation, a bereavement, or some other great shock or disappointment. It can happen to anyone, and not just to the psychologically ill.) By attempting to create a picture, a symbol of our fragmented condition, we are drawn back into the ordering and integrating magnetic field that all creativity provides. The attempt reawakens the courage to seek, gather, and reorient ourselves. When painting after a breakdown we often produce highly ordered pictures during this recollection phase as the fragmentation subsides – for instance mandalas or mandala-like images. The "fragmented" person is brought back into the healing radiance of the so-called "Mother Field".

Principles of Artistic Creation

Painting as a creative process is really a negotiation process between the painting materials, the artistic medium, colors, forms, and their position on the painting surface. This conflict resolution brings us automatically and without fail into contact with the laws of artistic creation, which are in themselves therapeutically effective. The laws that are set into motion, structuring and composing activities, finally place colors and forms onto the painting surface, thereby creating a coherent picture. And since colors and forms express emotions, we end up assembling ourselves by gathering together our conflicting emotions, our moods and affects into a coherent whole. We gather our opposites and sew back those parts of ourselves that have been torn away or split off. We re-form ourselves.

This integration process, which contains healing aspects within itself, is especially apparent in the following three principles to which every artistic creation must conform.

1. *the law of complementarity* (which applies to both color and form) in which one pole seeks, points to or implies its opposite pole

2. *the law of balance* which demands an aesthetic distribution of colors and images over the page, and

3. *the law of limitation* which dictates that the composition must fit within a certain frame.

According to these principles, whatever we depict in a work of art – be it fear, or rage or grief – must be inserted at a specific spot within the available space. A limit is thereby experienced by the painting subject. Additionally, our sight operates according to a sense of proportion provided by the human body: we exist in space and therefore experience an above, a below, a right, and a left. Everything that we paint must somehow be projected onto a flat surface, and yet the picture has to stay in balance, because our eye and our sense of balance won't endure it any other way and would otherwise judge the composition to be a failure. This sense of balance can also refer to a subtle or maybe volatile balance of energies where ideas oppose one another in great tension, analogous to the expression of counterpoint in musical composition. We can say that the prevailing rule of the painting surface is: every weight must find a counterweight.

All pictures contain some kind of proportion symbolism, which is predetermined by our experience. The painted surface somehow reflects the human body in space and also the human being in life. Insofar as we position our own themes or problems in this spatially symbolic field, we also orient ourselves: we organize our lives in response to our own real problems.

Spatial Symbolism

Recall Aristotle's theory about how things as they are come to be. He proposed four types of influence that work together to produce everything that exists, and he called these influences the four "causes": the material, formal, efficient, and final causes.

The Jungian tradition of picture interpretation has focused primarily on how spatial aspects in a picture are expressed: a focus that emphasizes their "efficient cause". We point out, for example, that what appears in the lower right corner of the picture is often derived from the motherly energies in the psyche. But the final cause in pictures has received little attention even though the creation itself of a picture requires a strong final impulse.

The following description of the painting process has been told over and over again by those of us who paint: First a color, a line, a form is placed into the picture expressing a particular mood or condition (a mood that can be discussed and interpreted as an efficient cause); but then we add a color or form or symbol which we feel is needed just now for completion, because we sense a need to modify the feeling that we brought initially. This addition will very often be a polar opposite to the original feeling, which brings the potential to change the painter's mood. This constantly retold description betrays the final cause of the painting process. This cause ought to be incorporated and even accentuated when interpreting the resulting picture, just as the final cause is emphasized and favored over the efficient in the Jungian interpretation of dreams. This is ultimately what heals us. When considering images out of the unconscious, it is their final cause that points to the future that completes and makes us whole.

We naturally interpret dreams under the double aspect of efficient and final causes, and we should interpret pictures in the same way. I don't question that this already happens in many therapeutic settings, but it occurs to me that thus far we Jungians have officially taught a classic interpretation schema for spatial symbolism as set down by Michel, that looks primarily at the efficient causes revealed in the picture but not at the final causes (I have worked on fine-tuning this schema myself[47]). A consideration of the final causes would include the artist's desires and needs. And experience shows that these tend to appear in certain spatially symbolic places within the image or on the drawing surface.

For example, a need or desire for security, for feeling grounded, for feeling down to earth can often reveal itself through protecting and sheltering symbols appearing in the bottom half of a picture and mainly in the bottom right-hand quarter (the traditional "mother" corner). In such a case a possibility is revealed – the artist's potential to become more of a mother to him/herself.

Or take the opposite pole: getting above and beyond ourselves. Our need and desire to do so quite often shows itself in the upper half of the picture closer to the heavens and mainly in the upper left quarter (traditionally the "father" corner).

A need and the desire for greater realization and higher consciousness very often reveals itself in the upper half of paintings, corresponding to the head and chest of the body and hinting at straightening up or reorienting oneself. This usually gets painted into the upper right quarter, corresponding to the right hand (for right-handed people), where activities are more conscious. The drive is to become consciously active in the outer world.

The expression of a need and desire to be able to lift something out of the unconscious, to go to the roots whether in one's own life story, or in human history in general, corresponds to the lower half of pictures in spatial symbolism. This area is equivalent to the belly and the pubic region, and especially in the lower left quarter we are furthest from consciousness but nearer to the left hand and therefore also the heart. The region of the feet and "the ground under our feet" is symbolized in the lower regions of the picture. If one has something activated here in this part of the picture, then in a sense, some access to the unconscious has been achieved, and what shows up in this place has become visible and understandable.

47 Riedel, Ingrid: *Bilder in Religion, Kunst, und Psychotherapie: Wege zur Interpretation.* Stuttgart 1989. "Michels Modell", p. 38 (referring to the bright coloration of the Pâques series).

Schema of Spatial Symbolism

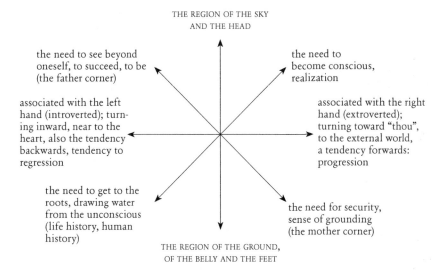

THE REGION OF THE SKY
AND THE HEAD

the need to see beyond oneself, to succeed, to be (the father corner)

the need to become conscious, realization

associated with the left hand (introverted); turning inward, near to the heart, also the tendency backwards, tendency to regression

associated with the right hand (extroverted); turning toward "thou", to the external world, a tendency forwards: progression

the need to get to the roots, drawing water from the unconscious (life history, human history)

the need for security, sense of grounding (the mother corner)

THE REGION OF THE GROUND,
OF THE BELLY AND THE FEET

The schema of spatial symbolism was originally derived from comparing hundreds of pictures. More recently, it has become clear that the schema actually corresponds to the bodily experience of being oriented in space, which we then project upon a flat surface when we paint.

The entire lower half of a painting space corresponds to standing on the ground, to steadfastness, to being down-to-earth (including our need for this). This lower half refers to the navel, belly, pubic region, legs and feet of a standing person. The symbolism on the lower right side of the picture can illustrate a deep-seated and nearly conscious need to go to the roots, to lower oneself down, or let oneself in. Less conscious tendencies would appear in the lower left, such as the wish to allow oneself to let go or fall.

The upper half of a painting corresponds to straightening oneself up, rising above the ground and holding one's head high, and thereby having an overview (including our need for this). The upper body – the waist, the trunk, the breast and the head – is projected onto this upper half of the painting surface. The symbolism in this region illustrates the need for an overview from a higher perspective, including the striving to look up, to overstep boundaries, and so a tendency to observe and then rise up.

Our body's experience of space not only differentiates according to up and down, but also according to left and right (there is also front and back in pictures that are purposely drawn three-dimensionally). These give a picture's bodily orientation a special accent: dexterity (for right-handers usually the right side) is nearer to consciousness, and clumsiness (usually on the left side) is less conscious. Whereby it makes symbolic sense that the left side, the side of the heart, transmits the feelings and emotions. Often the hand that does not work so much is fresher, more tender, weaker, and has a keener sense of touch. Areas of a picture are emphasized during the painting because the painter senses a stronger urge to "fill" them: this is for the painter somehow "fulfilling". Here the complementary energy of the picture begins to work on the painter. A picture painted out of the desire for what is fatherly will release energies in the painter while that corresponding zone is being painted. This energy can actually make the painter more fatherly.

Complementary Colors

The law of complementary colors is just as informative as the principles of spatial symbolism when looking at an artistic creation. Complementary colors summon, impel, and enhance each other: red summons green, blue calls to orange, and yellow calls out violet. This optic phenomenon, that the eye presses for an integration of opposites, seeks an overcoming of one-sidedness and an end to splitting off, is a physiological manifestation of the law of enantiodromia: a philosophical principle describing how every force that reaches its development generates a counterforce.

At the same time, complementary colors enhance each other's power of expression. When we cover an entire surface in a stressful dark violet, our eye and our mood will seek the light and freeing color yellow, as for instance in the picture painted by a 55-year-old woman (picture 2) which she named "Wise". The law of complementarity reveals itself even more impressively in a series painted totally in an introverted, mystical blue (pictures 22-30) and interpreted in a later chapter. The paintings in this series cry out for some orange. And that is exactly what the painter, a highly talented alcoholic, needed in order to save his life. In his addiction, he constantly sought to re-experience the free-floating life, symbolized in oceanic blue. This side of him was in a constant wrestling match with his orange side, the color which expresses facing the world head on.

2. Wise

Chagall writes in a poem that he must get up at night in order to put the still missing red on a picture, because for him, without this red, it was just "unbearable". One need not be Chagall in order to sense that a picture exclusively in yellow, green and blue-green needs a dab of red in order to become "whole". This desire of our eye, our color sense, rests upon the need for balance – a need experienced by our sense organs. Complementary colors evoke each other, and ultimately the whole wheel of color seeks to be successively realized. Where a color is locked out and cannot be used, some need will thereby increase. Because colors also express emotions, the physical/optical law of complementary colors corresponds to a psychic law that calls forth complementary emotions: After lingering long in Lent, whose liturgical color is heavy, dark, blue-violet, both the psyche and the organs of sight start longing for bright yellow-orange, the expression of Easter joy. Manessier's color choice in the "Pâques" is an example: the crucifixion is a violet background with an indigo-blue darkened sun, whereas Easter is a page filled by a revolving red-orange disk[48]. In this way the dark colors call for light ones; but the opposite is also true. As I already pointed out, a participant in one of my painting seminars stated: "I first paint black. Only then can the lighter colors properly express themselves and take off."

Complementary Forms

The form[49] best corresponding to the color purple is the tension-filled, heavy-burdened sign of the cross. The form best corresponding to the relaxed yellow-orange is the circle. Passion and Easter can thus appear together as in the Celtic cross. Sharp points, corners and crosses (for example jagged mountains and steeples) call forth rounded forms such as curves, ovals, and blobs (for example lakes). Closed forms call for open ones, dynamic forms seek languid ones, the vertical and diagonal seek the horizontal, and the "banished" calls for the "welcoming". These pairs could almost be divided into masculine and feminine with the masculine forms appearing in the vertical, the arrow, the wedge, the triangle, the diagonal; and the feminine in the horizontal, the bowl, the oval and the circle.

A further theme revealed in the creative process is the relationship between a figure and its foreground or background. Here we can pick up on the confrontation between the conscious ego and its emotional background as well as the artist's approach to perspective.

---

48 Ibid. "Manessier" pp. 225-258.
49 Riedel, Ingrid: *Formen: Kreis, Kreuz, Dreieck, Quadrat, Spirale*. Stuttgart 1985; as well as Itten, Johannes: *Kunst der Farbe*. Ravensburg 1962.

Coherence

Two-dimensional compositions demand coherence, completion, and a balance of energies. The colors and forms have to fit together. This demand brings the artist into contact with the self-regulating powers of the psyche: every attempt at a coherent creation evokes their sense of correspondence, balance, and completeness.

The reference point and organ of coherence is a stable ego. This is a prerequisite for coherent painting, and without it, one paints isolated elements that do not hold together as a whole. This is observable in the artwork of schizophrenics, whose ability to paint remains despite their strong psychiatric disturbance. According to Jung, this creative ability in schizophrenics reveals an autonomous region of the human psyche that can paint with an uncanny, idiosyncratic coherence. I will discuss this phenomenon further in the following chapter.

Even people with a strong ego structure usually have to paint an entire series before they can get this sense of coherence exactly right. The coherence of a composition is an analogy or reflection of an inner-psychic coherence. We could say that our creative activity is a way of experimenting in order to regain wholeness. Whenever a well-balanced composition is found, more is happening than just the experiment: in a successful sketch, in a clear model, what is desired has already become reality.

2. The Symbolization Process

Healing in painting therapy is partially due to the symbolization process, a sub-process within the larger creative process. Symbolization happens all the time, but it happens in a special way during creative activity. Let us be clear about how the creative process is carried out from a clinical perspective: First we relax. Then in this relaxed state we focus on a mood, an emotion, a bodily pain, a conscious problem or some other theme. In doing this, an image comes to mind that alludes to the complex or archetype underlying it. This inner image, this pictorial conception, will now be painted.

1. Through the colors a particular emotional tone will be expressed.

2. Through the forms a certain configuration and expressive structure will come together.

3. Through the concrete acts of coloring and structuring, the inner image will change and further develop.

The initial emotion or mood could be anything ... anxiety, joy ... but it changes during the depiction process. The emotion becomes visible in this creative activity; it becomes an object with which we can come into contact, even into conflict. In this way the rudiments of an underlying complex or archetype may become visible. The painting taking place is, psychologically speaking, a creative process, which for Jung means something very important. Being creative for him means above all that we bring into consciousness something that until now has been unconscious. "The creative process, so far as we are able to follow it at all, consists in the unconscious activation of an archetypal image, and in elaborating and shaping this image into the finished work."[50]

This process of creating something is itself an expression of the "transcendent function" of the psyche, the term Jung used for symbol-creating activity; it transports things out of the unconscious and into consciousness. The transcendent function is often misunderstood to have a religious dimension, but Jung meant nothing more than an "over-stepping" or "border-crossing" function that can produce a synthesis between conscious and unconscious contents, and which then finds expression in a symbol: "The shuttling to and fro of arguments and affects represents the transcendent function of opposites. The confrontation of the two positions generates a tension charged with energy and creates a living, third thing, not a logical stillbirth in accordance with the principle *tertium non datur*, but a movement out of the suspension between opposites, a living birth that leads to a new level of being, a new situation. The transcendent function manifests itself as a quality of conjoined opposites."[51]

In this context Jung describes how a symbol transcends: how consciousness and the unconscious take up opposing positions forcing a

---

50 Jung, Carl Gustav: *CW*, vol. 15, *Spirit in Man, Art and Literature*, § 130.
51 Jung, Carl Gustav: *CW*, vol. 8, *The Structure and Dynamics of the Psyche*, § 189.

third position to develop and become conscious in the form of a symbol pointing beyond (i. e. transcending) the opposition. "Thinking in terms of energy transfer, Jung compares this process to the collision of two objects. When consciousness and the unconscious clash because they have taken up opposing positions, the psychic dynamic comes to a temporary standstill as the psychic energy withdraws into the unconscious. There it constellates a third position, which includes the two opposing positions but also points beyond them. It is therefore essential that the unconscious be allowed to express itself so that the ego (which Jung calls "the abiding center of consciousness") can grapple with these expressions. It is about paying attention to the unconscious, portraying it, and understanding it. And it is about the question of meaning." [52]

An impressive example of such symbol generation through the union of opposites is "The Divided Face" (Figure 16), painted by a 29-year-old student. The face is divided in two and yet is a whole. The right side (traditionally considered the conscious side) is dark – darkened by everything that her life history up to now has brought her and is portrayed in the dead tree with a pitchfork leaning against it: the memory is of the early loss of her mother and the ensuing hard work living on a farm lacking a mature woman. A red, as if bloody cross pushes into the picture from above and threatens to crush the woman's head – it reminds the painter of her attempt to escape the desolation of that time by seeking a spiritual or religious home in a pietistic religious group. The group's moralization, however, brought on new stress. Her membership ended in heavy disappointment with the group. The left (traditionally the unconscious) side of the face is bright, and beside it are symbols such as the four-season-tree, which knows not only winter, but also the changes from blossom to fruit to harvest. Over this tree spans a rainbow, the ancient sign of reconciliation after a hard storm. This chapter is not the place to mine all the inner riches to be found in this picture; that will come later in this book. What is important here is to see how a symbol

---

52 Kast, Verena: *Die Dynamik der Symbole: Grundlagen der Jung'schen Psychotherapie.* New Edition Ostfildern 2016, pp. 28-29. Citation translated directly from German edition. English version translated from 1990 edition: Kast, Verena: *The Dynamics of Symbols: Fundamentals of Jungian Psychotherapy,* translated by Susan A. Schwarz. Fromm International Publishing Corp, 1992.

of hope emerges from her own unconscious. There is no denying how heavy the burden must be under which the young woman stands, but the picture also shows that she is producing symbols that give hope and perspective to her situation.

A symbol contains both memory and desire, a reminder and an expectation, a history and a utopia. The picture we just discussed, "The Divided Face," reveals both aspects: memory of a difficult childhood and hope of incorporating that dramatic experience into a greater whole that will bring healing. The picture not only mirrors the conflicts present in the painter, but also anticipates their possible solution. For the painter it is more a symbol of optimism, of progress, of a positive outlook on the future, than it is a regressive symbol of unresolved childhood conflicts. Possible integration and healing may become visible in a symbol and are even partially accomplished by the act of creating it. The reality of this process reveals itself in the enormous change in the woman's mood accompanying the creation of this picture. Symbols are vessels for emotions.

Within all of us there are inner images. And underlying them are a host of emotions, complexes, and crises. Through conscious confrontation with an inner image, we come into contact with that which underlies it. And by painting the image, we express its underlying emotion. Simply by carrying out a creative process we attain a state of mind whereby we are no longer held or overwhelmed by the emotion. Instead, we find ourselves above it in a way that we can approach and actively confront it.

The possibility of banishing an emotion through artistic activity is especially easy to experience regarding pictures of anxiety. If an anxiety can be captured in a picture, it has found its vessel, and the anxious painter experiences a first version of what it will be like to regain his or her composure. Anxiety is thereby immediately diminished. In a similar way, painting and creating can in some cases transform destructive and self-destructive impulses into constructive and creative impulses. This was seen in the case of a woman who was painting during a suicidal crisis and found she forgot her self-destructive impulse; she just kept trying to paint the picture as exactly as possible.

Fear can also be averted through attempts to capture it in a picture, simply being able to see the fear already works to diminish it. Expressing a hitherto invisible anxiety in picture form will transform something intangible and eerie into a visible object. As the fear diminishes even a little, more positive images and symbols can now be added to the painting.

Creating pictures can set emotions free, helping to discharge them. I recall one such cathartic process involving a woman full of rage over her father. She went into the next room and painted her rage in such a state of upset that she sometimes ripped and pressed through the paper. Her emotion was pouring into the pictures! When she came back to the group she was relieved and released. I also recall the arrested grief process of a daughter who had really loved her father whom she had lost 20 years earlier. Her grieving was finally engaged as she dared to paint the scene of her father's death, especially the moment that his coffin was borne out of the house. The fettered emotions that had not been allowed expression broke free in this picture, and the painter could finally take leave of her father.

To an extent we can get a handle on anxiety, and for that matter any other emotion, simply by symbolizing it. Why is this? Every picture has a frame, a limitation, a border. In painting, our free-floating anxiety can be localized and placed within limits. People who are enmeshed in the collective view will accept the edge of a sheet of paper as their limit just as children up to a certain age will generally stay inside the fence around their yard. With increasing maturity however, we begin to set our own limits. These limits act as boundaries making it possible for us to either include or to exclude; they provide us protection but can also restrict us. How the edges are observed in painting is therefore worthy of our attention. With some people the available space is far from being filled, while others burst their frames. Some painters choose their paper according to its height, or depth, or maybe even breadth, and this already has symbolic significance. The artist's stance toward reality, either accepting the limits given in life or setting one's own boundaries, correlates with the symbolic choice of the frame. Maybe life has become too narrow, or maybe I'm not yet ready to fill it out.

Verena Kast describes the central function of the symbolization process for the psyche thus: "The psyche is a self-regulating system whose regulation is made conscious to the ego by symbols and symbol-formation. It would be a mistake, however, to look only at the moment a symbol is finally born. We must look at the whole process. Comparison with the creative process suggests that what is essential for symbol-formation is really the illumination of a new idea. We glimpse it, and wow! We experience a new vitality. But this is only a beginning. This feeling or premonition may herald a long, tedious process requiring perseverance against uncertainty and frustration; one requiring the hard, conscious confrontation with our initial problem. Psychologically this means that the opposition between conscious and unconscious material must often be borne, observed, and endured for a painfully long time before a new symbol arises and with it a new purpose in life. Yet symbol-formation does happen. We just need to accept the illuminations that come – be they a dream, a fantasy, or a fascination with a projection – and let them work. They will provide the 'creative leaps' in our life."[53]

3. The Therapeutic Discussion and Interpretation Process

As we have already pointed out, the painting process itself produces positive effects, even when the picture is not later discussed. But painting therapy according to Jungian principles also requires discussion about the picture between therapist and client or among members of a painting group. This is analogous to other therapeutic discussions which process material originating in the unconscious such as dreams or fantasies. Using association and amplification, examining further symbols that occur to the painter during the discussion, and considering the broader religious and symbolic significance of elements in the painting, the therapeutic discussion seeks to unlock and interpret the picture. As noted above, Jung himself emphasizes

---

53 Kast, Verena: "Die Bedeutung der Symbole im analytischen Prozeß" in Barz, Helmut / Kast, Verena / Nager, Frank: *Heilung und Wandlung: C.G. Jung und die Medizin.* Zürich / München 1986, pp. 64 ff.

"... that the mere execution of the pictures is not enough. Over and above that, an intellectual and emotional understanding is needed; they require to be not only rationally integrated with the conscious mind, but also morally assimilated. They still have to be subjected to a work of synthetic interpretation."[54]

Simply to engage in creative activity can set into motion a process that releases significant self-healing energies and stimulates individuation. The therapeutic relationship adds to the creativity with an ensuing discussion that contextualizes the picture within the painter's life history and brings the painter's inner and outer realities together. The picture functions as a third party posited between therapist and client – it has been "painted between them" – as a courier that can go back and forth between the two. Then verbalization is required to isolate and capture the symbol: a particular symbol must be named by its own name, but just like Rumpelstiltskin, at first it keeps silent about its name. The particular emotion, problem or complex portrayed in the painting becomes fully conscious only by naming it. Only then does its meaning light up and show to which complex or constellated archetype the symbol is linked. The therapeutic discussion confronts the painter's ego with symbols that the hand has discovered and painted, thereby adding this material to the purview of consciousness.

The therapist should pay attention not only to the conscious contents, but also to the colors and form of the composition, and during the discussion may ask the painter: "What do these mean for you? Which feelings are you connecting with them?" We arrive at the essence of a picture most quickly by asking the painter a question such as "What in the picture was especially important for you?" or "What moved you the most emotionally?"

According to the principles of analytical psychology it is essential that the amplifying and interpreting discussion of painting therapy takes place as a concluding discussion and in the presence of the picture or picture series. It should only take place when the whole series is finished, so that the painter's independent confrontation with the resulting symbol or chain of symbols will be least disturbed. Again, this

54 Jung, Carl Gustav: *CW*, vol. 16, *The Practice of Psychotherapy*, § 111.

is analogous to the Jungian discussion of a dream that has given rise to an inner picture, but in the case of painting therapy we have in addition a concrete, outer picture before us. Very often the picture still belongs to the dream from which it evolved and derived its motif.

In a healthy therapeutic discussion the picture should not be picked to pieces. Every single stroke need not be interpreted and discussed. Rather one should work as far as possible in accord with what the painter finds to be essential. The goal is to make contact with an essence that has expressed itself here. We should respect a painter's timidity. An artist may avoid talking about one or another element in a picture, even adamantly refusing to discuss it. With too much pressure, it is likely that further discussion of the pictures, as well as the joy of painting, will become completely blocked. With pictures, only as much as the artist can swallow and digest in the moment should be discussed. I am thoroughly convinced, above all with narcissistically disordered patients, that an empathic discussion is more appropriate than a confrontational interpretation. Such patients first want to be seen and understood through their painting. An "interpretation" can irritate the trusting climate that makes the patient feel accepted, provides them with a sense of belonging, and characterizes the "mother field"[55]. Since the elements of a painting make visible the elements of the soul, in an empathic discussion we seek to notice, embrace, and find an appropriate language that carefully and faithfully translates what we see in the picture. The artist has vividly copied a soul image. Now we want to talk to the soul and not drag the discussion to some psychological meta-level. Above all, the discussion seeks to motivate the painter to find a language for the picture. This is especially challenging for patients who suffered psychological damage in the pre-verbal stage, because they often lack language for their emotions. Luckily, creating a picture is already a conscious act of translating hitherto unknown material. Compared to a "naked" dream where interpretation still needs to take place verbally, a painting is already in itself an interpretation. Painting is a conscious creative process in which some material has become conscious, and some symbolic connection of the opposites has already taken place. One

55 Schlottenloher, Gertraud: *Das therapeutische Potential spontanen bildnerischen Gestaltens*, p. 163.

need not rub the patient's nose in the new unconscious material. That can be offensive. "The painter has allowed her unconscious to appear in a picture, where she can recognize it."[56]

A painter requires "a relatively stable Ego structure"[57] in order for interpretation to have a positive effect. Only then can the patient understand and accept what is being said. Such structure is lacking in the case of personality disorders. It is, however, completely present in ego-structured people, for whom a confrontational interpretation is often desired, exhilarating, and encouraging.

If an interpretation would be tantamount to suggesting a disorder or deficiency, the therapist may be wise to withhold it. Instead, we can always do as Schottenloher suggests: "substitute the search for a solution, the resources, the self-healing portion, and the representation of the goal"[58] which are also available and to be found in the pictures. In this way we move away from the damage and towards the interior possibilities. This reorientation toward the potentials and possibilities that become visible in the painter's pictures is nothing other than Jung's final or prospective interpretation of unconscious materials. According to Jungian methodology, we allow our own feelings, associations and amplifications to influence how we discuss the picture with the patient, albeit carefully. For example, the painter finds a white snake to be rather scary. But a fairy tale occurs to us in which a white snake imparts the wisdom to understand every animal's language. We set against her rather negative interpretation a possibility of understanding the dream positively. In this way painter and therapist may come to a more common understanding of the artwork despite initially seeing the same picture completely differently.

We tend to interpret dreams on the objective level first, and we do the same with figures portrayed in a picture. Initially we assume that the figures depict actual people in the artist's life. But then on the subjective level we recognize that the figures reveal inner parts of the artist: a strict teacher, a passionate gypsy, even a loyal dog should be seen as aspects of the artist him/herself. The therapeutic discussion is essential to

56 Ibid.
57 Ibid, p. 162.
58 Ibid, p. 165.

ascertaining a picture's possible subjective interpretations. One should ask the artist such questions as: "What have these figures to do with you?" "What do they mean for you?" Indeed, a subjective interpretation only makes sense in conjunction with the picture's creator.

Every therapeutic discussion and interpretation process includes the following elements:

1. An atmosphere is constellated – the mother field – wherein an empathic and caring discussion occurs, out of which the creative work is born.

2. The artist describes how the picture came to be painted and what it means personally.

3. The therapist and painting group pose further questions and offer additional insights, observations, associations and amplifications.

4. The therapist and painting group interpret the picture or picture series in the context of the painter's entire life history and of the problem that the painting might be depicting.

4. The Art of Encountering and Relating

C.G. Jung's view that dreams are dreamed "between analysand and analyst"[59] applies analogously to a picture: it is painted between analysand and analyst. It mirrors their therapeutic relationship and is at the same time a message from the analysand to the analyst, from client to therapist. With Schottenloher, we could indeed call it "a present"[60] from analysand to analyst. This present requires no explanation outside the therapeutic process. Rather it reflects the therapeutic process and offers itself as a creative product of this process to the analyst. It is very important in this regard, to point out that in painting therapy the relationship between therapist and client is always carried out by way of a "third party", the picture that they behold and confront together.

59 Jung, Carl Gustav: *C.G. Jung Letters Volume 1 1906 – 1950*, edited by Aniela Jaffé with Gerhard Adler. Routledge & Kegan Paul, London. 1973. Princeton University Press, p. 172. Letter to James Kirsch, 29 Sept. 1934. "In the deepest sense we all dream not out of ourselves but out of what lies between us and the other."

60 Schlottenloher, Gertraud: *Das therapeutische Potential spontanen bildnerischen Gestaltens*, p. 166.

What heals here is not simply the relationship, but also the message that springs from that relationship. It arises from the unconscious of the client and is made visible by being painted into a picture. The therapist takes that picture on, becomes interested in it, and thereby constellates the mother archetype for the client – or maybe not in the case where the therapist remains distanced from the picture.

3. The Plants vs Destruction

A picture by the student who had earlier painted "The Divided Face", illustrates how a trusting relationship to her therapist was constellated even though she still felt trapped in her depressive and suicidal condition. In this picture (Image 3) – we call it "The Plant Verses Destruction" – a sitting figure (incarnating the painter) looks upon a skull representing her desire for death. But in her belly she carries another face that looks in the opposite direction. It looks to a living green plant with leaves shaped like helping hands (incarnating the therapist).

In a painting by another client (Image 4) the negative experience with her own mother imposes itself for the time being between the client and her nascent feeling of trust for the therapist in the form of an all-domineering spider. Note here that the disturbance to the therapeutic relationship does not present itself as a direct confrontation, but rather in a symbolic form. Luckily, even in early disorders, the therapeutic relationship can usually relieve such a disturbance: the negative mother in this instance has not been projected onto the person of the therapist, but rather onto the picture, where therapist and client can observe and overcome it together.

4. Spider

The analyst's first task in any therapeutic relationship is the constellation of a basis for trust. This provides a protected space between analysand and analyst in which creativity can arise. Jungians call it "the vessel." Next comes a keen awareness and therapeutic management of the transference and counter transference that always and everywhere are playing themselves out, whether we realize it or not. I can often read clearly in the picture just what the client is presently projecting onto me – now the healing plant as in the already named picture, later the dangerous spider creeping between client and therapist. Once somebody who painted a smiling spider wanted to show that his originally negative relationship to his mother had, through the encounter with me as therapist, become friendlier.

5. Leading the Horse Out

6. Black Horse

7. Blue Horse

8. Horse with Foal

It is also essential that I notice exactly how I am experiencing the picture lying before me. I can, for example, experience a picture negatively as uncomfortable, or shocking or artificial. I must maintain my composure, because my reaction has an effect upon the analysand. This is just as true when a picture touches me deeply in a positive way: perhaps the analysand has not yet completely accepted the picture. Most often it can happen that I intervene too early or incorrectly. This includes being too encouraging and thereby discouraging, because the analysand still doesn't believe s/he can paint to my expectations, which are implied by the encouragement.

In one particular case I was shocked by a client's picture from a dream in which she finds a horse – her vitality and also her sexuality – walled up in a cellar, and I suggested to her that she lead the horse out of the cellar in her next picture. Although she did so, she was overtaxed by my premature suggestion that she would be able to free the horse. She dared only a pencil sketch of this exodus (Image 5). This colorless representation functioned like a rough draft of an idea – an idea that the artist truly had in her head – but did not yet dare to realize as a graphic, full-color picture. Luckily, from my premature suggestion, she nevertheless went further with the idea of freeing the horse. She stayed with the emotions connected to the picture, on the one hand anxiety on the other a desire for freedom. This desire to reclaim her full vitality as a woman had been lost after the death of her husband years before. She painted another horse, this time a black horse (Image 6). She is admittedly a bit stiff but is affectionately trying to feed it. Then in the next picture (Image 7) she swings herself onto a blue horse. With the blue and with the title "Fantasy Horse" she is still somehow holding back the wildness of a natural horse. But a couple of pictures later (Image 8) her now brown horse has a young one, a foal, that happily encounters the waves of the sea. Finally we see her in the last picture (Image 9) in full gallop through the desert on a brown horse.

9. Gallop

What exactly does the therapist do during a painting therapy?

The therapist's first and foremost task is to create the therapeutic "vessel" in which the pictures can come into being. Haerlin calls it preparing the "mother field" which makes "holding" possible. Winnicott emphasizes how important it is for the patient to feel "held" so that out of this experience a creative process can dare to emerge. Next the therapist spurs the creative process on; primarily by making it understood how very interesting the clients' pictures would be. We might directly suggest that the client paints something, perhaps a dream, a fantasy, a mood, or a physical pain. A picture might also be sparked by a symbol, fairy tale, or myth … or perhaps a difficult relationship, even the therapeutic relationship itself.

The painting can be executed in the therapy session, at home, alone, with a partner, or in a painting group. Each picture should be discussed.

This is usually done right after its creation or after the last picture in a series, when several pictures have been painted in a single day or weekend. In the case of several pictures, whether a series by one artist, or pictures from several painters, they should be discussed one after the other. Only through such discussions will the picture language become plain language and thereby directly address or express the real-life problems of the artist(s).

Sometimes finished pictures lying on the table will themselves suggest further motifs to paint. Sometimes the therapist might suggest something further. The therapist may notice, for example, a problem either in the content or the form of a picture and suggest that the painter add something, continue something, or fill something out. Perhaps the therapist may suggest completely new motifs, colors, or symbols. We might also try leading clients in a guided imagination before a painting session. Possibilities include nature symbols or simply imagining one specific color. Exactly how all this is done will be presented in later chapters of this book.

One picture series (Images 18-30) resulted from asking a whining, complaining alcoholic to precisely paint his mood. The moment he accepted the assignment, his random bellyaching started to take on form and developed into a fascinating sequence of pictures described in a later chapter under the title "Fascination through Blue". The man yearned for some sort of oceanic feeling, so he actually lived in blue rooms. They were rather solemn, as if built from ice, water, and sky. In these rooms he attempted to compensate for his little ego. By painting this series he got onto the scent of his true desires that he had been trying to compensate through his addiction. He figured out how to assuage them by making contact with his inner images and their creative display.

Inevitably during the painting process a problem presents itself, which the painter then attempts to resolve. Indeed, the painter can hardly stop until it is resolved. Painting therapy is an efficient way to the solution. It aids and abets the inner work going on in the soul whenever someone paints; and this inner work is an essential part of every single painting process. The creative process will often begin with a relatively harmonious picture, as in the following example. But soon a disturbing moment comes when its antithesis presses forward and the opposites stand crassly across from each other, producing a high tension that longs to be balanced and resolved. Although oblivious to this process, nevertheless every painter can access the creative resources of the unconscious and thereby keep imagining until a viable resolution is reached. We can access the soul's images of healthy human experience, such as the necessary separation of parents from their children. The soul's images ensure that the painter's own picture for the accomplishment of the problem at hand will be found. That happened in the following series:

10. House with Bright Straw Roof

This series was executed in one weekend by a mother in a painting group and shows how painting can spontaneously initiate a problem-solving process. The problem was still in the so called pre-therapeutic or the prophylactic arena. The series illustrates how the mother overcame a gnawing worry about her son, who when he was eleven years old, had painted what she saw as a lonely, thatched house. She herself describes how she came to paint the series of pictures that weekend:

"Themes for the weekend were the motifs: house, fire and water. During the active imagination concerning "house" a watercolor appeared to my inner eye that my then eleven-year-old son, the middle of my three children, had rendered: a thatched house with a straw roof. Since the exercise was supposed to be about my own image of house, and this one was, so to say, "in the way", I first painted it in order to be rid of it and so get on with my own house. I painted it the way I remembered: alone on the height of a mound in the sea (Image 10). I remember distinctly thinking: "This is definitely not my house. I never felt so alone and unprotected." I painted a second picture (Image 11) and for a long time wanted to change it until it would be my own house. Only on the third try did I hit upon just the house that pleased me – and it pleases me still today (Image 12).

11. Hallig with Dyke

"The fourth picture (Image 13) was not the result of an active imagination. Rather, I had conceived the idea to combine water and house with each other – perhaps it was also formulated as an assignment for the seminar. As I began to paint, I intuitively realized the truth and the meaning of my creation. The picture seemed to be painting itself. It made me feel happy and at peace and gave me an answer to the question

I had been wrestling with: "How could I endure and allow the loneliness I perceive in my child's life, without clinging to him?" Suddenly it dawned on me that despite the current awkwardness and distance in our relationship, deep down we were "through and through" connected: the sea floor symbolized the solid ground of our extended family and reassured me that my child would not get lost. And yes, I realized that the present distance from him was necessary so that he could become independent. The water not only divided us from one another, it also joined us and gave us a clear and constant view of the ground. I was happy to have found a picture symbol that clarified my relationship to my children. This picture accompanied and comforted me as an expression of inner truth through the difficult years of my children's puberty, and it still does!

12. Frisian House

"When I got home after the weekend, of course I immediately got out my son's watercolor in order to see how it really looked. I was astounded and breathed a sigh of relief! There was no loneliness and isolation, no lack of protection! A very cozy straw-roofed house, someone standing in the door, somebody runs toward two animals, a sea-worthy boat with outboard motor and small radar antenna lies tied up on the shore! He had established himself on the island but could also leave there again according to his own wish and whim.

"I was relieved, but I must confess, also ashamed, I had projected something onto my son that was completely unreal. I thought I knew him and was astonished how I had misjudged him!"

13. Connected Halligen

Summary

The therapeutic effectiveness of painting therapy rests upon four interlocking mechanisms. To conclude, I wish to make explicit what makes each mechanism so effective.

1. The Relationship Process. It may well be that the most critical step in the relationship process is for the therapist to develop a relationship of trust, thereby constellating a positive "mother field". This expresses itself primarily as an atmosphere arising between therapist and client and in turn gives the client a sense of being born or carried. It is this that makes the creative process possible. The painter partakes of the positive energy available from both the "mother field" and the therapist. Such energy enables the painter to risk creating. The painter dares to become the active creator of a picture and has a corresponding sense of his or her own destiny.

2. The Discussion and Interpretation Process. It is absolutely essential to establish and maintain a discussion within the gentle and empathic atmosphere that has been established. Such a discussion makes ever more conscious the communication from the client's unconscious. This communiqué was previously delivered in the form of a picture that already combines conscious and unconscious content. Now, a language must be developed around the picture in collaboration with the artist. This language must remain close to the picture and yet be capable of making transparent the psychic processes that produced the picture.

3. The Symbolization Process. The painter must imagine coming into contact with the rich experiences, powers and forces of the unconscious. The painter's imagination plays itself out before and during the act of painting, displaying resources from the unconscious. These resources – or forces at work in the painter – reveal the problem in a more comprehensive context, which enables the painter to see it on a higher level and finally to "outgrow" it.

4. The Creative Process. Finally, we find the essence of the creative process is both construction (the symbol-making work with color and form when structuring and filling in a picture) and destruction (the dismantling of entrenched patterns). Such creativity translates into a restructuring of the outer and inner space of each person. Here we find the *ego complex* in its relationship to the all-embracing *self.*

Part II:

The Painting Series and its Interpretation

The picture functions as a third party conceived
between therapist and client – it has been "painted
between them." It is like a message, like a letter
passed back and forth between the two.

Introduction

by Christa Henzler

As we have already made clear, a series of paintings can come into being through a single person's active imagination. But a series can also be initiated in a group by using guided imagination. We will be exploring this thoroughly in a later chapter.

Experience has shown us that during the painting of a series, a "theme" usually emerges for each painter. This theme both initiates and illustrates an inner-psychic developmental process. Jacobi writes, "We could never observe more distinctly than we can in a series of pictures by the same painter the alternation between ordered and disordered phases (normal and dissociated states). Nor could we so clearly discern the emergence of an interior impulse produced to abrogate the painter's interior chaos by giving it form and shape".[1] Here Jacobi is suggesting the diagnostic value of a painting series.

Basically the same interpretation criteria apply for both single pictures and painting series. With a series one can additionally notice and compare the way pictorial elements are first presented (form, color, location, etc.) and then pinpoint when they have changed. Also when and

---

1   Jacobi, Jolande: *Vom Bilderreich der Seele: Wege und Umwege zu sich selbst*. Olten/ Freiburg im Breisgau 1969, p. 114. (An Italian translation is available: *Dal regno delle immagini dell'anima percorsi diretti e vie traverse per giungere a se stessi*, translated by Murrau, Marina Pia; Edizioni Magi, Roma 2003).

where picture objects have been added or left out is meaningful. Special attention should be given to changes in coloring, and it is helpful to follow each color throughout the painting series.

My experience of interpreting pictures has taught me that in every series a "picture message" is directed to the artist. I have learned to seek out this "message" and thereby discover the theme that the series brings to expression.

"To want to explain and interpret images out of the unconscious is a dangerous undertaking which should only be attempted very carefully. The images will frequently explain themselves. Often they are just snapshots of a current condition which later loses its significance. But some images carry greater weight: they illuminate basic tendencies and situations which can affect their authors' entire lives and destinies."[2] Here Jolande Jacobi is hinting at the possibility of understanding an image in its entirety if we approach it not just methodically, but also intuitively.

A methodical approach is most useful when we first let our intuition blaze a trail to unlock an image's contents. Intuitively gazing at an image allows us to notice the shape of its feelings and moods. These might include fright at seeing a burning house, liberation, appearing "meek as a lamb" in an idyllic family scene, or trepidation. As interpreters we must pay careful attention to how the image affects us personally. In this way we minimize the risk of a false interpretation from projecting our own unresolved inner problems and complexes onto the painter of the picture.

We should investigate the kind of processes that give rise to a specific painting: did the picture take form as it came out of the artist's hand? One student so aptly described this kind of painting as: "… it just slipped out of me". Or did the image already exist as a definite picture in the painter's mind before the paint touched the paper? If the latter is the case, then we should ask what was originally intended, and compare it with what actually came to be. Such questions cannot be answered by just looking at the pictures; they can only be clarified through discussion with the artists themselves. Picture interpretation can only really

2　Ibid, p. 149.

take place in dialogue. To make this clear I will continuously let the painter speak in the following pages. For example, during an interview Ms. E. described that for her, whenever she paints, a completely different picture appears than the one she originally imagines; but it is exactly this fact that causes her to reflect.

We should ask which feelings and emotions were experienced during the painting process. Were there interruptions? If so – at which point in the picture or in the picture series did they arise? Such differentiating questions about development are important, and the pictures themselves already include parts of the answers. Their expression became partially conscious during the painting process. Further questions will then arise, made possible by a well-aimed and accurate interpretation.

In this connection the question of the inner censor is important: how much censorship was imposed by consciousness during the painting process? Basically it can be said that those pictures which just "slip out" with little or no conscious censorship arise from deeper levels of the unconscious than those painted more consciously. They often include more archetypal material. In such cases it helps to have a good knowledge of possible collective meanings that such a picture might reveal. As Jacobi puts it: "Insofar as archetypal motifs are on hand, their more collective and general aspects must be looked into so they are not reduced to a purely personal problem."[3]

3   Ibid, p. 102.

Painting Against Death

Pictures of a Suicidal Crisis by Christa Henzler

This series illustrates graphically and eloquently how active imagination[4] in the context of painting can inadvertently translate into nothing less than an act of survival.

Judith, a 29-year-old woman, was first confronted with a deep-seated problem while taking part in a short-term self-awareness group. Through guided imagery followed by painting, she came up against a suicidal impulse that had always lurked within her, but now suddenly flared up and became enormously powerful. When the self-awareness group disbanded, Judith withdrew into social isolation because of this psychological pressure, and she began to paint intensively. A series of fifteen paintings resulted, which spurred her on to new stages of development. I have chosen five from this series for discussion here.

Judith wrangled intensely with her paintings; it was very important for her that she understood herself in their expression, which was often very difficult to do. She did as Jung recommends with active imagination: she let the images emerge from within and immediately began to deal with

4 Kast, Verena: Lecture manuscript about "Imagination" in the winter semester 1981/82 at the University of Zürich; now contained in Kast, Verena: *Imagination: Zugänge zu inneren Ressourcen finden.* Ostfildern 2012. (First printing Olten 1988). See also Kast, Verena: *Imagination als Raum der Freiheit.* Walter-Verlag AG, 1988, translated into English as *Imagination as Space of Freedom: Dialogue between the Ego and the Unconscious.* Fromm International Publishing Corp, New York 1993.

them artistically. She withdrew from all social commitments for almost two months during which she had contact almost exclusively with just one therapist, with whom she attempted to figure out the pictures.

14. The Family Tree

In the week after the last self-awareness group meeting, she found herself under enormous mental stress as she constantly took account of her life. At the end of this first week her first picture (Image 14) took form: a mighty black tree taking up almost the entire painting surface.

Judith "drew up" orange-brown paint into its roots that were also originally painted entirely black. *"There I had this feeling that orange-brown
symbolized life, which I still had in me. I did this only after I had first painted
the tree entirely black."* From a limb on the left of the tree a branch loosens
itself or breaks right off. It looks like an entire tree, since it is so big and
full of limbs. Out of the break flows dark red, and also on the branches
are small red leaves. Blood? Judith describes how she painted: *"I actually
only wanted to paint a branch breaking off, like in the middle of the picture.
But this branch kept getting longer and thicker. It kept branching out, and I was
completely astounded in the end as I saw that I had somehow painted a second
tree. I had only wanted to paint one."*

On the opposite side of the painting from the second tree, a tear falls,
blue with an orange and yellow nucleus – a frozen tear? It is dropping
onto dark, eerie-looking mountains that have been rather softly painted.
In fact, they remind the observer of stalagmites, whereby they express
a "deadly" loneliness. Judith painted blue-black clouds on the upper
border, out of which an eye with a red pupil gazes from the upper right.

This strong, powerful tree in black, the color of mourning, of problems, and of threat – is it really identical with Judith?[5] Is it not older and
mightier than she in her still young life could be? It looks more like the
"family trees" we often see in tree symbolization. Its broken-off limbs,
its darkness, and its heavy, forked branches speak of a sad, difficult and
oppressive history. In contrast, the left arm of the tree, which hangs
upside-down, becomes ever softer and more differentiated in its crown,
plus it is sprouting reddish leaves. As Judith beheld her picture, she
was no longer so sure whether she should identify with this dark tree
in the middle. After all, it was the small, more tender tree that had so
easily flowed out of her hand. She had painted it with strong emotional
feeling. What further suggests that this upper left tree symbolizes "her"
personality is the breaking off from her family tree.

At the time, Judith felt very strongly that the young tree would per-
ish, that it wouldn't live on. Judith was asking herself heavy existential
questions such as: "Why and for what should I live?" These circulated

---

5   Riedel, Ingrid: *Farben in Religion, Gesellschaft, Kunst und Psychotherapie*, Stuttgart 1983
    (Eighteenth printing completely reworked, expanded, and reformatted in 2008);
    p. 158ff.

continuously through her head. The relationship between the two trees made it clear to her that if she actually committed suicide, she would radically sever herself from the family tree and from an oppressive history. But she would simultaneously be sacrificing herself on the "family altar". By painting the left branch breaking off, she could sense how important that second tree was to her. She expressed it in the tender, fine branches and their little red leaves. *"The red leaves and the red at the break are expressions of pain for me,"* said Judith. But is this not, actually, an expression of a stirring self-worth – that she would feel pain over the destiny of this, "her" tree? And doesn't the red express vitality and passion and even a certain opposition to making herself a victim of the family?

For the friends who stood by Judith in this difficult crisis (although she constantly pushed them away) she painted the big, shiny, blue tear with the orange and yellow nucleus. Judith explained the bright colors of the tear as corresponding to the friends whom she associated with life. But she could not yet see that that these were also her colors that she too was bound up with the colorful energy field of blue with its emotional strength. Also the untarnished yellow with the orange expressed a source of light that compensated for so much black in the picture.

In the so-called mother corner, stalagmites grow up against the tear. When her mother was mentioned, Judith reacted movingly and admitted that she had lost her mother in puberty through cancer, which she had experienced as cruel and inhumane. Since that time she has pondered whether one can only avoid such an inhumane death by a freely chosen death. Then it occurred to her that it was mostly the bond with her father that had hindered her suicide. By looking at the so- called "father corner" we noticed that the young tree exactly in this locale breaks painfully from the bloody "father branch". Looking at the stalagmites in the mother corner, rising stiff and alone from the hard ground, through which no feeling can press, it became clear to Judith that she could not really grieve over her mother when she died, because the family members who did not know how to handle emotions, left her very alone. The eye in the upper region of blue clouds according to Judith stood for the fact that she looked at herself critically in her situation.

The overall impression is dominated by the black of the tree and to some extent the stalagmites. This black expresses Judith's big problem with her family history regarding grief and remonstration.

From the center of Judith's second picture (Image 15) a strange head with bared teeth and bloody eyes stares out at us. Judith intended it as a skull, as one might guess from the two large crosses protruding from the forehead and the receding cemetery atop the skull. In black one can make out a border between the cemetery and a triangle standing on its tip in the region of the brain. This skull, whose nose and cheekbones remain black and white, is otherwise bathed in a deep, dark blue defined by a thick, black border. From the left, out of the brown undergrowth an orange-brown hand with blue veins reaches toward the skull. To the right of the skull is placed a bottle. The color of the bottle is supposed to indicate its poisonous contents: a strong alcoholic drink in which a bunch of white tablets are dissolving. *"The poisonous green label indicates this,"* remarked Judith. The entire lower section of this landscape-formatted picture is taken up by brown undergrowth.

15. The Bull of Death

Judith wanted to portray the suicide situation with this picture; *"To lay one's hand on oneself,"* as Judith named it. The hand that perpetrates the suicide, the poison bottle as the method, the undergrowth as the place where she wanted to die – in her existential crisis Judith again and again sought refuge in the undergrowth. She sometimes stayed there until late into the night. This would be an appropriate place to die, in deep darkness and loneliness.

The skull with its cemetery symbolized death for Judith. However, looking objectively at the picture, what really "jumps out" is how lively this supposedly dead skull looks with blood flowing through its eyes, its teeth bared, and "cross horns" growing out of its forehead. Doesn't this skull look more like an angry bull that's gone wild and wants to wrest itself free from the hand of death that is reaching toward it, or set itself against the expected deadly destiny? Judith became aware of her own "inner bull" while discussing this picture, and the scales fell from her eyes as she was confronted with her own monstrous potential for aggression.

As I plunged myself into the picture, I suddenly had the feeling that this bull sprang out of the undergrowth wildly determined not to let this happen to it. Thus it stood for a part of Judith that reared up against the suicidal impulse. Perhaps it stood for the body that did not want to be poisoned. Judith stood in this tension-filled ambivalence that came to such strong expression in this picture. *"I could neither live nor die, because whenever I sought radical death, something in me fought against it. But I did not feel carried and held by life either."* This is how Judith described the situation.

At this point she could hardly eat without throwing up. She took this as a sign that she would encounter death, so she ate nothing more, and drank only fluids. She thought that by weakening her body she would come to the bottom of her question about life and death, and the decision to die could ripen. But the bull's head with its aggressive expression finally provided cause for a "delay".

It's true: the bull stands for the will to live, to fight, to resist. But with its strong, aggressive expression it also looks very destructive and unyielding. Judith came to a momentous insight regarding her self-destructive tendencies: could it be that her aggressive energies were being directed against herself in service to her own destruction and annihilation, rather than directed outwardly? This picture kept prolonging the "delay" and let Judith feel the ambivalence ever more strongly between her will to live and her desire to die.

This tension also expresses itself in the way the head is colored: red and blue stand here in a tension-filled relationship. The red that Judith selected is the color of blood, which is also connected to her experience of pain. But it also expresses vital life energy – it is a living color. Judith painted the "bull horns" and the blood vessels in the eyes blood-red. The cross is a Christian symbol standing for a deep-reaching transformation through death. Concerning the redness of blood she writes, "It is over and over again about the experience of pouring out and sacrificing vital life. It is not about a discarding, but rather about fully entering into eros, into battle, or into sacrifice. The completeness of this offering leads near to death or through death to renewed life."[6] Does a deep desire for a renewal of life express itself in Judith's red cross – a desire for a new, deep feeling of life? In any case *"the red gave me no peace"* she herself said. It confronted her with her aggression and with her desire for a thorough change in her attitude toward life. Thus red is a "close color", a color that startles, that confronts, in which one cannot get lost as is possible in blue. *"I could sink into the deep sea-blue,"* Judith mused, documenting this in another picture that she painted, where she cowered in the calyx of a flower at the bottom of the sea. (I have not presented this picture since it does not illustrate a clear step in Judith's psychic development.) These eyes with red veins and these red bullhorns are painted upon a deep blue and partially black-blue background. They are thereby in constant danger of being sucked down into this deep blue, just as Judith was in reality. (It is worth noting that the sea in its all-devouring depth stands symbolically for the unconscious.) Whenever Judith would give in to her death wish by letting her unconscious powers steer her thinking and acting, her red Godparent had to take a stand. But this stirred her aggressive and vital powers against herself. Her inner longings then became disconnected from life and bound to death.

6   Ibid, p. 25.

16. The Partitioned Face

Judith's fourth picture (Image 16) is an example of an explicit segmentation. A black wedge, which becomes a black line, divides the picture vertically into two opposing halves. These halves are divided horizontally into upper and lower quadrants by the placement of the individual items in the picture. A woman's head connects all four quarters of the picture. Its left half clearly belongs to the left side of the picture, which appears lighter and friendlier. The right side is dismal and "problematic". The right side of woman's face is bathed in deep dark red and lined with black veins. It is reminiscent of a skinned or scalped or in any case a very wounded face, and is framed by black-blue, shoulder-length hair. A blood red, upside down cross presses onto the top of the head (notice the parallel in the last picture) and appears to be leaking blood. Red streams flow from the cross and collect in a black triangle that "shoots in" from the right. This black triangle becomes the limitation for a bare, black-brown tree growing out of the lower right. On its right side a black pitchfork is stuck in the earth at its roots. The entire right side leaves a heavy, oppressive and threatening impression. It is therefore a relief to turn to the colorful, bright left side. Also here a tree grows up from below, and it can grow all the way up and sports all the colors of nature in-so-far-as it is painted as a "four-seasons tree". Judith did not anchor it as firmly in the earth as she did the right tree, but instead it lives with its entire strength while the other appears as if it were dead.

Above the "Vivaldi-tree", as Judith called it, is a rainbow (Antonio Vivaldi composed a violin concerto with the title "The Four Seasons" which meant a lot to Judith). The left half of the woman's face looks very serious and collected as if it knows about the right half.

In its vertical bifurcation the picture speaks for itself: quite obviously the right side reflects a complex problem. The left side compensates for the right by depicting an inner desire. Judith herself recognized remembrance and desire standing beside each other in this picture, but could not imagine these two worlds ever being brought into harmony. *"My reality was expressed in the right side, but it had nothing to do with the left. The left was merely an expression of my delusory and dubious hope for a livable life."* This was her opinion of the picture during her crisis situation, and it is true that it reveals a split into two worlds that includes something brutal. This is clear from the black, wedge-shaped triangle driving into the woman's hemispheres. And of course the woman is identical with Judith. Is this pointed, black wedge just an expression of Judith's self-torturing tendencies that feed themselves on the thoughts coming out of her head? Did she think this split completely through? The actual picture does not depict an unbridgeable abyss separating left from right, but simply reveals memories and a huge, entrapped desire. On one hand it is true that Judith's memories and inner desire are separated, but precisely through her face they are placed next to each other.

Judith very much devalued the left side, although it takes up exactly as much space as the right. Instead, she was fixated on the right half of the face with which she identified. At that time she could not yet see that by painting this picture she had become capable of bringing together the opposites of past and present (and in a wider sense also death and life), which she so strongly felt within herself. And she could not yet imagine just how much she needed the left side in order to withstand the right side. She didn't realize that it was possible to create a work of art, and by doing so to also create within herself a counterbalance to compensate for her oppressive past experiences. She needed this counterbalance in order to look her past in the eye, and she did that for the first time without compromise in this picture. In it she found three symbols: the tree, the triangle, and the cross. In place of the eerie stalagmites of the first picture (Image 14), which Judith associated with her mother's terrible illness and morbidity, now stands a wounded, earth-colored mother tree whose growth is seriously hindered by an invasive triangle. The triangle stabs from the right side into the woman's blue hair. (Hair stands for energy and strength in many cultures.) Not only does it inhibit the tree's growth, it is likewise something dangerous and threatening. Where does this threat come from? What does this triangle symbolize for Judith?

The right side of the painting usually symbolizes the outer world and is called the "you-side" (as opposed to the "I-side"). From there one is attacked, wounded, or oppressed. When asked about this, Judith admitted some serious experiences. After her mother's death she came under the tyranny of a male attachment figure whose brutality sometimes got out of hand. What happened to her gives the triangle in this picture a very powerful meaning. It stands for a negative patriarchal family domination under which Judith's mother (recall the growth-inhibition and woundedness of the tree in the lower right corner) as well as her daughter, had to suffer. For Judith's mother was reared by a tyrannical and brutal father. So it is becomes clear on the subjective level that the masculine in Judith as well as in her mother took on very destructive forms. This is what incited Judith's self-destructive tendencies, finding expression in her suicidal impulse; and in her mother's susceptibility to cancer. In this connection the pitchfork makes sense: a man once threatened Judith with one, and so now she supposes it to be the murder instrument.

Across from this corner of oppression and pain, Judith places the "four-seasons tree". It is growing straight and tall, spreading its branches wide, has the possibility to continue growing, and sports the colors of all four seasons. It stands for Judith's desire for wholeness and natural unfolding of her personality. She reports that *"still today this tree gives me strength, for it symbolizes not only my desire for self development, but also makes it clearly imaginable that after every winter the spring will come again."*

The left side of the face reflects the grave doubt and great seriousness she had during her suicidal crisis, when the dark side of her past still had to be overcome. But then the cross that had already appeared in the second picture is now banging against the dark, right side of the face, and is turned nearly up side down. "To set something on its head" is a metaphor. It means looking at something from a completely different perspective. But it can also mean to oppose something that until now was the case, as illustrated by the common German saying: "And even if you stand on your head, I won't do it!" Both meanings made sense to Judith. *"I settled the score with the Pietists."* This was one meaning of the cross on its head for her. *"... in so far as I could without a guilty conscience put aside their moral values and norms, which they falsely deduced from the Christian cross. Also in the picture I could let the cross empty out ... which I think for me at that time meant winning freedom. Under the moralizing authority of the Pietists I could never deal with my suicidal ideation, in the sense that I actually wanted to understand why these ideas kept awakening in me. It was never allowed, and that was bad for me."*

Judith had worked a couple years as a Baptist Sunday-school teacher for children. To set the cross of Pietism on its head and to let it empty out was for her an act of liberation. Although it stands as an ancient and universal symbol for warmth, light, life, liberation and protection, in other words for the overcoming of every division[7] ; it had to be placed on its head in the context of Judith's life. Yet it worked as an ancient symbol in Judith's case anyway. It pointed her beyond Christianity to a source of ceaselessly regenerative life. The symbol affected her imagination and creativity such that her suicidal ideation became conscious as a deep inner need for transformation. Could such spiritual transformation only take place because she allowed in the suicidal impulse? Did she even have to pursue it? Should she not have fought against it? Would that mean that only through this transformation, which made possible for her a new self-understanding and a new relationship to the world, could she make peace with herself? The rainbow placed opposite the cross is a

---

7   Rosenberg, Alfons: *Einführung in das Symbolverständnis: Ursymbole und ihre Wandlungen.* Freiburg in Breisgau 1984, p. 128.

symbol of peace and reconciliation[8]. It stands over the four-seasons tree in the picture's region of desire.

The way all of the symbols in the painting relate to Judith's self-portrait (they all touch her head) raises the question of whether overcoming the suicidal impulse needed to go through her head. This seems to be the impulse's inner logic. And it is confirmed by the fact that Judith never attempted an actual suicide, but only struggled with the possibility. But right up until the painting of this picture her struggle had been neither consoling nor constructive.

Through this picture it became clear to her that creative expression and thinking presented her with the possibility of probing her problem and asking questions. Moreover, it also became clear that she was struggling with her past.

3. The Plants vs Destruction

Judith's next picture (Image 3, p. 43) was the seventh in the whole series and was painted after almost four weeks of fasting. Again it was

8   Oesterreicher-Mollwo, Marianne: *Herder-Lexikon Symbole*, Freiburg im Breisgau 1993, p. 131. (Available as a French edition: Oesterreicher-Mollwo, Marianne: *Petit Dictionnaire des Symboles*, 1992).

divided into two opposing regions, one lighter and one darker, but this time by a 3-centimeter-wide, diagonal black arc. It runs from the upper left to the lower right, but does not go all the way to the lower right corner. Rather it hits the bottom of the picture a bit sooner. A deep black wedge sticks out of the black arc at about its midpoint and jabs a woman in the upper spine as she cowers in the left corner. She is crouched holding her head in both hands and faces left toward a shadowy skull. A second face is painted into her body and is looking in the opposite direction toward the right side of the picture. There it sees beyond the black arc a green plant with robust green leaves spreading out over the entire right side of the picture. The shapes of the leaves resemble hands in various hand-gestures. This hearty plant grows from the lower right into the upper right and, because of the close-up perspective, it appears to grow right out of the picture. In the upper left, by contrast, our gaze falls upon a "night city" in which no window is lit up. Perhaps it is a ghost town that has died out, abandoned by all forms of life.

In the center of the picture a "winter tree" stretches out all the way to the lower boundary of the picture. It is rooted in blue ground, is in contact with the black triangle and the woman's body and hangs down like the left tree of the first picture (Image 14).

Comparing the two pictures, we notice that both are divided into two parts, this time not vertically, but diagonally. But what is especially noticeable is that Judith reverses the content of the two parts. Now it is on the right side that a plant grows vigorously and spreads green leaves of various shades over that entire portion of the picture, whereas on the left an inner world "darkened by dead night"[9] seems to pervade almost two-thirds of the entire painting surface. What does this reversal of sides mean? What underlying experiences could prompt Judith to now paint a shadowy skull instead of her "Vivaldi tree" and a lush verdant plant instead of her deep dark past?

This vital plant with its "hand leaves" is on the "you side" and appears to depict a current and "close" experience Judith is having. It is connected to the outer world and at the same time vigorous enough to supplant those grievous experiences of long ago. When asked about this

9   Sachs, Nelly: *Fahrt ins Staublose: Die Gedichte der Nelly Sachs*. Frankfurt am Main 1961, p. 308. The translated poem *is* *"Journey into a dustless realm"*.

Judith spontaneously admitted that she had distanced herself from her good and true friends, thinking only about death. It was her relationship to the woman with whom she regularly discussed her pictures that she portrayed as this plant. The "second" face that Judith painted in the breast region of the crouching body unconsciously reinforces that connection. It looks toward the plant. And the face is directly related to the veins of the plant's lower left leaf by their mutual color. This means that Judith not only acknowledges the plant's "hands of friendship", but she can also experience herself within this relationship. Yet Judith paints herself overtly as a cowering woman sunken within herself and turned toward the shadowy skull. Here again the compensatory principle is at work: since on the right-side life is able to assert itself, Judith can on the left side turn and face her inner image of death and allow her death fantasy to play itself out.

Here the meaning of the diagonal division becomes clear. It heightens the contrast between the lower left and upper right corners. Because of the curve, the lower left is almost twice as large as the upper right. The long, black wedge further amplifies this impression. Judith paints herself as a woman in the lower left corner who is looking into the lower left corner: we know from experience that this region often represents the unconscious. But the second face is looking toward the upper right corner, which is often the region of consciousness. This depiction is not just about inner compared to outer – introversion and extroversion. Nor is it just about Judith's inner desire compared to her dark past, as in the last picture. Rather, this picture depicts an additional extraordinary state of tension between consciousness and the unconscious. Judith appears to have come much closer to her existential question about self-chosen death, because in this picture she looks it directly in the eye. After all, she was in a very weakened condition due to her weeks-long self-starvation. Now she paints a deep tension, sadness, and inner conflict via her cowering woman with a second face looking in the opposite direction.

This tension is not just expressed by the diagonal division of the picture, but also by the violet color of the women's bodies. Heimendahl assesses violet as the most disunified and ambivalent of all colors in that it indecisively carries the red pole and the blue pole within itself. Or as Cooper puts it, we see in violet the color of transformation and balancing. In either case violet is the color of creative tension in some of its variegated gradations, but in others it expresses a torturous stress.[10] Judith's violet mixture moves the observer to a torturous tension that she haphazardly tries to neutralize by reaching for its complementary color, yellow, to paint her "breast head". I found that very pleasant for my eyes.

Even as a beholder I could feel the tension in this picture. Judith describes it thus: *"Because of my strict fasting, I came literally and somehow inevitably nearer to my question. Logically the question became more urgent, since at the end of my fast stood the possibility of death: a couple of tablets and the weakened body would hardly resist. But there was a bigger conflict within me: because of my pictures and my direct, consequent and exclusive conflict with my "no longer wanting to live" I could no longer avoid the philosophical consideration of the meaning or meaninglessness of suicide. It was damned serious. I felt myself often torn between that which I wished from life – for I had very big expectations from life that I believed could not be fulfilled – and that which I believed I would find in death: namely my peace."* To my question about her life's ambition, she answered: *"I want to have an inner fulfilled life, not only to function, but to experience tenderness in my life, I want to find the meaning for my life, to know why I exist."*

Maybe Judith can once again discover the personal meaning of and tenderness for her life when she descends into her inner darkness, as this painting appears to express. And what does she find there? Pictorially she stands here across from death and perhaps the weird, abandoned "ghost town" has something to do with it. The town is a place of communal life, of doing business, a place of encounter, of wealth and enjoyment, in a word – of life, as it reveals itself externally. But it is also a place of isolation, misery, poverty and loneliness. In Judith's picture it is empty of people, dark, dead, as if burnt out.

What does this town have to do with Judith's experiences? What does it bring in the context of the picture? Does it perhaps have something to do with Judith's entry into the world, or does it stand for Judith's being cut off from the outer world? The green plant on the right, however, and also the tree in the middle seem to speak strongly against this, as

---

10 Riedel, Ingrid: *Farben in Religion, Gesellschaft, Kunst und Psychotherapie*, pp. 134ff.

does her second face that does not turn its gaze to the "dead" town. These questions we asked ourselves and through them could get off the ground with the ghost town. Judith had often "played theater" as she put it, and added: *"I have traveled to several cities, lived there, formed many contacts, functioned outstandingly in them, was friendly, helpful and loved, but in myself I never felt at home; often I was empty, as if burned out, confused – but nobody was allowed to notice this."* Judith's inner experience is reflected in this burned out night city, in the same way she found herself in the outer world and in her relationships. The graphic imagination that in her ghost town, Judith could submerge herself, comes very close to the image of suicide. I understand this to be an absolute self-alienation, a "having lost oneself", being completely unrelated to oneself and to others. And with such a life-feeling one must either be dull or suicidal.

Diagonally down from this night city grows another tree. It appears to be rooted in the clouds. In India people imagine that the tree of life is rooted in heaven and grows into the earth, the reality, into bodiliness[11]. Is that what Judith's up-side-down tree means? If so, it would be another counterbalance to her thoughts of death, to her *"becoming ever less"* as she expresses it. The eyes of her inner face would also see this tree.

The painting in its entirety speaks of Judith's existential test like no other before.

Judith's fifth picture (Image 17) came to be after she had already fasted for six weeks and was in a completely weakened condition.

It appeared that something essential was forced into the center in Judith's psychological process. This is expressed by a single, central, graphic element in this picture. What is evident is a tree, but no normal tree. It is a seeing, a looking tree. This tree is given eyes in every direction with large, violet pupils surrounded by dirt-brown "branch hair". These round, wide-open eyes, with the surrounding brown "branch hair" awaken associations of an alert animal. This impression is strengthened more through the two mighty outer, upward-stretching limbs that give the eyes and the "branch hair" a protective frame and simultaneously appear to be two outstretched arms.

11 Oesterreicher-Mollwo, Marianne: *Herder-Lexikon Symbole,* p. 24.

17. Emaciated Tree

The tree appears to be loosening itself out of the earth, and a watery blue from the background washes the root system. There are still earth tones (brown, grey, and black) recognizable in the root areas that lose their intensity in many places because of the watery blue.

The tree is reminiscent on the one hand of the great, heavy, black "family tree" of the first painting (Image 14) in its wintry barrenness, but on the other hand of the up-side-down tree limb with its brown, finely branched structure. These two related trees of the first picture here come into their own as they become one, while still bearing some of the black woundedness of the family tree. This is expressed for example, through the right lower limb stump. This limb stump refers to a heavy loss that Judith has endured. It is probable that it refers to the death of her mother, since it is painted in the "mother corner" of the picture.

It is again a barren winter tree. However, with these two round eyes and the consistently upward-reaching direction of the branches, it gives a very lively impression. Often such winter trees are painted in harsh and difficult times, but these are often the times in which self-encounter is possible, for in winter the tree reveals to itself its own structure. Judith's tree, although a winter tree, appears to express much more than just tough times in which nothing can bloom at that moment and no leaves unfold. By the wide-open eyes Judith grants it a bodily aspect. The tree looks at her, and does so directly, unmediated. Does it look sad, shocked, or accusing? In any case it is no friendly look. The finely arranged branches surrounding the eyes, and the two black-brown outer forks lifted upwards heighten the impression of it being a body.

The brown-branched limbs, essentially finer and more differentiated than the other limbs, remind us of hair standing up on a cat's back, and the two upraised outer limbs look like a person throwing up the arms. I have a feeling this gives the picture a strong presence, an immediate urgency. What is urgent, what is going on? Does this "tree glance" express an immediate situation? Judith said of it, *"This tree came to be at the end of my sixth week of fasting. I was extremely weakened and could hardly stand up. I cut back severely on my fluid intake, and that accelerated my weak condition. I was mostly in a daze. In addition, I suffered a very painful dental procedure, which was difficult because of my condition. A tooth had to be pulled, but then the hole abscessed. I had crazy pain, but the tablets did not work. And then this picture came to be. When it was finished, it went through me like a bolt of lightening: I understood immediately what it meant. My body was looking at me, disappointed and full of panic. I was deeply touched, looked down at myself, looked at my grey face, the deep rings under my eyes, sensed my absolutely depleted strength, and knew suddenly that I was too young to die."*

The determination to live on did not somehow enter Judith's mind; it did not flow from a decision of her will; she had not thought it; rather it came primarily as a direct, unmediated, experienced life-impulse. It was instigated through this picture, through this "body tree", which was being loosened out of its fertile soil and the anchoring of its roots. Judith had to give in to her death wish to the very end, probe her death fantasy to the very depths, in order to again allow life.

Judith's psychic process affirms Hillman's thesis that the death impulse must be seen as a version of the death experience, which is a necessity of life for the human soul. "Suicide is the urge for hasty transformation. This is not premature death ... but the late reaction of a delayed life which did not transform as it went along. It would die all at once, and now, because it missed its death crises before."[12] Judith's own evaluation of her suicidal crisis sounds like this four years later: _"I had to go all the way to the end in order to again find a new beginning. Through this crisis I have learned that I did not mean radical death by my death fantasy. It was basically a freedom fantasy. And so I have only gradually understood that I actually wanted to live a different life."_ When I asked her how her life went after this crisis, she replied: _"Right away it was as if I had to learn how to live again. I stood on very wobbly legs, not just physically. I learned in the weeks, months, yes years afterward, first that I myself belong to a fulfilled life. I mean by that, I had to be ready myself to confront my history, my life, and also my own destiny. In intensive therapy I encountered people who energetically placed themselves in the path of my tendency to escape and thereby revealed to me that it isn't enough just to say "it doesn't matter" whether I exist or not. The situation became clearer and clearer to me that I wanted to run away. Most importantly however is that I can now understand myself better: in my fantasies, in my feelings and also in my feelinglessness. I can do this openly, even when there are many other problems. There were also more difficult aspects, but never again in this radical form. Painting remains very important for me. It has become my possibility to express when something is unclear in my head or in my belly. But also I simply enjoy interacting with colors."_

I chose these five paintings from Judith's collection because as I said before, each one of them led to a new stage of development, or at least made possible a new level of consciousness. In the first picture (Image 14) it became clear to Judith that her suicidal fantasy was not simply a coincidental product of her psyche, but rather was bound up closely with her family history. The second picture (Image 15) confronted her with her aggressive energy, which she often directed against herself. Because of this picture she understood that suicide could be the same as an act of aggression directed inward. The third picture (Image 16) reflected a conflict with her past through which however, her desire

---

12 Hillman, James: _Suicide and the Soul_, 2nd edition. Spring Publications Inc, Woodstock Connecticut. New edition 1997, p. 73.

was also awakened. The fourth painting (Image 3?) shows the current condition of the crisis most precisely, where Judith must soon come to a decision, a decision that she makes in the fifth picture (Image 17).

It was important to me to demonstrate with these pictures how a life crisis can be handled through painting out of the unconscious. One can really say in the end that Judith painted her way through this existential crisis.

Fascination with Blue

Images of an Addiction

With the title "Fascination with Blue" I want to present a further picture series, painted by a 37 year-old commercial artist during a one-and-a-half-year therapy. The series was painted in only three weeks and marks the turning point of the therapy. This man painted with the color blue in all its nuances and symbolic meanings. For example in German *blau sein*, literally "to be blue", means "to be drunk", and the French "peur bleu", literally blue fear, means "to be terrified". He painted until this color transformed itself into red-orange, a color of inter-human contacts and a joyful turning toward life. But before I get into the interpretation of this picture series, I want to make a few remarks about the man's situation:

He came to therapy because of depression and anxiety that were causing a shaking in his right hand. The quivering hand might suggest that the anxieties could be the result of alcoholism. In addition to being a commercial artist, he painted and made woodcuts in his free time. The shaking overcame him primarily during the exhibition openings when he presented his creative works. These exhibition openings naturally meant a lot to him, but he became worked up every time as he was presenting himself as an artist and thereby exposing himself to public critique.

As regards alcohol consumption, his drinking pattern was that of the classic quarterly binge drinker, every four to six months. It always flared up in the incubation phase of his creative work: after he had collected and mentally arranged his creative ideas, they caused something like an "infection" in him. Because these ideas half slumbered and half rumbled in his unconscious and more or less fed off his unconscious during this phase, they often incited an agonizing condition akin to labor pains in a pregnancy, where the creation wants to be born. Very often a fear of failure, demoralization, and doubt about his self-worth or artistic ability would emerge during these times of "advanced pregnancy".

Everyone who works creatively knows this tense condition. Research into creativity identifies this as the second phase in every creative process. But this man, because of his depressive disorder, could usually not endure this phase, so he took up a habitual over-consumption of alcohol, which he otherwise kept within bounds. This was clearly alcohol abuse. For every creative person, the results of such abuse are unfortunate. Namely, the alcohol drowns the sprouting creative idea. It was difficult to convince this man to stop drinking, despite his fear that it would cause his hand to shake. His alcohol abuse greatly hindered his work and then brought him shame at his exhibition openings. Yet in the in-between-phases he was months long sober. It was therefore almost a stroke of luck that he had an accident that forced him to spend several weeks in a clinic, where he had to be weaned from alcohol.

If this one-time withdrawal from alcohol had not taken place in the middle of a depth-psychotherapy with my colleague, what happened next would probably not have been possible. This man was actually addicted to the flow of vitally creative ideas. Yet for some reason he couldn't fully admit or accept his creative talents. He somehow rejected his gifts, although they were indeed there, and as a result was constantly falling into depression. He then drowned the depression in alcohol. For this reason, this man's alcoholism and his deeper addictions could only be successfully treated by encouraging his true creative work. Courage is what finally healed him: courage and real trust in himself. He became a liberated, creative artist, who made a good name for himself in his region.

His therapy was at first irregular: he was erratic in his coming and going. But a turning point came the moment he took up his therapist's suggestion that he paint his usual attitude toward life. Although he did not feel inspired at the time, he did make an attempt.

The first picture (Image 18) depicts him as tiny, bent forward, and without visible feet, arms, or hands: his means of movement and action are clearly imperceptible to him at this time. He stands on a ground more yellow than green. It could be the desert floor. A gray mountain towers over him with its summit stretching into the upper left region of the picture. The painting expresses his attitude toward life: burdensome, oppressive, indeed "like a mountain."

18. Like a Haunted Mountain

19. Under Black Sky

That the summit looms distinctly in the picture's upper left may well suggest that this mountain, which represents the artists attitude toward life, is related to difficulties with the father. We know from experience that father issues often appear in this quarter of a picture. It might have to do with a specific demand imposed by a father, or a highly stressful expectation that a son internalizes and takes on. The high mountain in this painting symbolizes the high achievement that was expected of the artist earlier in his life, and which he now expects of himself. This self-imposed pressure is now crushing him, because he has never resolved it, even if he could have. It is worth mentioning here that depression is often depicted as a pressing down or crushing. The color gray may indicate indecision, lack of courage, or confession. This man wants to be – indeed has to be an artist; and yet he doesn't have confidence in himself. As he himself puts it, he has become "only" a commercial artist. His frequent self-devaluation of course, pushes him into depression.

The horizon above the mountain, the sky above, is even darker than the mountain itself: slate gray with a trace of powder blue. Does this bode for even worse weather? Does it indicate, for example, a definitive darkening of the situation into deep depression hanging over him like this sky? A further color is worth noticing. The red with which the painter characterizes himself, functions like a signal: he wants to be noticed, he wants the therapist to notice him, he wants the world to pay attention to him, no matter how tiny and stooped he portrays himself! This red is also a colorful way to express an SOS call. But above all it shows that at least he is still aware of himself. Vitality and a libido are still alive in him. Vitality and libido are usually symbolized by red, the color of the blood and of fire, and thereby the warmth of life – and that is why red is the favorite color of children.

The second picture (Image 19), painted perhaps one day later, is clearly related to the first. But it shows distinctive changes. The painter, portrayed again as a red person, now stands completely in the fore-ground directly at the bottom of the picture, literally on the lower edge of the paper. Young children often paint in such a way that their figures stand directly on the bottom edge of the picture. This shows that they do not yet have an individual standpoint, but rather use the one provided by the paper. Our artist's standpoint has become very small – smaller than in Image 18. In fact he is in danger of completely loosing his standpoint. At the same time this disappearing standpoint has itself acquired the color red, and therefore a signal character. Any observer, not just the therapist, should notice that he is in danger of loosing the ground under his feet. At the same time the head of the red man is lifted up; in Image 18 it was still sunken and remained unnoticeable because it simply fused into the sack-like body. Now rudimentary arms stretch upwards as if seeking help. The mountainous image of the first painting, with its weighty, demanding attitude toward life, has become broader and rounder. It could still be a mountain, but it might also be the high, arched ceiling of a cave or the interior of a cathedral. The light gray of the first picture has become very dark and contains strong strokes of black, but also of blue. The dirty gray of the beginning, the depressive sadness, has transformed into dark black-blue tending toward blue – a rather solemn, even tragic tone. It is as if this person stands under a tragic history or a somber destiny, which he experiences in a space which one could almost call religious. The sky over him is in pure black, and that is a color of absoluteness.

One can look at this picture in two ways. On the one hand, it could point to a grandiose idea that dictates this man's life as an over-compensation for his narcissistic wound. In this case, he understands himself as being tragically assigned a task that he cannot fulfill. But we can also look at this painting as reflecting a deep, authentic inkling that he really does have a destiny. However, for as long as he does not fulfill it, or chooses not to realize it (although his talents press him to do so) this purpose towers over him like a tragic doom.

Image 20 indirectly supports this second perspective, because here the human figure starts to move. Comparing the figure with that of the previous picture, one sees that irritation and inner motion begin to stir. By painting Image 19 the artist apparently steered himself in the direction of progress. The mountain-like or cathedral-like image in the first two pictures has metamorphosed into a floating, swirling vortex. The entire sky is set into motion. It is like the swirl of creation, the spiral beginning of all material being and of all life. It resembles both the unfolding leaves of a tender fern and the churning of a mighty cyclone.

The spiral's blue untwists its black at the nucleus. Blue is reminiscent of the sky with its emotional-spiritual, transcendental symbolism. Until now the center of these paintings has been a complex of grey-black, a depression in the face of the artist's burdensome destiny. But those colors begin to move appreciably here and to mix with emotional-spiritual soul energy. Such a transformation of energies is also suggested by light traces of violet – the color of creative tension and metamorphosis.

Under this wildly moving sky we again see our little person. He, too, is beginning to move. Now with arms and legs that enable him to propel himself and to act, he is flailing his arms as if awe-struck or appalled. The exterior heavens in some way represent his interior heaven; what does it expect from him? Will it suck him up in its churning movement? The ground beneath the painter, his standpoint, has grown somewhat and is dark red, which differentiates it from the orange-red person. The artist has clearly become a little more conscious of himself since painting the last picture, where figure and ground completely bled into each other.

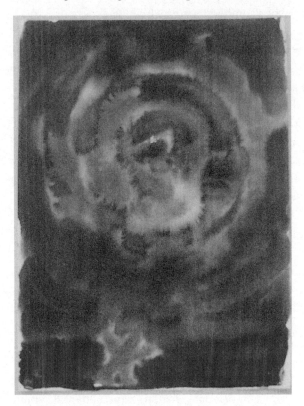

20. Vortex of Creation

In Image 21 our little person gains still more ground. The energies in him and over him appear calmer and more collected. But the picture is still filled with forceful, dynamic tension. The creative whirlpool has thickened into a primarily violet heavenly body. This is the color of transformation, and in the church is the color of the passion of Christ. Traces of black give this heavenly body plasticity and sharp contours. The artist has found his passion in both senses of the word – fervor and suffering. He is called to be a creatively active (passionate) person, but if he does not live this out, if he disowns it, it will twist him with unbearable pressure, that will drag him down into depression (passion as suffering). In this picture he stands directly under the heavenly body, his star of destiny. He is still stooped and a bit sunken into himself. But his figure is more contoured than in the first picture. Now he stands almost in the middle of the picture. In the first three pictures he was standing more to the left, symbolically pushed in the direction of unconsciousness. Those pictures mirrored his waking life where he found himself living more unconsciously than consciously.

21. Celestial Body

Indeed he was barely conscious of himself. The current figure is still red, drawing attention to himself as before, both from himself as well as from others who might look at the painting. He is standing on blue ground, which is lighter than the ground in his previous paintings.

Perhaps it is glass, which would be transparent but not very load bearing. The deep, dark, blue sky gives the impression of being far mightier than his small, barely structured ego. At least his vocation to creativity is now depicted as a mysterious star above him and no longer as a gray mountain. The first painting series ended with this picture, having taken just a few days to paint. It was succeeded a week later by the next series.

22. Stooped Over

With Image 22 the artist applies himself anew. He has gained much ground and now stands on a fresh green strip of lawn. His conscious living space, his standpoint, has become much clearer than it was before and is characterized by hopeful, vegetative green. This ground is clearly demarcated from the dominant blue sky, which represents the heavenly realm of fantasy and spirituality, but also for the artist a demanding realm dictating his creative vocation. The blue burdens him so heavily that he is bent down – perhaps because he still doesn't completely accept it, but rather forbids it, as the diagonal slash inside the picture might be suggesting. He is standing in the middle of the picture, which always means that he also puts himself at the center. But he is looking left, the direction of the past, suggesting regression. He protects his head with his arms. The arms are therefore not free to work nor the head free either to gain perspective or look for anything, or generate ideas. The sky again burdens him as a very compact force, as *"peur bleu"*, as blue fear.

23. Under Heaven's Burden

Image 23 resembles Image 22 so much that we might ask (as with a picture puzzle) how many differences to Image 22 can be found? First we see the man. He no longer just droops to the left, but now actively sets himself in motion toward the left. His head appears freer, but also emptier than in the previous picture. He is simply left inside the un-painted white. The painter has set himself into motion in the direction of regression and the unconscious, slowly allowing his usual depression to become overpowering. The sky has changed from the clear ultrama-rine of the first picture back to black-blue touched with a bit of powder blue. What I find above all to be the most meaningful transformation from Image 22 to 23 is that the sky begins to sink down onto his back, illustrated by long, inverted, curving strokes. The man takes his vocation upon his shoulders and bears it under heaven as a heavy burden.

24. Giant Atlas

Finally in Image 24 the sky, with everything it symbolizes, becomes again completely blackened and lies upon the man's shoulders like an overpowering, dark, cosmic stone. At least he has turned himself forward and now stands frontal before us like Atlas, the giant who carries the world on his shoulders, or like Sisyphus with his inescapable boulder. We are supposed to see how much he suffers and how he must bear everything! Again the hands and feet have not at all been suggested, completely left out of the picture. This man who takes the whole world upon his shoulders is at the same time recognizable as one who can neither act (for which he needs hands) nor move forward (for which he needs feet!).

Here we see him as someone caught in the throes of a really grandiose idea. He bears his heavy vocation like the savior of the world. With his art he doesn't want only to express himself, he wants to paint essential and momentous themes; he wants to explore new possibilities of expression that were not known before him. He himself admitted in a discussion that he understands his artistic creativity as akin to that of a van Gogh or a Dostoyevsky or even *"as a Christ-like passion, a participation in making sense of and saving the world."* He thereby over-reaches and over-extends himself and afterwards must humble himself so much that he can only bear it by drowning the humiliation in alcohol. Although he may not have been conscious of it, in this picture he at least gains a broad, bluish-green stand point, and bluish-green can stand for steadfastness. Unfortunately, this picture (which ends the series of the second week) betrays a grave danger that the self-imposed burden of the painter's pretension will break him down, which could cause him to regress, fall back into depression and with that resume his addiction.

In Image 25 a peculiar countermovement takes place that we see often in therapy. Jung calls it *enantiodromia*. It is an interior movement that occurs when one pole of a complex has completely exhausted, plumbed and played itself out. Image 25 shows the creative impulse coming not from above, not from the heavens, not from fantasy and great ideas, but out of the earth, the vital sphere that is grounded in the motherly. Here the black-brown earth heaves up. Brown, being the color of the ground, and so of Mother Earth, is also often the color of constraint, of braking, and blockage. Here the earth buckles upwards from a momentum originating very deep down, a mighty pressure out of the earth's interior which makes the ground vault like a phallus, like a penis. From the pressure coming from deep in the earth, deep in the body, this phallus arches up: symbol of the creative potential surging out of this man. The pressure can and will come up from below, from the vital sphere, and not from above out of the heavenly sphere. A sky-blue strip of the heavens surrounds the black-brown phallus, enfolding it like a ribbon. The sky gives him space by opening itself like a cupola.

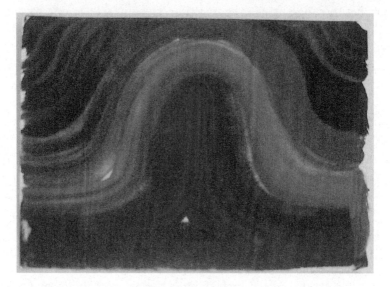

25. Phallus out of Earth

Image 25 appeared so promising in view of the painter's new entrée to the creativity which wells up from below, from his base. But his access to the brown of the earth and the motherly breaks away again, as if he didn't trust it.

In Image 26 the phallic image metamorphoses: it gets bigger. And it becomes glassy, transparent and blue, as if made of ice. The painter has elevated himself. Said differently, he has become high. The creative impulse of Image 25 returns in this painting as a psychedelic high painted under the influence of alcohol. Our figure now stands insecurely upon the dizzying height of a blue phallic iceberg.

26. Phallus out of Ice or At a Dizzying Height

He stands deliriously upon the same mountain that in Image 18 he had allowed to tower over him. But how much danger he is in, standing up there! He turns toward the left on the tip of this phallus looking down light-headedly. Instead of accessing the creative powers of the phallus within himself, his ego dances around the tip of this iceberg like a child delighting in scaring himself with dangerous feats. The little red man's head has grown larger in relation to his body, like one expects in the drawings of three- to four-year-olds. The bodily proportions correspond to those of a small child, revealing just how much the artist has regressed and how little he is really in control of the situation. He looks almost like a sleepwalker captured and controlled by an eerie blue force field. In his intoxication the artist has managed to compose a dreamy, exotic, transparent space of pure blue from his creative unconscious – a remarkable portrayal of the "blue condition" in which every constraint dissolves and one experiences a sort of floating, yearning, pulsing state of mind that points both beyond itself all the way to the sphere of the transcendent, and at the same time inward to dissolution into nothingness. Because it can lead to visionary experiences, creative people who are addicted to inspiration have often sought to bring on this blue condition with the aid of drugs and alcohol – above all the psychedelic drugs hashish, marijuana, and LSD. Unfortunately such visions usually disappear when the high is over. They can't be maintained into the final creative phase, where they can be documented. As the wave of potential creativity crests, the images get wobbly, like our little red man. He remains important to himself but cannot avail himself of the potential creativity. He cannot capture the vision and bring it into reality.

The blue space of Image 26 is quite nuanced. The further toward the left one goes (the zone of the unconscious), the lighter the space becomes. The further to the right one goes (the zone of consciousness), the greater the darkness becomes. At the time of this painting, our painter is obviously standing completely in the realm of unconsciousness. At least the picture depicts a division between the upper and lower halves. Above is still separate from below, but it is not a qualitative difference. Everything is plunged into and dissolved into darkness above as well as below. They are colors of the unconsciousness and of dreams. The painter's ego complex is neither coherent nor contoured enough to distinguish itself from the unconscious, which here expresses itself in black. From very deep below, out of fathomless depths, emerges this ice phallus like the tip of an iceberg. Even more frozen creative energy than we may expect lies below.

In Image 27 the red man on what I call "the blue ice phallus" begins to wobble. The *"peur bleu"*, the "blue fear" has taken hold of him as a panic as he realizes just how ungrounded he is. He orients himself more toward the right, meaning that he is trying to find balance on the side of consciousness. This is further revealed by the light coming from the right. There is a break in the blue that works itself in from the right. The entire blue space seems to be wavering when compared with Image 26, as if it is dissolving itself in waves of water and ice. The tip of the blue phallus has become smaller, and thereby the man's standpoint is also smaller: his situation becomes more pointed – more acute. In the lower left side of the picture, which often points to the abyss of the collective unconscious, the blue has thickened into midnight blue. This abyss appears really threatening, so that the man's attempt to counterbalance himself toward the right is quite understandable, if not actually promising. According to his bodily proportions, he is more mature here than in Image 26.

27. The "Blue" Fear (also The "Drunk" Fear)

In Image 28 the bodily reorientation toward the right, the direction of becoming conscious, finally takes place. Also the wavering phallus of ice becomes more like a stairway, perhaps also of ice, which the man in red is attempting to climb. The man's arms stretch forward, indicating that he is trying to feel. This indicates a proactive impulse to do something positive in order to extricate himself from his precarious, sleepwalking situation. The ground upon which he stands no longer resembles the tip of an iceberg nor the tossing sea, but rather is painted with calm, broad, horizontal strokes. This ground has the appearance of horizontally placed blocks that would really then be load-bearing, even when made of ice. Immediately around the man the blue has lifted, illuminating his path.

28. The Turnaround

There is much in this picture to suggest that our artist has been seeking, and can now find a way out of the *"peur bleu"* or "blue fear." We glimpse the possibility that he may now be able to extricate himself from the fascination with Blue altogether, from the high that hooked him over and over again making him an addict.

29. Confrontation with Himself

In painting Image 29 a radical change in the painter's perspective occurs, which he brings to expression in the perspective of the picture. Until now we have seen frontal or profile views of the little man in which we are obliged to look at him and pay attention to him, but always from afar, perhaps 50 meters away. Now we look with him, over his shoulder, at five ghost-like faces which are looking at him. Some are painted without a mouth, some without developed eyes, thus partially incapable of speech or sight. Are these reflections of himself? He wanted to say "yes," it appeared so to him. He had tried in the painting to face himself in order to see how he really is. He recognized himself suddenly, soberly, in his entire incompleteness. He recognized his inability to perceive what was really confronting him and to bring it to creative expression, although that indeed should be his vocation. Instead of such real creativity, he had always been drifting off into a drunken high, which was naturally easier to achieve than the full expression of a creative thought.

Such real creativity would mean enduring and experiencing all the stresses of the incubation phase. The bright symbolic color blue is in this picture muted and darkened with grey-blue, the color of sobriety and more depressive than visionary. The loud color red, so often used to depict himself, is not present in this picture. He neither wants to capture anyone's attention nor set the scene to be about himself. He shows no narcissistic need to point to himself and his personal world. He wants only plain, sober self-awareness. After painting this picture of self-awareness was as if the lure and fascination with the drunken condition was intercepted and smashed along with the *"peur bleu"*, the "blue fear", the fear of self-dissolution. By plumbing and sounding the blue depths through experiencing, painting and discussing, the blue finally played itself out and was exhausted.

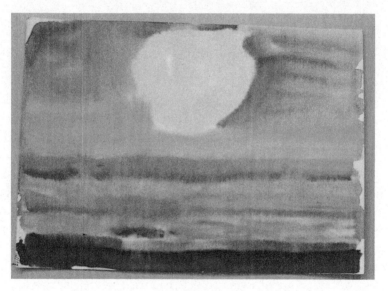

30. Sunrise

As the law of complementary colors dictates, when one looks too long at one color, the eye longs for its complement. In our series, blue was the predominant color for a long time. Now in Image 30 the switch to orange, the complement of blue, finally occurs. Jungian psychology's law of enantiodromia works in a similar way. Our painter's condition of extreme introversion and passive fascination with the unconscious mutates in this phase into a condition of active turning to the outer world, becoming conscious, and creating things. The insight phase that had partially divulged itself in Image 29 now becomes realized in Image 30. Knowledge and conscious enlightenment are represented here by the old-new symbol of a circle of light, yes, a sunrise. What was already suggested in the use of red that characterized our little man in his neediness is fulfilled now in the red-orange sunrise. In the beginning our artist was able to recognize himself and then expose himself in his neediness. Now in Image 30 he attempts to connect to a greater source of creative energy than himself. This creative, near-to-consciousness source is symbolized by the sun, which is vastly more comprehensive than his ego, yet it shares with him its energy to become the source of his creative powers. He doesn't need to portray himself as teetering atop this energy source as he did atop the great phallic energy symbol. Rather a broad, green-brown surface, a real standpoint, is available upon which he can act on reality. The brown of that first earth phallus, which thrusts itself out of the ground, is used again in the green of this ground, which we know from earlier pictures of the ground.. In the red-orange of the heavenly light – representing both insight and creative energy – and in the green-brown of the earth, upon which he can stand and act, this man finds himself. He finds his way to artistic activity, which has now fulfilled him for seven years. Since he dared and realized, he has been able to outgrow the depression and at the same time the alcohol dependency that concealed it. Both have lost their appeal.

Blue has remained his favorite color, as it is for so many of the great painters, Chagall for example. It no longer swallows him, but rather he can use it as the color that expresses his contact with the unconscious, with the spiritual depths, with dream and vision[13] . This man grew beyond his addiction – not through sobriety – but through inspiration and courage to visionary creativity, and through it he came to the root of his blue desire to the boundless.

---

13 Riedel, Ingrid: *Farben in Religion, Gesellschaft, Kunst und Psychotherapie*, pp. 48-59.

Finding Oneself by Letting Go

Picture Series of a Cancer Patient

In the context of therapy C.G. Jung envisaged that the patient should paint as independently of the therapist as possible. The images should take shape and be painted at home without the therapist suggesting motifs or giving technical advice. They should spontaneously emerge out of the unconscious, which is why we call the whole process "painting out of the unconscious." The image idea can emerge from a dream or from the imagination, or can be inspired by the previous painting. In that case a picture series comes into existence. Jung understood the painting process itself to be a form of active imagination, because while we are painting, the most varied forms and faces spontaneously appear. Figures just take shape on the drawing surface before we have consciously decided what they are supposed to be. Jung therefore thought it best to wait until the picture was completed, or even better a series of many pictures, before the analyst and analysand start discussing and interpreting the works of art. In exactly this Jungian sense, I wish to present the following series of paintings. The works were painted out of the artist's own unconscious without motifs being suggested; and the works were discussed only after each had been completed.

It was a case that deeply affected me then and still does today. Therefore, my own therapeutic abilities were significantly limited. I was to professionally and competently accompany a 50-year-old man with cancer whose body was literally breaking down before our eyes. Everything rested upon my ability to work together with him in order to trust, and if possible to unleash, the last creative and self-healing powers of his psyche.

The man, together with his wife, came to me after the wife had discovered during their summer vacation that his melanoma cancer, which had long been in remission, was again beginning to metastasize. Both of them were alarmed, but especially the wife who worked for a dermatologist. They knew that he might have only a short life expectancy.

I am no physician; I am a psychotherapist. Therefore, they came to me not to be healed, but to be accompanied. Above all they needed help to brace themselves against what was coming at them: the possibility of a swiftly approaching death. Perhaps they came also to clarify their own relationship. In contrast to his wife, the man appeared calm and collected, if not reserved. He was a tall, thin, ectomorph with red-blond hair and light skin. Although he acted as if the whole thing did not yet bother him, he was actually full of unbounded fear. He sat there as his wife agitatedly explained everything – almost wordless and spasmodically restrained.

It seemed important to me above all to bring this man into contact with his own feelings. This might enable him to put a face on both his diffuse fear and also his hope. Then he could start to sort them out. To verbalize all of this did not seem to me to be the method of choice. He was neither accustomed nor at all motivated to talk about his fears. I asked him what he had always enjoyed doing in life, and especially what creative activities he had tried. It came out that he had always enjoyed painting in his free time. True, he had neglected it in recent years, but he always came back to it. We agreed that in this time of crisis he should resume painting, and should paint whatever was occupying him, whatever came to mind given his condition with its accompanying moods. We would then, from time to time, discuss the resulting pictures. This is exactly how C.G. Jung understood painting from the unconscious, and what he had recommended as both a therapeutic medium and a special way to individuation.

I can only present the essential pictures of this case, since covering them all would fill up the whole book.

The first painting, Image 31, revealed the man's reserve and almost compulsive structure. It was painted with acrylics very carefully and exactly. There is a house, possibly standing on an island, since in front of it runs some water, which keeps the observer separate from the picture, and in the upper left, beyond an elevated dike, is the sea. Several elements make the house appear very protected: its meticulously painted roof tiles, a fence boarding the front yard, and not least a beautiful tree standing in the center of the picture still full of vigor – the man's tree of life.

31. House Surrounded by a Dyke

Conspicuously the tree's shadow is falling to the right in such a way that the light has to be coming from the left exactly from the region he had so strongly shut out with the dike. In paintings done by terminal patients the struggle with death often reveals itself as coming from the left, as Susan Bach has proven in countless comparisons of pictures from dying patients[14]. Also on the left is a jetty (or wharf) stretching out into the sea, into the infinite, even though this corner of the picture

14 Bach, Susan: *Life Paints Its Own Span: On the Significance of Spontaneous Paintings by Severely Ill Children.* Einsiedeln 1990, pp. 11-12. See also the reproduction and

appears barricaded and even damned up. It appears that the house is empty, even abandoned. Though the doors stand wide open, there is nobody there. The wide, brown road could almost be a plowed field. The color brown can express, among other things, self-consciousness and blockage. Next to the road are a wagon and a pile of firewood waiting to be loaded. In the pasture a cow, a nourishing mother animal is still there. In the background we see a yellow crop of ripe grain. Something here has become ripe for harvest. The bench turned toward the grain invites us to stay a while, to reflect upon this field of grain. We have a picture before us expressing the feeling of security experienced by the artist during his last vacation, which he is now trying to maintain at all costs. But the signs of disturbance cannot be ignored. Already the whole scene seems to be separated from the observer by a moat, as if it were an island heavily protected from the open sea.

32. Ripe Grain

discussion of her spatial schema in Riedel, Ingrid: *Bilder in Religion, Kunst und Psychotherapie: Wege zur Interpretation.* Stuttgart 1989, pp. 32ff.

In Image 32 we see that the ripened grain visible in the background of Image 31 has now shifted to the foreground. Harvesting ripe grain is symbolic of his current condition and the theme has become conscious to him. In this image the house stands much further away and in a valley. No longer an island house, it is now a farmstead in Hessen, where the painter lives (although in reality he lives in a city apartment). This fantasy farmstead is again meticulously, carefully, almost compulsively painted. Its three buildings might be expressing the current living situation of the family, namely father, mother and twelve-year-old youngest son. The two older children have already moved out.

The house is again protected, this time by two wooded slopes upon which firs stand like guards. Two roads are indicated. One leads from left to right through the picture, passes the main building, and connects to the other two buildings. The second road bends around the base of the left mountain heading, like the wharf of Image 31, toward the upper left – a region that the painter both avoids and seeks. It is the sky that is so striking here. Not even visible in the first picture because of its perspective from above, here it takes in a large space and presses down like a funnel between the flanks of the mountains all the way to the farmstead. The lower layer of sky is whipped up by the wind, and through the white and yellow clouds blow tattered brown clouds that may represent the melanoma. The yellow color here corresponds to the ripe grain below. The upper sky is clearer, bluer, more peaceful, with long, horizontal clouds floating across. Could this mean that our painter becomes more serene at the highest level of consciousness, even when the middle of the picture is churning, and at the base (the ground level) he is still trying to maintain his safety? The sky, which we also call "the heavens", symbolizes human destiny. In this painting it has become visible over an Earth ripe for harvest. And the house, the painter's earthly dwelling, now huddles fearfully between the protective mountains decked in fir trees. The vigorous tree with its open crown in the first painting has here become a forest of firs. They are lined up like a platoon of vigilant soldiers who have tightened their ranks: literally a mobilization or mustering of troops in the plant kingdom. The sky likely reveals just how stirred up the man is on the inside, even though he is trying to appear on the outside to be still very much in control.

We have before us in Image 33 the utmost self-control, expressed with meticulousness reminiscent of the old masters. Indeed our painter is working here in the style of his beloved Dutch masters and demonstrating his own technical ability. Yet the painting engenders such a sense of coolness and distance that my first glance left me almost chilled. Yellow is completely absent and only traces of red can be found on the roofs of the house and mill. Furthermore, the house and mill are set far back on the horizon, suggesting an ever-increasing distance from coziness and comfort. In several of his late paintings, as death was drawing near, van Gogh lightened his colors with ceiling white, as our artist does here. The result is a definite cooling of the coloration.

33. Poplars on the River

This picture is so composed that the observer is placed in the front right corner of the painting on the riverbank. A small path is visible leading further down to the water but also up the slope, perhaps all the way to the white bridge and black structure. The bridge crosses over to the other shore where the white mill stands with dark blades. From there one can follow the river's current down to the three tall poplars. Only the lower portion of their trunks is visible in the picture, the upper portion rising into the upper left quarter of the picture, into what Susan Bach calls the "zone of eternity". These trees are transcending the drawing space of this picture. The third tree, whose trunk ends in a fork, reminds one of the Germanic rune meaning "life" and is almost stepping out of the picture. Perhaps most significant is the direction of the water: it flows from right to left, backwards, in the direction of regression and introversion, toward the collective unconscious. It streams through the drawing space toward the painter and observer taking over the largest portion of the picture's base line. Its left bank is edged in black, marking it as threatening. The reflection on the water is exquisitely executed: mill, bushes, trees and clouds shimmer on the water's surface and everything pulses with the movement of the waves and the flowing of the current. What does this reflection in the river express symbolically? The particulars of life are reflected in something comprehensive, the disparate elements flow together. It is the flow of life itself and the stream of memories in this man's interior – in the depths of his psyche – that are reflected here. All this can indeed be symbolized by this stream of water. With this picture, the painter begins to look back over his life, to summarize, to bundle his experiences together. At the same time everything is beginning to flow. While the man's life-current flows toward the lower left into the zone of the collective unconscious (which in this case could also mean the "zone of death"), a subdued light reflects off of the poplar trunks from the upper left (the "Zone of eternity").

Finally there is the mill. Even though it does fit naturally into a Dutch landscape, one must marvel at how appropriate a symbol of this man's painting process it is. The analogy here is that the ripe grain is the man's ripened life that can be processed through milling/grinding/ suffering and be, as it were, transformed into a new state. That is how this man, marked by his sickness, at first attempted to interpret his suffering, and why he chose to paint the symbolic theme of the mill on the stream of life. For the time being however a cool sky with broad, sallow clouds presses over the landscape, and above all over the mill. The sallow ceiling white which is mixed into all the blues and greens of this picture reminds one of frost which has settled upon all the colors of this picture.

The afflicted man's wife had also begun painting right away, and she did so with far more emotionality than her husband. Expressing herself in painting was something new for her, and so her technical ability was of course not as developed as that of her practiced husband. But from the first painting, her pictures possessed a strong expressiveness and a natural emotional strength. Interestingly, she also attempted to find and to paint a way across a stream. It is, after all, an ancient symbol of decisive life transitions.

34. The Way over the Stream

In Image 34, the sun, the moon, and all the stars are hovering over the lush bank on the opposite shore, inviting her to cross over. The sun is standing directly across from her. But contrary to the painter's initial intention, the path does not lead directly to the sun. Rather, she senses while she is painting, that the accessible land somehow ends and she must turn. She must go back and follow the bank of the stream, but she doesn't yet know where. The movement of the painting is again in the direction of the collective unconscious, and interestingly there are also three trees in her picture, this time standing under the orange-violet of a darkening sun – or is it the moon? In her first painting, this had also been the direction of movement, first past two summer trees in a blooming meadow, then to a third tree upon which a white frost had settled. This woman's path however eventually leads back into the land of the living. We see this in another of her paintings, Image 35. There her path circles behind a mountain lake, then on past the left side of a lake, past a dark church, over a brown bridge with explicitly drawn railings, and back to the village over which the sun stands. Although a carefully painted, inhospitable range of snow-capped mountains looms in the background, the painter succeeds symbolically to portray a way around the problem (signified by the deep lake). One walks around (circumambulation) until the circle is complete. Here the symbolic circle is doubly formed by both the path and the lake. Like a mandala it is able to center the painter and bring her again to herself despite her troubled soul.

35. The Way around the Lake

Up to this time, the man had exhibited a tacit reserve and emotional restraint, not outwardly expressing his pain and anxiety in the face of dying. Two things enabled this to change. First he was animated by the images he was painting and discussing. But then he also had a dream: a group of white-haired monks, each one carrying a young, black-haired child in his arms. The children were only a few months old, and the monks were taking them into their monastery on a cliff.

This dream very much unsettled him, and he decided to paint it in oil (Image 36). He used this durable, long-lasting medium because he felt that the dream with its resultant painting were essential for him. Only a special, careful, valuable, long-lasting creative work would do. It could also be that on some level he felt that the message of this dream was intended to outlast him.

36. Monks with Children

The sixteen monks in his painting wear earth brown habits and have snow white hair. Each of them gently carries a child. These lively children, each with a head of black hair and each sporting a yellow romper suit, almost glow with vital energy. Does this dream, and its resulting painting, underscore the pain or the comfort contained in the situation? Is the main message that the group of monks (symbolizing the painter's own quasi-abdication of the world) is bearing away all youth and all future possibilities? Or is the main point that the monks (who are oriented toward the eternal) are becoming invigorated because they are receiving this charge of lively energy into their monastery? If the second is correct, it would also mean that the man's own inner monk is being animated by this youthful energy, that part of him which participates in the eternal while renouncing the world. The dream certainly did awaken the painful realization and the deep, terrible recognition that his future possibilities would be taken away from him and that he did not have long to live. But it also awoke the monk energy in him – the power to fulfill his eternal destiny. These were neither kidnappers nor robbers taking the children, but monks. Thereby the religious dimension of his suffering became conscious and real for this man sick with cancer. But the pain also remained, stirred to full strength for the first time by this dream and his painting of it. Eleven children are visible although sixteen must have been picked up, since every monk carries one. The number eleven in pictures often indicates a problem which the artist experiences as unsolvable at the moment, just as the number eleven is indivisible or indissoluble. The number of monks, however, is sixteen, a number indicating completion and wholeness. The man's problem concerning his future prospects and developmental possibilities, symbolized by the children, is not yet solvable. But in the arms of the sixteen monks a new level is hinted at, where a solution may indeed be possible.

The man did not paint sixteen monks on purpose, which makes this explanation even more likely.

As with the stream in the previous picture (Image 33), the monks move with the children toward the lower left corner of the picture, following the path to their monastery on the cliff. This may suggest a pull into the collective unconscious, which here again could well mean a pull in the direction of death. But the path forms, with two other paths in the painting, a triangle pointing into the upper left, the "eternity corner" of the picture. One path leads past a row of houses with empty black windows, as if the place died out. The houses seem to stare at the observer as if out of hollow eyes. Then there is the monastery sitting on a cliff. It takes up almost the entire left edge of the picture and is reminiscent of a decayed tooth or brittle bone – a merciless reminder to the painter that metastasis has been found in his bones. Finally, the yellow that is mixed in with green in the grass, repeats the lively yellow of the children's romper suits, but it is replaced by a deathly white in the foliage of the trees, where frost has suddenly come on. In this picture life and death are battling with each other. And judging by the direction of movement down and to the left, death has begun to gain the upper hand.

All the affright caused by this painting and the dream behind it shook loose something liberating in the painter. His emotions, up until then blocked and held fast, loosened up. Fear, grief, and anger that such a destiny should confront him at 50 years old broke out from him. But with this came also intense feelings of love for his wife and for his son, and the knowledge that the life they had lived with one another was precious.

37. Sailboat beneath Turbulent Sky

Then Image 37 appeared, casting all previous paintings into the shadows because of the freedom, the daring expression, and the dynamic of its painting style. Red was completely absent in the last two paintings. Now both the sky and the cascading water are churning with wild, passionate yellow- red. The stream shoots up at the painter as much as at the observer from under the arches of the bridge and spreads out. The heavens are torn open, exposing a sliver of blue that repeats itself in the water's reflection as if to emphasize the direction in which this stream is gushing forth. A torrential waterfall has been added to the painter's stream of life. He knows that he does not have much longer to live. He senses that soon he will have to cross over to the other shore, a shore that happens to be green. Upstream a heavy black bridge with five hollow white arches crosses the river. It forms the backdrop of the scene, reminding us of our mortality. Someday every one of us will have to cross it and make that transition.

38. Boat by M, 12 Years

The painter has now taken heart. He has unrolled his sail here in order to throw himself personally into the wind of his destiny. "O Lord, give everyone his own death", wrote Rilke. The sail is noticeably light and is very carefully painted. Four gold-yellow triangles lie concentrically within each other – the dynamic of three is embedded in the calm of four. They are edged in blue-violet, green, red and white. This sail has a centered structure completed by all the colors of the rainbow. Its triangular shape reminds us from afar of the protecting eye of God. The way the sail pattern is centered allows both painter and observer to give order to churning emotions. This is the usual effect of clearly structured graphic symbols, which tend to take the form of a mandala. In this painting turbulence and serenity stand like counterpoints in the face of approaching death, much as in a contrapuntal composition. At first the opposites were irreconcilable, but they come together in the symbol of the boat. The hull expresses the painter's decision to meet the unavoidable head on, while the sail with its concentric design expresses the painter's ordered, interlocking, inner powers.

This man's decision to paint himself as accepting the unavoidable was taken up by his son, who in these days celebrated his twelfth birthday. After he saw his father's painting the boy painted his own boat (Image 38). The ship is completely centered in the drawing space. With its bright white hull and crimson sail it exhibits great intensity. As the helmsman in yellow sailors' clothes this boy is proactive. The picture expresses his remarkable volition to take over responsibility for himself.

He has set his initial and his age "M. 12-years-old" twice on the hull and also on the sail, almost like an oath.

He is very young for what is coming at him, separation from his father. He knows it all too well and he fears it, as we can ascertain from a sea that completely encapsulates the boat and reaches all the way to the heavens. But as the boy asserts through this picture, he has already survived twelve years. He is proud to be initiated and included by his father and mother in everything that is coming at the family. He feels like a young man in his initiation ordeal, which demands his utmost courage, and which he has chosen to endure so that he can mature. His youth, his inexperience and also his awkwardness are expressed in the white of the boat. From time immemorial white has been the color of initiation and initiation garments. In the red of the sail we see his pain, his anger and also his courage to face them all.

This boy will loose his father early to a terrible sickness. Of course he has moments of doubt along the path. But it was evident and impressive that just when his father was finally able to admit his own feelings, the boy also found his way to an openness which is the entry to the depths of his own feelings. It unlocks the unconscious powers that can carry him even now. It is also moving how the father gained insight into the boy's picture, recognizing that it was somehow an initiation for his son. This didn't happen through talking, but rather through the father's painting of an unusual picture. Image 39 depicts an Indian who could be both the initiate and the initiator in one. For this man an Indian is a person who can bear pain and look death in the eye; but also a medicine man who is bound and initiated into the inner and mysterious powers of nature and the mysteries of death and life.

39. Indian

The gaze of this Indian is tremendously hypnotic: he is full of fear, deadly fear, but at the same time he looks far into the distance, into another dimension, he transcends the earthly horizon. The black eyes and the black hair stand in stark, express contrast to the earth-toned ochre of the face and to the intense, vital red of the mouth with its connection to the red necklace. If the mouth has something full of life and also longing for life, the red beads of the necklace remind me more of blood, of wounds to remember. This man now is inextricably bound (symbolized by the chain around his neck) and he is marked (with the red). But at the same time he is held up, honored, decorated and in a special way headed on a journey into passion (the initiation par excellence). Colors of intense vitality, of suffering and of pain stand closely together.

40. Landscape of Pain

The violet background (violet as a tension color between red and blue) finally means transformation and also an experience of mystical depths. In this passionate, expressive picture the man expresses his readiness to accept the transition to the zone of death and place himself in the resulting great transformation. In addition to the masculine clarity of this expression, the soft, feminine contours of the Indian's face are not to be overlooked. Now the painter also makes room for his feminine side – softness, affectivity – in these last weeks of his life. A step toward greater wholeness is achieved.

After this picture of "readiness to suffer" came Image 40 that is painted completely from pain. A trickle of red runs like blood down the long trunk that stands to the far right of the picture portraying the spinal column of the man who at this time is overcome with excruciatingly painful metastasis. The towering tree, whose crown is lost in the heights beyond the limits of the paper, stands to the right in the picture so that it completely blocks the way and the view to the right, the direction of the outside world. Realization and action in the outside world and the external reality are no longer possible. Inwardly, however, the space is open. A broad landscape spreads in ochre and green, which crosses the horizon on a green hill. But there are also red traces in this landscape like blood drops and pain points. The interpretation of pink, which in the entire series of paintings only appears here, means acceptance of soft, tender skin and body sensitivity, irritated again and again through the bodily pain.

It is worth noticing how zones of deep blue open up in the sky over the green hill and also through the tree branches above the mountain. They take on a half-round shape, like waxing heavenly bodies. It is as if a window or a bull's eye is opening into eternity. Indeed symbols of eternity often appear in this zone.

The last two paintings of the series to be titled (Images 39 and 40) are also the only ones in portrait format. This is the orientation of straightening up or standing up, of being raised or righted, that accentuates the tension between above and below, between heaven and earth.

The next picture, Image 41, was done in landscape format, suggesting the ground, lying down, resting, and giving oneself over. This picture's perspective is so chosen that our view of the ground glides over grass and reeds and the lower part of tree trunks landing directly upon the water with its reflection of the trees and upon a rowboat lying ready to take off: a boat for only one as the single bench indicates; a boat with no rudder that indeed no longer needs a rudder. It reminds us glaringly of a coffin, which in Switzerland even today is called a *Totenbaum* (tree for the dead). The earth at the boat's stern appears to have been excavated making a place for the boat. It suggests a freshly dug grave. The boat waits unambiguously ready in the takeoff position pointing towards the lower left, which was also the direction of the monks' procession: the direction of inward retreat, into the past, into the origins and into death. The arrangement of the trees is peculiar. Sometimes there are two standing together, sometimes one alone and in the upper left, four stand together. Does this suggest the extent to which this man lived in the security of his family (wife and three children), especially in relation to his wife before his way led him more and more in the last months into the isolation of facing death? The lower right of a picture often suggests both mother and security. In this picture we see a pair of trees standing nearest to us. Also in the middle of the picture a pair of trunks dominates, and are even doubled by the reflection of the water.

41. Canoe

The power of the relationship reaches even into the perspective of this water of death. In the "corner of eternity" a quaternary of trees is

visible. The quaternary is both a symbol for completeness and completion, which here is foreshadowed. Near this realm of eternity but further
receded away from both the painter and the observer, a house appears
again, or rather a bungalow, maybe painted red or perhaps made of brick
and roofed with straw. It is like a last station where one is still at home
in this world. Much like the late pictures of van Gogh, painted shortly
before his death, this picture attempts a "near-the-earth perspective",
as if the painter wants to hold firm to the earth, hanging on and yet at
the same time ceasing to do so, as his body entrusts itself in death to
this earth and again becomes dust. Rest, knowing, and decisiveness lie
together across this picture. The intense royal blue shines here not from
the sky, but from the depths of the water, from the depths of his soul.

42. Coastal Landscape

Two more pictures came into existence before this man died in
March. He had come to me in early autumn after he had discovered that
his cancer was back. Both of these pictures express a peace that is already
hinted at in the choice of landscape format: the attraction to the earth
that simultaneously widens the view of the heavens. The coast painting
(Image 42) gives a free perspective of the sea and sky. Here the corner,

which in this man's first picture (Image 31) had been so obviously blocked by a protective dike, now lies open before us. A sailboat with mast but without sail lies ready with the bow pointed straight in the same direction where in Image 31 the wharf had pointed. The boat lies between the second and third of seven stakes that may well measure phases of time which this man still had left (he still had probably two to three months left). In the picture's foreground nearest to both observer and painter, are portrayed dunes and clumps of bushy grass. The zone of security in the picture's lower right is completely overgrown with them. The bush in the left foreground is surrounded by a brown rectangle that again reminds us of a grave. There are long shadows, the longest of which stretches from this clump of dune grass. It is as if what is about to happen is already casting its shadow. The light now comes from the region of the lower left that we attribute to the collective unconscious, the realm of the inner world, the origins, and also of death. "That is where the eternal light goes"one could say in the words of an old Advent hymn. For here something is arriving, even when this man is getting ready to take leave.

The last painting that the man was able to create, the image of a sunset on the ocean (Image 43), came about six weeks before his death. It expresses pain and sadness but also intense love of the life he must leave behind – with its flaming red around the sinking sun. The path that leads directly away from the dunes describes the inevitability of this process. It is again bound by black fence posts sealed by a cable both to the right and the left. Here he must go down to the sea, to the setting sun. Five and six posts border the path on either side: the painter had indeed at this point only five to six weeks to live. The path is etched in yellow and surrounded by dark green clumps of grass. Yellow as the grain found in Images 31 and 32, that reminded us of the harvest time of ripe life. Here however, the yellow is the sand. The path leads over the dark places of the upper sandbanks, the threshold of pain and death, and also through and away from it out into the open sea, a path of light to follow that is also shown by the sun. Above the red farewell fire of the sun, the heaven is light and transparent. A stripe of yellow-gold light takes the yellow of the sand path up into the heavenly sphere until it opens up into the delicate light blue of limitlessness.

43. Sunset at the Ocean

This man's path, set out and expressed in his paintings, reveals an intense spiritual development realized in the months before his death when his suffering from cancer could no longer be held back. At first rather inhibited and blocked in his feelings, he now shows a great freedom and expressiveness in the creation of his pictures. The meticulous accuracy and stability of the initial pictures gives way (after the monk dream), to a more generous dynamic and expression of passionate feelings like fear, pain, and agitation; finally coming to rest in accepting the inevitable, with a serenity he gains when painting one of the great old and yet forever new symbols of infinity: the ocean reflecting changing phases of light, in this case the sunset.

Relationship and Dependence

Pictures of a "Mother Complex" Case

Symbols are so important for therapy. Yet Jungians often mystify the process of how they come into being to such an extent that we almost don't ask about their formation. It is as if they just spring spontaneously from a completely indescribable "unconscious." But careful observation of the therapeutic process reveals that new symbols always occur precisely at consolidation points in the analytical relationship and not approximately somewhere. They are constellated by the relationship. On the other hand, this symbol creation can also be blocked by certain relationship situations. These may be caused by either or both parties and are often very hard to see through. For example, an analysand may project an unconscious complex onto the transference/counter-transference relationship with the analyst in such a way that it can only be experienced in the transference/counter-transference.

With this next picture series I will try to illustrate how personal and archetypal energies constellate and transform in the transference and counter-transference of an analytical relationship. We note the special consolidation situations in the analytical relationship that arise with regard to symbol creation.

I shall call our patient Marga. At the time she was a 34-year-old social worker. Before we began our therapeutic work, she belonged to a painting group led by another woman. Whenever the participants could select which subject to paint, Marga always chose a certain collective symbol.

She kept repeating it but could not say much about it; because she couldn't connect it with anything in her own personal life. Marga always painted orbs – orbs that usually fell into water and sank. The leader of the painting group did not understand this motif and finally expressed her impatience over such a stereotype: Marga should finally cease with this painting of such orbs...

44. Blue Orb

Marga was deeply hurt by the group leader's impatience, because Marga's own mother had never believed that her daughter could do much. Therefore she was very easily wounded in her feeling of self-worth.

Because her orb motif had not been recognized as the sign of a complex nor understood as a symbol, it kept recurring. Conversely, experience shows that whenever constellations that underlie complexes are recognized and understood, the stereotypes dissolve themselves.

In our first therapeutic session Marga brought such orb paintings and reported how impatient her painting group leader had been. Together with her, I tried to hone in on the meaning of this motif. The orbs somehow reminded me of the heroine's golden balls in the Grimm's' fairy tale "The Frog Prince". In that fairy tale they fall into a well, leaving the princess devastated. The ball symbolizes the princess's youthful completeness, her self. Therefore it is really the princess's self that has fallen into the well. The fairy tale underlines just how precious the orb symbol is by making the balls golden. But Marga's orb in Image 44 is soft blue, glassy and transparent, in other words very fragile.

Already here in the symbol of this orb that she must paint again and again, her relationship to her self is fermenting, as far as was then possible. Where we make contact with our self, there we come into contact with the meaning of our existence. Therefore the orb is also about the dimension of meaning. It slips away from the princess and seems to disappear into the depths of the water – the unconscious. So too, Marga's quest for her self and her search for meaning that is so important in life, was not recognized by her painting teacher in the orb symbolism. The teacher had not caught her ball, and so it fell into emptiness. I somehow seem to have caught it in our first session.

Thereafter Marga painted some pictures in which the orb motif evolved into a golden ball that fell onto solid, weight-bearing ground instead of into water (Image 45). This ball then started to sprout roots as her self-seeking began to root itself in our therapy. The ball became ever more penetrated with roots (Image 46) and finally it cracked open. This freed a new symbol that Marga could, for the first time, apply to her own life: the picture of a mother holding a kicking baby in her lap (Image 47). Notice the pieces of the broken orb still visible and swirling around the mother and child.

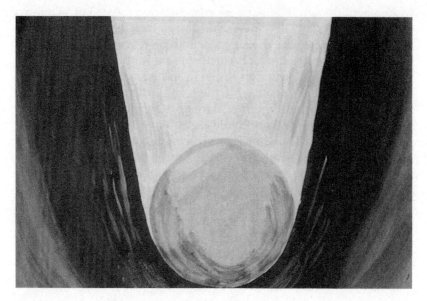

45. Golden Ball

46. Ball with Roots

Here is an archetypal picture, the symbol of the Great Mother with a child sitting under the tree of life. In contrast to the orb motif, Marga could immediately recognize her personal life theme in the mother motif. It made her aware of a question about feeling safe with the mother and with life itself. This is her basic problem, and will become the problem of our therapeutic relationship.

What follows is a close-up of the analytical process between Marga and me. After some dramatic transference and counter-transference reactions, some very clear points of transition appeared that were characterized by the formation of new symbols that Marga then painted. She painted spontaneously out of an inner need so I never had to encourage her. The result was more than a hundred paintings. I will select only the most important ones among them: six picture sequences that graphically illustrate the creation of new symbols.

47. Mother with Child

In presenting this case I refer to Verena Kast's theory about the necessary conditions for the creation of new symbols. Kast writes: "Our complexes, with their accompanying affects and stereotypical behaviors, are patterned by our childhood relationships. As long as these complexes remain unconscious, they dictate the analytical relationship and frequently result in a complex-laden, collusive transference/counter-transference situation. Only when the complex constellation of the relationship is emotionally understood, and when the other person in the relationship is understood as an inner part of oneself, can the complex "fantasize itself out." Then further symbol creation is possible."[15]

Thus everything depends on creating the conditions under which a complex can fantasize itself out. To do this we must first examine and really understand the transference/counter-transference situation hidden in the complex constellation. Thereby two things usually become visible: the childhood caregiver involved, and – little by little – the child role that the analysand is playing in the inner life of the analyst.

First I want to sketch my analysand's childhood experience of her mother, since it formed the basis of her negatively colored mother complex and strongly affected our therapeutic relationship.

Marga was an unwanted fourth child in a family where alcohol was abused. Her over-taxed mother became ill early on and was constantly rejecting her. In order to keep bread on the family table, the mother took a job in a restaurant, pouring drinks and sometimes imbibing herself. The worst thing for Marga was when her drunken mother would just look through her, not even recognizing her anymore. This not-being-seen was the basic experience of her childhood and prevented her from developing a good sense of self-confidence. As a child she was seldom entrusted with tasks because she was considered clumsy and untalented. Her mother never backed her up in the presence of others. Whenever something came up missing or broken in the household, Marga was always the first one suspected. Thus she lived in constant stress and anxiety.

This child's expectations of her mother were completely unfulfilled. Therefore a constant fear of being disappointed lurked within her. No matter how well-intentioned people approached her, she feared being unwanted, and felt as if she were in the wrong place at the wrong time, or somehow behaving unsatisfactorily. In line with this childhood situation, Marga placed a huge expectation on my motherliness in the

---

15 *Kast, Verena:* "Umschlagspunkte in der Analyse" in *Zeitschrift für Psychologie* 20/3 1989, p. 178.

analytic relationship. At the same time a great fear of disappointment possessed her and expressed itself in an anticipatory retreat each time even a little bit of closeness appeared between us. She herself admitted a great fear regarding me. She feared that she might overburden me and disappoint me, and then get on my nerves, because she was not fit for an analysis, and that I would drop the case. Often real warmth developed between us during a session. But afterwards it was as if a thread was snipped and all at once she could no longer sense me nor access me. She would then get the idea that I had withdrawn from her.

Often she spoke of her fear of becoming dependent upon me, since she felt so needy for a sense of belonging. This desire to belong combined with the fear of dependence had been a theme of her entire childhood. She herself expressed it in this way: *"During my childhood I was always trying to be nice to women in whom I saw some little thing that showed promise for giving me warmth. My heart was continually starving for that."*

In my counter-transference a strong motherly feeling for this dear child, so disadvantaged by life, was there from the beginning. My ever-renewed attempts to emotionally warm her up, to assure her of my affection and express my confidence in her maturation process were increasingly met with new reservations. She could not drop the suspicion that I would discard her and leave her as soon as I got to know her better. She must really be completely unworthy of such attention from me.

Quite honestly this put my readiness to understand her to the test. I felt constantly undervalued and frustrated in my attempts to show her my openness and acceptance. What Verena Kast describes as a characteristic of such constellations is exactly what happened here. It was a complex-laden situation with a collusive transference and counter-transference. From the outside it must have been apparent "that the behavior of the analyst was dictated in a most polarized way by the analysand's behavior. Even when this process is conscious to the analyst, the behavior cannot be altered. A pattern of relationship repeats itself stereotypically."[16] At first such a complex appears to be inextinguishable. It can be unlocked only when its essence is grasped both by the analyst and the analysand, and when they both understand its make-up and its

16 Ibid, p. 166.

genesis in the childhood relationship pattern. Then the complex can be grasped more deeply than was previously possible, especially on the emotional level. According to Jung, a complex arises from "the clash between a demand of adaptation and the individual's constitutional inability to meet the challenge." [17]

In our case, this complex-producing process, in which an individual could not accomplish an adaptation challenge, may also be looked at as a relationship process. The adaptation challenge must have been a requirement of the earlier attachment figures (psychological parents). Therefore the complex that emerged from such a collision would not just be a quality of the individual disposition of the affected person. Much more, it would also be a quality of the relationship history, forming the relational behavior of her childhood. From this starting point the knot can be untangled.

Because such a complex comes into existence in a childhood relationship between an attachment figure and the child, it can split off in the analytical relationship and re-establish its original poles – at one end the analyst as an attachment figure posing adaptation requirements, and at the other end the client in the former child role.

As long as the underlying complex causing this constellation is not understood, it can happen that the analyst and analysand behave toward each other like the attachment figure and the child. But it can also turn around so that the analyst is the child and the analysand the demanding attachment figure. In this form the collusive transference/counter-transference is much harder to see through.

How was it in our case? On the one hand Marga was an un-appeased child, full of expectation, and fixated on being disappointed; and I was the over-taxed mother who wanted to make everything right, but could never do right considering her excessive expectation. But on the other hand, I was the one who wanted to be understood and recognized by Marga for all of my efforts, and so I was that child, and she was the absent attachment figure who didn't trust in me, who encountered me exactly as her mother had encountered her, and was capable of making me sad and angry. Very gradually at first myself and finally also my

---

17 Jung, Carl Gustav: *CW,* Vol. 6, *Psychological Types,* §926

analysand began to grasp the polarized roles of her childhood history that were working within her and causing our collusive relationship: she was projecting onto us the mother-daughter relationship of her childhood. And so after nine months of analysis she painted a mother whom she bound in a sack and put out in the desert (Image 48), a mother which as "Mrs. Squid" swallows her (Image 49), and finally a mother who lets her fall into an abyss as Marga trustingly reaches out her hands to her (Image 50).

48. Sack in the Desert

49. Mrs. Squid

In these paintings Marga could recognize her childhood affect that flared up again because of the abandonment, the anxiety, and the rage she experienced in the counter-transference. It was the same affect that again and again had boiled up in the face of an inadequate mother. Slowly she began to recognize that the aggressive one, who was abandoning her by withdrawing from the relationship, was not only to be seen in me, but also in herself. She began to understand how she was preemptively seeking disappointment with this behavior. Indeed, in each case she was the first to pull back from the emerging closeness, thereby constellating the feeling of abandonment. She started to grasp just how often she abandoned me. So in Image 51 she jumps into an abyss where a demon is waiting to swallow her. This demon is baring its teeth and holding its waiting mouth wide open for her. In the face of this picture she is able to ask whether a part of her self is not also hidden in the demon, and not just in the active jumper.

50. The Step into Emptiness

In what follows, I will describe the essential steps of this case and the new symbols illustrating each step. By "new" symbols I mean symbols that were not tangible before, and which unlocked new emotions, new behaviors, and new hope. In the course of this therapeutic process I recognized six turning points or consolidation phases that I wish to present with their corresponding picture sequences:

Right at the beginning of our analysis the patient was painting stereotypical orbs. The first turning point came early on, just after we emotionally understood the abstract collective orb motif. Immediately a new symbol, the concrete mother-child symbol, was released. This for me was the map for the diagnosis as well as for the prognosis of this case (Image 47).

51. The Leap into the Abyss

The second turning point was the transition out of the symbiosis that had marked the first nine months of our therapeutic relationship. The orb, symbolizing imprisonment in the negative mother complex, continues to lurk near the lower left quarter of the picture – the region of unconsciousness (Image 52), but then comes the new symbol (Image 53) of a hike together. The mother grasping blooming blue flowers is a positive element in this therapeutic stage. The painting is no longer a static, stilted repetition of the archetypal Madonna motif of Image 52, which betrays the archetypal mother image being projected onto the therapist. Rather, Image 53 is a picture of being underway together that reveals itself in the similar profiles of mother and daughter, in the goal-oriented focus toward the right of the picture, and also in the emphasis on the shoes that express the mother's ability to march. Of course the relatively small child is still carried in a backpack.

52. Madonna with Lead Ball and Flower

53. Wandering

This transition was made possible after Marga, despite her ambivalence, admitted her desire for a mother, which at first she was ashamed of. Now she could feel understood by me. As we learned in our talks, Marga's only pride was her very early independence from home. Therefore, it was especially difficult for her to admit her need for attention and her wish to regress. But these were necessary in the service of her ego-development.

The third consolidation phase in our relationship made it possible for Marga to review her now-conscious childhood abandonment history and realize how this history was reflected in our therapy history. This initiated a long series of paintings and simultaneously relieved the pressure of projection on the therapeutic relationship.

54. Plant between Ravens

She wrote a fairy tale about part of her life during this painting phase, and new symbols appeared in addition to those pictures of her being banished or devoured (Images 48-50), which I have already shown. A new, more positive symbol creation took place whenever I would hit the nail on the head during our sessions. Cognizant of the banishment she experienced as a child, we discussed her renewed fear of being banished from our relationship. That discussion resulted in Image 54 in which a little plant sprouts up between two ravens, which perhaps symbolize her parents. This is an image that unites opposites and exhibits a hope that despite everything, something new will sprout up, also in our therapeutic relationship.

55. Tree-Mother

A further picture followed (Image 55) suggesting just how quickly that tender little plant was able to develop. It is a tree-mother. A first green leaf appears in its branches, again between the two ravens. She is holding a bear out to the tree-mother, a transition object to comfort her in her abandonment. In the tree-mother symbol – which naturally includes the therapeutic mother – Marga again finds a symbol of the archetypal mother that is so necessary for life. Her recurring fear of being devoured was already graphically illustrated in the "Mrs. Squid" (Image 49) mentioned above. This is a negative aspect of the Great Mother, in whose body we at one time rested as in a cradle, and against which we also kick out. It is also a negative aspect of the unconscious. In this painting she is no longer so very small as before. I point out to her during our discussion of this picture, that I can very well understand her kicking out against this constrictive closeness, and that apparently she no longer feels so tiny as before.

56. Carried by Wind

Her stature is repeated in Image 56 that she brought to the next hour. In it a strong wind – a creative happening, an up-lifting power – takes hold of her, carrying her away from the symbolic situation of being inside the squid and into the openness of the desert. But she again feels banished in this sudden freedom. She seeks renewed protection in the cave (Image 57).

57. In the Cave

At least it has a view out, a perspective. She felt very disoriented after painting this picture and writes: "*... still I feel empty and alone. I no longer know where to go nor even where I am.*" Again she is sitting there, rescued but alone. However her perspective has increased in that the view stretches into the depths of the painting. This awareness of space in paintings is always a sign of expanding consciousness. A path is visible, contradicting Marga's statement that she no longer knows where to go. Also there is a vibrant golden-yellow sun, which until now has not appeared in this series. With her choice of the cave symbol Marga indicates that from now on she can accept a sheltering space without becoming overly afraid of being too close. Here she is no longer swallowed up inside "Mrs. Squid" (Image 49), but rather a window with perspective remains open.

58. Under the Protection of the Cloak

In the last painting of this series (Image 58) a little impishness shows itself, indicating that the situation is no longer as completely hopeless as she kept wanting me to believe. On the same day that she painted the cave she went on to paint the figure of a mother whose mantle is spread invitingly wide open. Marga, again as a child, peeps around it.

Her humor dares for the first time to show itself – humor in the face of her own typical behaviors which she can now better see through. All the new symbols of this sequence suggest new ways of handling old fears. The child image is continuously growing in these pictures, despite occasional setbacks. The mother image, because of her growing trust in me, signifies her growing trust in life and so is also an image of her own interior. Comparing all the images of mother and daughter in this series shows that Marga definitely finds herself in both figures.

In the fourth consolidation phase of our therapeutic relationship we became ever more aware of two chronic tendencies in Marga: her constant need to call our hard-won trust relationship into question, and her frequent relapsing into the negative mother complex. But achieving this insight created a new threat for us. Because she now recognized her constant calling of our relationship into question, Marga began to experience herself as "bad". Now she saw herself as unbearable and so figured that I would at some point just cut off the therapeutic relationship. Every time this happened I would try to demonstrate to her that this constant questioning of our relationship could be explained by the constantly on-the-rocks relationship with her mother. It developed out of the fear that she had developed in childhood of suddenly being dropped, especially if even the smallest fault could be pointed out.

The discovery and acceptance of her own shadow was an especially hard bone for Marga to chew. But increasingly she succeeded in recognizing her mother's shadow within her own shadow, and she did figure out how to understand it and take responsibility for it. Declarations of mistrust like those she expressed toward me, she now noticed in her attitude toward her friends. This was especially the case with her housemate, who at the time was the only close attachment figure she had. Luckily Marga recognized that she was stretching this friendship with her often- expressed fear of sooner or later being left by her friend. Whenever she noticed this mistrust in herself Marga found it contemptible, and she reacted with self-hate. It was in this phase of our therapeutic relationship that Marga began to take note of her own aggression, in other words her shadow, and to paint it.

59. Teddy-Devil

I named Image 59 her "Teddy-Devil". It expresses just how archaically Marga experienced her shadow. It is a childish and therefore exaggerated image which became ever more humorous to us as time went on. Eventually her shadow side ceased to be so despicable to her; rather it simply belonged to her life history. This is revealed in the next picture (Image 60). It is the picture of a mother, and it represents me as therapist as well as herself in her motherly possibilities. Now the little Teddy-devils crawl around in her lap like children who simply belong there.

The fifth consolidation phase of our therapeutic relationship saw Marga's most difficult crisis. Postponed or canceled therapy appointments had always been a big problem for her. Every time I had to cancel it threw her anew into an abandonment crisis. Although she earnestly desired that I replace these missed appointments with new ones, she never told me why she so desperately wanted them. At the time I really could not manage it, no matter how good my intentions. Despite all the trust we had thus far built up, the negative mother complex always got reactivated. Marga felt abandoned by me not only for the moment, but generally. Image 50 came at this point, the painting where she steps into an abyss, a ravine, into emptiness and feels that the therapist has let her fall.

60. Little Devils in the Lap of the Mother

I didn't want these images to be true (at the time they seemed exaggerated to me), and I underestimated the existential distress into which Marga plunged when I canceled an appointment. I could not hold her with enough empathy. She therefore fell into her complex--actually she jumped into it on purpose, as Image 51 clearly depicts. And she plummeted into the toothed jaws of her own self-torture, which didn't let her go for an entire series of paintings. Up until the beginning of my summer vacation, in which I would again be leaving her for several weeks, we struggled to understand every little rejection that had released such a powerful reaction in her, realizing that abandonment had indeed been the theme of her childhood as well as of her whole life. The crosses on the body of the toothed monster meant both the anger and the feeling of abandonment she felt at the death of her father two years earlier, an asphyxiation death that had really shaken her. I am not going to discuss Marga's father problem anymore here because it was not further played out in this phase of her therapy. Suffice it to say that the feeling was of abandonment by both parents – the father had not noticed or protected her either.

61. In the Desert

By remembering that empty look with which her mother had looked right through her on certain occasions -no longer recognizing her-, I decided to really look at her and take her seriously. I saw how abandoned she felt and I shared that with her. Only in that way could I reach her. Finally the spell broke and she could again feel that I understood her in her disappointment at being abandoned. Now Marga made up her mind to hold out through the aloneness of my vacation. She dreamt: *"I am painting in a group. As I show my therapist the picture, she is very astonished at how I altered the picture just as I was finishing it. She gives me more attention, and that does me a lot of good. She says that she is amazed at how I can repeatedly change and transform the picture. She really likes my picture."* This dream showed that she did feel noticed and accepted by me, and that in the end she would be able to alter the situation. It led to another painting (Image 61) in which a girl kneels alone in the desert as if praying, but full of expectation and turned toward the light.

When I got back from vacation she told me that my going away and my long absence were *"a hammer"* for her. And a hammer actually showed up in one of her paintings. She laid before me a sequence of five astonishing paintings that she had painted during my vacation. I shall now describe them.

62. Orb with Embryo

The first painting (Image 62) shows another one of those orbs falling yet again into the water like those she had constantly painted at the beginning . But now this one almost seems to be enfolded by the wings of the spraying water. The orb is reminiscent of an amniotic sac, and inside it we find a black, shadowy human figure, like a *Homunculus*. At the beginning of my vacation Marga had regressed again, and so was in the amniotic sac – a regressive situation that is also full of hope.

63. Fall

Then it was as if she dared to cast a glance into that mirror which reflects nobody but oneself; I was away at the time. Image 63 resulted. Suddenly a part of her begins to plummet backward, sucked down toward the so-called "mother corner." But she is actively undertaking this bold adventure as if daring to spring backward from a diving board. She hurls herself into the depths of her mother/abandonment complex to confront it actively, throwing herself against it with her full weight. This jump's direction of movement is powerfully traced in dynamic brushstrokes. Marga is not only utilizing completely new symbols, she has adopted a fantastic new painting technique as well. To her right a face appears, a lion's head. It signals the outbreak of lion energy, sun energy, from the midst of her doubt; the rise of pride, anger, and a feeling of power. The painting presents a triple face: one steady, one jumping, and one a lion. At the same time it is an energy explosion with red and yellow flames shooting up between the black like a volcano. The lion in Marga (her zodiac sign is Leo) has been released!

In contrast is the figure of the mother (it could also be the therapist) in Image 64. She looks like an angry witch or shaman smoldering with monstrous energy. Her fire red dress corresponds to that of the falling figure in the previous painting. This is also a picture of the therapist in Marga herself, who has gotten angry, but is full of energy. This can be healing energy. While she glows with all this energy, a black sun hovers over her, indicating that she acknowledges consciously her feeling of abandonment.

In the next painting (Image 65) the hammer appears. It stands for the heavy blow of being abandoned by me during my vacation. But something remarkable has happened. Naked, riding the crescent moon like a canoe, bristling with the fiery hair of the lion's mane that first appeared in Image 63 she approaches the hammer. Before her waves a patch of red, reminiscent of the witch, which she holds out toward the hammer like a red cape. With the energy of a lion and the rage of a witch she confronts the hammer, the very thing that earlier would have destroyed her. What supports her here is the moon canoe, a symbol of her newly-won femininity. It bears her like a boat across the black-blue waters, the depths of the unconscious.

Fourteen days later the last painting of this series finally came (Image 66). No longer in a canoe, she now glides naked through the water as an adult. The difference between this strong female body and that vaguely formed little homunculus in the amniotic sac (Image 62) cannot be missed. Here is peaceful power. Safety and security radiate out of the soft semi-circle into which the woman's head pops up, and it looks remarkably like a rainbow, that ancient sign of reconciliation. In this picture the black is tinted with a lighter color and no longer dominates the bottom of the painting. Instead of suggesting the fathomless depth it appears more like a retreating storm being pushed back by the rainbow.

64. Shaman

What had happened? The insight she gained into the psychodynamics of her abandonment complex in the sessions before my absence carried her through the vacation time. Her regression into the amniotic sac caused fear. The fear expressed itself in the backward-falling figure. But with that came also rage, pride, and power – lion energy. These provided a counterbalance to the fear, i. e. to the suction of her backwards fall. The therapist who had so often abandoned her became a witch; and the energy of such a witch empowered the patient. The rage of the witch, the courage of the falling/jumping figure, and the fire of the lion combined themselves in Marga, giving her the power to march against the hammer. At the same time, she is in her lunar vehicle, in the certainty that her femininity will now bear her safely over the depths of the unconscious.

65. The Hammer

She came to the first session after my vacation astonished at herself and proud of the paintings she was able to bring me. Although my going away was *"a hammer"* for her, she could proudly say, *"Was I furious with you! But the connection with you was never broken."* That is what was new.

66. The Swimmer

Marga's abandonment complex had finally been able to "fantasize itself out" in this series until completely new symbols and energies came up. This is proof that despite all her feeling of abandonment, she had felt understood and even carried by me before my vacation started. She recognized in the witch and in the hammer her mother's rejection, and she wanted to distinguish these from her therapist. But perhaps even more valuable was that the symbols of the hammer and the witch no longer had to be projected, neither onto her mother nor onto me. Rather she could claim the positive power contained in these symbols for herself.

I have briefly retraced a long and sometimes protracted path and I cannot today guarantee that there will be no setbacks or recurrences. After all, recurrence is a structural and not a hopeless characteristic of our work.

That being said, recurrences can also develop into a *Circulus vitiosus*, a vicious circle. I experienced this for a long time at the beginning of my relationship with Marga. What I learned from this experience – and this is my thesis – is that it is only possible to break this cycle, to open up this vicious circle, if we can emotionally decipher the pattern of the relationship in which we find ourselves stuck with our analysand. We do this through persistent repetition and through being empathetic with ourselves as therapists – using empathy to feel what is honestly going on inside us. Only then can we discover what is going on between us and our analysand. We discover which emotions are bound up in the two of us – emotions that were probably already there before the present difficulty.

If we succeed in communicating this to our analysands in ways that they feel understood and accepted, confronting the problems together with them as a "we", then new symbols can emerge and give rise to new emotions and solutions.

How did personal symbol formation and archetypal symbol formation interrelate in the just-described therapeutic process? We could look at it this way: without the formation of archetypal symbols, this poor lonely child would never have been able to overcome such a history of abandonment by her parents. The archetypal symbol of the Great Mother was present from the very beginning, but hidden inside the orb, that core symbol of the self. The Great Mother was so important because she contained the witch energy as well as clarifying and liberating powers. Our therapeutic relationship (which was itself symbolic) enabled and encouraged Marga to create and understand trans-personal symbols. Through our relationship, Marga found the archetypal mother with both her good and evil aspects, and could gradually recognize the light and shadow aspects both in herself and in me. And finally she became able to accept this reality as part of the human condition: as part of our relationship, and as part of every relationship.

Under the Sign of Sophia

Pictures of Feminine Self-Discovery

The following series (Images 67-73) did not arise during therapy. Rather, it illustrates how to make contact with the unconscious and let symbols freely constellate outside the therapeutic context.

Elisabeth Weth came to know analytical psychology more than a decade before she painted this series. She had trained as a child and youth psychotherapist, which included undergoing a training analysis. After her training she continued accessing her own unconscious by painting the images that arose during her active imagination. She did this ever more independently of her teaching analyst, and in so doing she practiced what C.G. Jung conceptualized as a particular goal of imagination and of painting therapy: to let the inner images become the guides to individuation, independent of psychotherapists. Weth became increasingly refined at sensing what was constellating within herself that fostered her inner development, then letting images arise within herself and dialoging with them.

After reaching the age of fifty, several themes started constellating within her: the question of feminine wisdom, a serious review of her life, and a surmising about the events of the world. (It should be noted that in her youth she got along well with her father.) Bound up with all this, a question resurfaced about a primordial feminine identity not derived from the masculine. It is a theme that comes up in many women today.

It is, in fact, the theme of an entire generation of women. But it takes shape uniquely in each individual.

Elisabeth Weth became particularly fascinated with the biblical symbol of Sophia (Wisdom). She had heard about it in a lecture expounding the profound poetic images of the Old Testament, and so she tried to understand it more exactly and to paint it. In so doing she was surprised to find herself feeling very much mirrored and understood by this Sophia symbol. Weth also recognized within herself what the lecturer had called a "split in the feminine" wherein the earth side and the heaven side have been torn apart. Reared in a Christian household, the earth side of her reality was difficult to access during her youth, and the spirit side was taken up with a religion derived primarily from the masculine. Now the youthful Sophia began to fascinate her. Sophia had accompanied God the creator from the very beginning as his co-creator. Weth now recognized that female Wisdom is involved in all creative work. She is present during creation as one who plays and dances and really inspires. This liberty and ease of Being – God the playful and dancing One – had been inaccessible to Elisabeth up until then, but the longing for it, this other side of Being, of the *Dasein*, had always been there. Now her encounter with the figure of Sophia gave Weth a sort of permission, liberating that other side within her. It was probably easier for Weth to accept the figure of Sophia because it comes out of the Old Testament of the Judeo-Christian religious tradition. Yet it was little known until the advent of feminist theology. Today we can almost speak of a new discovery of this figure, especially by women theologians.

It may be important to remind ourselves at this point that archetypal symbolic creation does not always have to arise spontaneously out of our own unconscious in order to touch us and grab hold of us. In the present case, Sophia was an already formed image. Within Elisabeth Weth was an inner constellation directed toward feminine wisdom, a desire for it. Weth was already primed to open herself up, and as she encountered the ready-made image of Sophia, the desire was activated and set into motion. Weth's desire became experientially bound up with Sophia's image. In this way it became "her image".

The Old Testament tells us of Wisdom's lonely quest: she wants to know how she can come to Earth and to humanity. Since Wisdom became "her image", we can ask what this quest might have meant in psychological terms for Elisabeth Weth. She may have put it, "How can this archetype incarnate itself (literally take on flesh) in me – in my very self – so that in the future I can in everyday existence live in accordance with Wisdom even in my body?"

Weth learned indeed how to live in accordance with this Wisdom. She paid increasingly more attention to her needs, to her inner rhythm between exertion and recuperation. She learned to distinguish important things from unimportant. She made more time for things that she absolutely wanted to accomplish and also things she found to be fun, for example painting her interior images. In other words, she started doing what she truly valued, despite all opposition from everyday life and the vocational sphere.

"Her image" of Sophia gradually developed into a fruit tree, another symbol from the Old Testament. In this image Weth's encounter with Wisdom begins to bear fruit. The tree image develops still further during the painting series, taking on the shape of a woman. In a certain way this tree is Elisabeth Weth herself, a fifty-year-old woman who can now become fruitful in new ways. Thus she allowed her desire for feminine wisdom and for playful, dancing creativity to express itself as Sophia. To a large extent she incarnated this desire by painting it. But another desire was also being fulfilled: the desire to be accepted as the darling of a fatherly creator who shared her ideas.

Some time later Weth came across the Pelasgian creation myth and discovered herself yet again, this time in the figure of the divine woman Eurynome, who does not derive her existence from some higher-ranking masculine principle. According to this myth, all creatures and essences exist because of Eurynome's creative dancing. Further, they must then be hatched, and so incubation is required for what was creatively fertilized by wind and snakes. To this end Eurynome changes herself into a bird.

Again, mythical images that Elisabeth Weth first heard about in a lecture enabled her to make sense of what she happened to be dealing with personally at the time – the development of a new self image paramount to a re-creation of her self. The mythical images gave her insight into this new self that was emerging out of the purely feminine. It was a self who, like the goddess, loves to dance over the waves of chaos and the unconsciousness thereby creating for herself both an inner and an outer world. One might say that Elisabeth Weth began at this time to dance creatively over the waves of her own unconscious and the movements of her inner images by adopting a new, very free, creative style. She altered the way she painted. One can see that she became freer in painting the Pelasgian series (Images 75-82) than she had been when she painted the Sophia series.

She became free both in the way she painted and in the way she related to religious tradition. The Pelasgian creation myth of ancient Greece is not bound up with the Christian theological tradition of her father, which could no longer serve as bridge nor barrier. Rather, it is a creation myth out of a feminine religious tradition. Although very new to her, she found it definitely liberating. The world that comes into being in the myth is a new reality. It is born out of the dance of a goddess who wants to spend herself in the travail of a labor necessary to give birth to that which she had fertilized in the dance. In emulating this goddess Elisabeth Weth awoke to the creative woman in herself, a woman who conceives inner images out of the primordial feminine spirit, out of Sophia, out of playful and dancing inspiration. She patiently bears these images until their delivery, namely until she can paint them. She often bore such images within herself for long weeks so that she could then paint them all in a single process over several days.

Being captivated by a creation myth, in this case by a feminine one, always means that one is struggling to give new birth to oneself, to understand oneself anew. For Elisabeth Weth it meant establishing a new foundation in the feminine principle, in Sophia, in a self-understanding no longer derived from a patriarchal basis of creation. It meant nothing less than a new orientation in religiosity. When Eurynome emerged as her new foundational principle, Elisabeth immediately understood herself differently as a creative woman. She realized that she takes images from the dance of life and from the imaginings of the spirit, and she gives birth to them in the form of her paintings. From that time on Elisabeth Weth dared to understand herself as a woman who has pictures to paint and a woman who has something to say about herself and beyond herself. It hardly needs to be added that with this new daring, she always succeeded in outgrowing and creatively handling any oppressive feelings that might surface regarding both the plight of her special school children, or that of our world.

67. Loneliness and Desire in the Split in the Feminine

The Sophia Series

Images 67 and 68 were painted on the same day, January 1, 1987. They came about, as already mentioned, under the influence of a lecture about Sophia by Hildegunde Wöller. As Elisabeth Weth listened, the figure of Sophia caused a constellation of the wisdom archetype in her that evoked so much emotion that she was compelled to express it. And so during the first week of the new year, the experience developed itself into the Sophia Cycle. Elisabeth Weth was deeply stirred by an expression that Wöller had used: "loneliness and desire in the split being of the feminine." It became the title of her first painting and also inspired a later painting called "A split in the feminine has occurred that we still know today. The great Mount Earth, the earth goddess, has been sliced through; the lower part with the cave becomes the underworld, hell; the upper part with the summit becomes heaven, the cloud throne ... Sophia however, it is said, suffers alone upon her cloud throne; she would like to return to Earth and dwell with humanity."[18] (Image 74). The painting series does not begin right away with the figure of Sophia, but rather with the original earth goddess, with the one who was so cruelly split. Elisabeth Weth makes herself clear that the goddess's story is both her own story as well as that of all women coming out of the Judeo-Christian tradition.

The great Mount Earth of the earth goddess is not crosscut but long-cut in Image 67; the one complete Mount Earth has been split into two mountains, like two breasts. They are painted light blotchy brown, especially the left one, over which rises a silver crescent. It is the waning moon, and it almost gets lost in the flaky brown sky. Out of the sky from precisely that place where in Christian iconography the patriarchal god and spirit father of heaven used to be, two hands are reaching down. Like the hands of Noah from the Ark, they release a dove – a dove of peace and at the same time the bird of Aphrodite. Its course is set for a steep descent down to the other mountain, from whose depths outside of the painting's drawing space, two black arms reach up imploringly for help. This region in a painting often symbolizes the mother. Red fire-light blazes between the hands. In front of them, nearest to the observer, three flames are licking upwards. To this three-flamed fire corresponds a three-branched tree. It appears to be a growth symbol connecting the two mountains and attempting to bridge the unfruitful duality between the two aspects of femininity – the one spiritual, the other connected with the earth. One branch is longer than the others and is growing toward the mountain of the Mother Earth. Like the three-branched tree, the three-flamed fire could also be foreshadowing a possible meta-morphosis in which the rigid partition between the heavenly and the earthly aspects of the feminine transforms. There is no question that in this picture all of the painter's libido flows toward the dark feminine figure of Mother Earth, who is caught up in the fires of transformation. This dark figure in turn expects from Sophia, who represents her bright

18 Wöller, Hildegunder: "Die Weisheit und ihre Verwirklichung durch die Frau" in Pflüger, Peter Michael (Editor): *Wendepunkte Frau-Erde-Gott*. Olten/Freiburg im Breisgau 1988.

superior aspect, some sign of reconciliation and peace. And the dove of Noah is dispatched.

All indications point toward a union of opposites leading toward the integration of an essential aspect of the feminine, depicted here as the dark Mother Earth. In describing her life history the painter reported that she felt darkened and repressed under the superiority of her father's religion. She also had the impression that her mother was often very exhausted. Before painting Image 67, she had never been able to positively constellate her parental complexes. In the following picture, however, the dove comes to the nucleus of Mother Earth's cave. Now contact with the feminine earth archetype can get underway.

68. Life and Growth Happen from Within

She called Image 68 "Life and Growth Happen from Within." It was inspired by a vivid description in Hildegunde Wöller's lecture, where she had said: "The mountain upon which God sits enthroned is a symbol of Mother Earth. She gave birth to her son in a cave. He is now enthroned upon her summit as if in her lap. Mother Earth herself is essentially directing from within all that happens. She lets things sprout and bloom, is surrounded with animals that she leads with a light touch, is crowned by stars, and her foot is bathed by the waves of the sea."[19]

The first impression of this picture already reveals its theme: the brown mountain of Mother Earth. It absolutely over-arches the entire breadth of the landscape-formatted paper, filling it so full that only a small portion remains for the sky – just enough to let us see the lower half of a gold-yellow sun, symbolizing "the son of Mother Earth". He is now "sitting on her summit as if in her lap". We can safely assume that she bore him in a cave because he is still bound to the dark brown earth by his golden umbilical cord that reaches to the placenta deep in the mountain. This placenta is an egg within an egg: dark, egg-shaped, with gold objects arranged in its middle and to the right. It is the focal point and energy center of the painting. It is Mother Earth herself symbolically "directing what happens from within". Out of this energy center "it greens". One bush flourishes just to the right of the yellow "umbilical cord" and a smaller one sprouts out of the golden egg. These two bushes stand in the far left of the painting's lower right quarter. Out of this region, things novel and heretofore completely unknown often emerge. The bushes are bearing little yellow blossoms. The painting's warm golden-yellow produces a contrast to certain other colors in the brightening surroundings, above all to the brown, but also to the green and finally also to the blue. This creates the color tone or atmosphere of the painting. Red is still missing here, and the blue in both zones is rather withdrawn compared with the brown.

Dominating the colors is the brown of Mother Earth, but with it also the gold-yellow of the lights emanating from her. The stars crowning her were a special idea of the painter! They are placed like lights in the vault of the earth cave. The mountain simulates an entire cosmos, which includes the four elements. That is why the artist painted Mother Earth "surrounded by animals". In the left part of the cave is a completely light space with a flying dove. It symbolizes the element of air (spirit) and represents the bird kingdom. Representing land animals and mammals as well as the element earth, something like an ass or a cow with an udder is grazing. And finally in the lower right, where "her foot is washed by

19 Ibid.

the waves of the sea" darts a fish, representing the element of water. On the summit of the mountain, the son of Mother Earth herself is depicted as the sun and the element of fire.

69. Sophia Plays on the Globe

A picture has been generated that takes the entire cosmos inside, into the mountain cave of Mother Earth. It is a painting that depicts liberation for this woman who had long lived under a dominant father figure and a weakened mother aspect. She has become free to take a feminine view of the cosmos and of the cosmos within her own female soul. With the warmth of its colors and its vaulted earth formation the image quite resembles a body.

Image 69 was painted on January 4 and portrays her according to this description from the Old Testament:

> The Lord begot me,
> the firstborn of his ways,
> the forerunner of his prodigies of long ago:
> From of old I was poured forth, at the beginning, before the earth.
> When there were no depths
> I was brought forth,
> when there were no fountains or springs of water;
> before the mountains were settled into place before the hills, I was brought forth;
> While the earth and the fields were not yet made, nor the first clods of earth.
> When he established the heavens I was there,
> when he marked out the vault over the face of the deep; When he made firm the skies above,
> when he fixed fast the foundations of the world;
> When he set the boundaries of the sea
> so that the waters should not transgress his command; Then was I beside him as his darling,
> and I was his delight day by day,
> playing before him all the while, playing on the surface of his earth;
> and I found delight in the children of Adam and Eve.
>
> (Proverbs 8:22-31)

The central figure in Image 69 is no longer Mother Earth, but rather the youthful, playful and daughter-like Sophia. She is the muse or anima who inspires the creator. The painting format has changed from landscape to portrait suggesting that the feminine image has stood up. In the foreground, left of the playing Sophia, the dark, heavy orb of the Earth lies upon the black-blue ground. This globe is painted in brown tones nuanced with red, blue and yellow. In alchemy these are the colors of the not-yet-formed "*prima materia*" or prime matter. In the center of the painting is the bright figure of Sophia in her lilac dress with long, wavy hair. Taking elongated, dance-like steps she paces off the vastness of space. Her hands grasp a golden ball that hovers like a cosmic body. It could be a universal self-symbol placed in the light. Or it could be the waxing moon surrounded by a colorful halo that repeats in brighter tones the colors of the earth ball. The color spectrum of this rising moon symbolizes the spectrum of the painter's feeling. She is becoming increasingly at home with the feminine. She holds the golden orb playfully. It symbolizes her self and her highest values.

Mario Jacoby claims that golden balls and orbs in fairy tales are always symbols of the "mobile self" which hurries ahead of the ego drawing it along behind itself. The moon waxes in the upper left quarter of the painting, the traditional location of the father or the masculine god. Here a feminine symbol has replaced him.

The colored clouds of the cosmos are painted in violet tones, complementary to the predominantly gold-yellow of the moon's halo. These clouds deepen into completely blue tones that beautifully enhance the lilac of Sophia's gown. Violet is the color of creative tension and metamorphosis, the color of transformation. In the violet here we see the transformation from black-blue and black- brown toward red, the vivacious color of life. When we compare this painting with the previous one, we see that the painter is now mixing red into the other colors. For example, the gold-yellow of the previous painting has increased here to become really gold. The green that was growing and blooming in Mother Earth's cave is at first lost.

We are now in an open cosmic space and no longer in the cave; a space of freedom and creative play has become accessible to the youthful Sophia.

With the archetype of the playful Sophia being constellated in her, a playful mood comes over the painter – a feeling of joy and the ability to just let things happen. At this time she rediscovers her old enthusiasm for movement and dance. Her detachment and ability to let go even express themselves in the way she paints. In her earlier works she had almost exclusively used pastel sticks, but as the Sophia theme constellates within her she switches to thin, fluid watercolors and she holds the paintbrush loosely in her hand. She unselfconsciously lets the colors run together over the wet surface so that a free play of forms comes into existence and passes away.

If a man had painted such a picture we might surmise that his anima had worked itself loose from the mother archetype. In the case of our painter, it was an aspect of her feminine self that had long been hidden in her rather oppressively accented mother image and overshadowed by her superior father image. It gets newly constellated as the playing, creative, young woman. We see this over and over again in so-called "daddy's girls". It is typical that the feminine aspect of their spirit very conspicuously constellates at a certain unmistakable point in the developmental process. Our painter's Mother Earth by this time had already become able to positively constellate itself.

Images 70, 71, and 72 stand in close connection to one another in theme as well as in color and form. Their color scheme is based on the triad black, blue, and rose/violet. Yellow and red are introduced in Image 71, and green reappears in Image 72. Already in Image 70 the spiraling movement begins which by Image 72 forms the major impression.

The artist based Image 70 upon a text from Jesus Sirach: "I came forth from the mouth of the Most High and blanketed the earth like a mist. My dwelling was in the heights and my throne on a pillar of cloud. I wandered the celestial sphere alone and strode through the depths of the flood" (Jesus Sirach 24:3-5).

This emergence of one thing out of another, Sophia out of "the Most High", is compellingly portrayed by the artist in the form of a spiral. Soft violet light breaks through the bleak neutral light of original creation. This soft violet may well represent Sophia's youthful development. She blankets the earth like fog or a fertile, moist vapor whose colors give the painting a misty, damp atmosphere. The fog's gray, blue and soft violet are the colors of undifferentiated unconsciousness. The concentric movement of the colorful spiral is Sophia's lonely wandering through the celestial sphere, exploring the vast reaches of the cosmic heaven alone, measuring by stepping off the wide spiritual expanse. This lonely exploration is, of course, also that of the artist. In the lower segment of the picture (the lower left quarter represents the attitude toward deepest unconscious) are the depths of the flood through which Sophia strides. The sphere's breadth and the waters' depth that Sophia in her loneliness measured off, are the cosmos of the spirit and the soul, but likewise depict the great exploration going on in the soul of the painter – her inner Sophia.

70. Emanating from the Mouth of the Most High

Image 70 is the portrayal of Sophia proceeding "out of the mouth of the Most High", "dwelling in the heights" and striding "through the depths of the flood". She is of cosmic proportion. We may well surmise that she is coming forth out of that blacked-lined celestial body in the picture's upper left, the traditional place of God the Father in symbolic religious pictures. Why would this image be black? Is a certain problem bound up with it? Could it be the problematic of the shadow which the traditional image of God the Father is casting over the life of this "daddy's girl" so that "the mouth of the Most High" appears black here? Out of this "mouth of the Most High" Sophia comes like a rose colored breath that solidifies into the curving scarf. Sophia sits directly across from the Most High, face to face, on the same level, the image of a powerful cosmic woman. Sophia is a much more concrete figure than the Most High is for the painter. The curving lines with which the scarf cradles her head continue in the broad sweeping spiral movements across the entire breadth of the painting and reach all the way down to the lower left corner, to "the depths of the flood". These spiraling rose-violet lines originate in the first breath and represent both the mist with which Sophia blankets the earth and her measuring or pacing off the celestial sphere. The spiraling movement also establishes a pattern, one similar to an egg or a womb, which is the symbolic promise that something can be born out of this swirling. Something fruitful can come into being.

71. Celestial Body over the Earth

The next painting (Image 71) takes up the egg shape again, this time laying it broadly across the whole picture in landscape format. This egg has taken the black heavenly body of the last painting into itself, plus a new gold-red one. It also contains the violet mist, and the earth together with its trees and people. It is as if the cosmos should and could be incubated anew in this egg. The gold-red celestial body is placed symbolically at the same place where the head of Sophia was in the last picture. We see symbolically a warming, feminine celestial body positioned across from a dark, cool fatherly one in an egg shape that attempts to bring both together anew, father and daughter, "the Most High" and Sophia, like two poles of the same reality. But both are clearly still floating above the brown of the earth with its lifeforms; they are separated from it by a multi-layered seam of cosmic mist. Lo and behold, we can make out a road leading out of Mother Earth's darkness, rising from the lower right up to him who is above.

72. Double Spiral

The calm with which everything in Image 71 lies in layers, with the upper clearly separated from the lower, comes into powerful motion in Image 72. The creative-dynamic spiraling movement from Image 70 grabs hold of the two opposing poles, the dark and the light heavenly bodies, and binds them in a double spiral. The dynamic from the dark pole (the unconscious) unwinds itself into the lighter, more conscious one. The triple spiral unrolls itself, and then re-rolls into a five-fold spiral. The colors expand from only black and violet into a wide spectrum of yellow-orange, red-violet, blue and green. Most importantly, this spiraling movement manages to bring the people (or trees as the case may be) into itself. They were previously outside Sophia's spiraling circle under a layer of mist on a flat plane (Image 71). When Sophia measured off the entire celestial sphere, her movement was sweeping. Now it also becomes fruitful because out of her cosmic loneliness she has succeeded to come to humanity, or to pull them into her creative dynamic. The violet path, which led below to humanity in Image 71, here takes on the shape of an open archway. Psychologically, the artist's gripping; isolating complex has opened itself, giving her free access to humanity, to contact with others and also to herself. The emotional energy produced by the Sophia archetype has enabled the painter to break through her former isolation, opening herself to relationship and affection in the feminine spirit. "The desert could become a garden" is what the painter named Image 73. By using the subjunctive, she was most certainly including herself. It is a picture of the not-yet that she paints here, actually a picture of hope. She lets herself be inspired by the following Old Testament text (Sirach 24:12ff):

"I struck root among a respected folk like a cedar … like a cypress and like rose bushes around Jericho… I am the mother of noble love … and of sacred hope. Come here to me you who desire me, and satiate yourselves on my fruits."

Sophia has come to humanity and struck root there where "the Lord" had reigned alone until now. The painting is of a fruit tree depicted like a woman with out-stretched arms. It is a female version of the "universal human" and C.G. Jung would say that it is also a self-symbol. It stands in the middle of the painting, hanging heavy with fruit. The two central fruits remind one of breasts, and repeat the warm yellow-red celestial body in Image 71 that stood for the cosmic Sophia. Now they are being given to the people so that they may taste of wisdom and knowledge, the fruits of love.

73. A Garden Can Come from the Desert

"I am the mother of noble love,
of honor, of knowledge
and of sacred hope."

This Sophia-become-tree is like a new tree of paradise. The story of the fall would have to be rewritten in view of her, for this tree is not forbidden, but rather invites with wide-open arms. To paint it meant for the artist finally allowing herself to take something for herself from the fruit of life. The time of eternal prohibitions and guilty conscience is over for her. Sophia has become a human tree, and around her neck, like a diadem, the bowl-shaped moon. This is how the moon looks in the Sinai desert, where the painter had some really deep experiences a few weeks earlier. The gold nuggets laid among the roots are the Shekhinah, the "Splendor of God", which has now been crushed into a thousand divine sparks and distributed into all the world, as the Hasidic tradition teaches. The text mentions tall cypresses, and so the painter has placed two of them like sentinels to the right and left of the Sophia tree. Under each blossoms a rose bush. The most important love relationship of the painter's life, which she had to renounce, is somehow "repealed" in this erotic Sophia tree symbolism. The tree obviously forms a cross. But its limbs spread out broadly, too broadly, considering the landscape format of this picture and considering the celestial origin and relationship that Sophia originally possessed. Has the painter here stripped Sophia completely of her celestial attributes, except for the moon? Has Sophia now become too strongly "grounded" because the painter wants to connect her with human reality? Given her rich fruitfulness, the Sophia tree appears to have relatively few leaves. Might this be a sign that the tree appeared a bit too soon: that it had to bear fruit too quickly, before it could naturally mature and unfold its leaves? Or since the painter was 52 years old when she painted it, perhaps it is an autumn tree? In that case the fruit can ripen still longer, although the leaves have already fallen. Finally, the head seems relatively underdeveloped. It usually indicates how connected one is with spirit. Here it looks more like the top of a decorated Christmas tree.

74. Placenta over the Empty Mountain

The creation of the Sophia tree was in a certain sense forced, which precipitated a resultant regression, discernible in the next picture (Image 74). This was not at all untypical for the painter. With the Sophia tree as image of Hope, she had somewhat overtaxed her ability to hope. This plunged her back to where she had started in the first painting, into her original "being split". The text which she chose for this last picture in the series comes out of the already-mentioned lecture by Hildegunde Wöller which also refers back to the split: "The feminine is split, and we know it still today: the great Earth Mountain of the earth goddess has been sliced through, the lower part with the cave becomes the underworld, hell; the upper part, the summit, becomes heaven and the world throne. Several myths recount that here, in between, the space is opened up for humanity."[20]

Again she paints the great Earth Mountain of the Earth Goddess in brown, but this time the slice through the middle is horizontal. The split tellingly resembles a vagina or a mouth, and in it can be seen objects representing human beings. "The separation was necessary in order for humans to become conscious," says the myth, and the painting illustrates this in its own way. The painting appears to say that suffering under the "split of the feminine" was necessary. It seems to have been necessary in order for the artist to become conscious. But the cost for it was high. Too high, suggests the painting. The dark cave in the belly of the mountain is empty and hemmed in right and left by dead trees that suggest the destruction of the environment. These contrast with the living cypresses that flanked the fruitful Sophia tree. This devastation reveals a personal experience of the painter in a certain area of her femininity. At the same time it is a collective problem: "The lower part of the Earth Mountain in the course of history has become mere raw material available for plundering …"

Especially peculiar, however, is the upper part of the mountain. Like a dangerous growth in lurid red some object covers the summit. It lies like a misplaced placenta (the cave belly is empty) upon the "upper Sophia". An egg shape surrounds this red object. Can anything fruitful grow here? Or through this switching of places, this turning inside out,

20 Ibid.

is something made impossible? What the body should protect has now been placed on the outside. Is an un-clarified mother complex maybe growing here on the upper Sophia, in the spiritual realm, as a result of the earlier "split in the feminine"?

The painter herself sensed the incongruity in this outcome, and as soon as she had enough time, she sought out a new myth for herself; she undertook a new creative process; and she began painting a new series. This time she painted out of the Pelasgian creation myth of ancient Greece. It is as if she wanted to start once more at the outset in order to establish a beginning that existed before the split in the world, which was continuing to tear at her in her self-understanding and from which she was still suffering.

The Pelasgian Creation Myth

It was in August of the same year that she began anew. As mentioned, she was now letting the ancient Greek Pelasgian creation myth take hold of her. Always when something new crystallizes in us symbolically, it is like a new beginning, like a new birth. Creation myths present such beginnings symbolically making them especially suited for helping people experience their own self-renewal and self-creation through the mythological images. This myth begins right away with a "goddess of all things" instead of a father-bound daughter goddess, as in the Sophia myth.

"In the beginning was Eurynome, the goddess of all things. Naked she raised herself up out of the chaos. But she found nothing solid upon which she could set her feet."[21] Image 75 was painted to this sentence on August 4, 1987, again using a thin watercolor technique on wet paper. Out of the brown chaos, which from the heavy black of the depths to the soft violet of the heights grows ever lighter, the naked Eurynome rises. She stands in something like a crescent moon with her feet still in the dark. Her hand is raised above her eyes as if scanning the brightening sky. The psychological expectation still seems to be that the realm of light will

21 Seifert, Theodor: *Weltentstehung – die Kraft von tausend Feuern.* Zürich 1986, pp. 39, 54.

be in the upper left, the symbolic place of God the Father. However, nothing more than a slight brightening of the chaos is recognizable. The goddess of all things, whose figure resembles the youthful Sophia of the previous series, no longer needs a God the Father, and also no Mother Earth, in order to exist. She is born out of herself. In the same way, the painter's ego, or rather the self, in its autonomy is born anew here. It is freed from both the father and the mother imagos that have enclosed and controlled it until this time.

75. *"Naked she arose out of the chaos"*

"But she found nothing solid upon which she could set her feet. She therefore separated the sea from the sky and danced alone upon the waves."

76. Eurynome on the Waves

So continues the Pelasgian myth, to which the artist painted Image 76. Eurynome dances and moves in concentric circles, unrestrained and sure, over the waves of unconsciousness. We are reminded of the great spiral figure from Image 72 of the Sophia series. Now soft, violet half-arches create a sheltering vault above Eurynome. Again the figure very much resembles the playing Sophia of Image 69, but she has lost that childish, daughter-like character. This Eurynome, goddess of all things, is an adult woman. She is also alone but secure in her dancing and harmonizing with the rhythm of being. This is brought out in the way the arches nearly join themselves to form a circle.

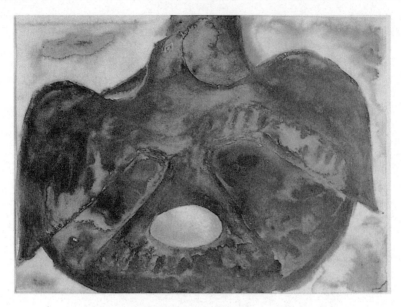

77. Eurynome as Dove

To Image 77 belongs the following text:

"Then Eurynome took on the form of a dove,
lighted upon the waves
and in her time laid the world egg."

Eurynome is here painted as a dove (Image 77). She reminds us of the messenger dove in the last series dispatched between "the Most High" and Sophia. But in this painting, the dove is an embodiment of the goddess and not beholden to any "Most High". Poised as if in flight, standing and facing toward the right – the direction, by the way, of becoming conscious – the dove lays the world egg. This takes place seemingly in a dark container – an alchemical vessel? A womb? This white egg, tinted with soft pink, contains a creation that can now become fruitful, mainly because it is in the right place here, inside the protective vessel. Now something can really grow and be born one day. We have an image of hope. And more than that, the egg has already been laid and the placenta is prepared for what is about to happen.

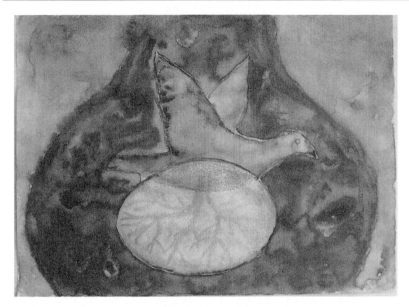

78. Dove on the Egg

In Image 78 the painter goes over the whole process yet again. This time the dark gray dove fits more naturally together with the deep purple vessel. Both are painted in the colors of creative transformation. It is as if the dove is both protectively sitting on the shining, white-silver egg and at the same time in flight above it.

At this point, in order to complement the Eurynome story, the artist included another ancient Greek myth about the world egg:

"In the beginning was the night:
a bird with black wings.
This primordial night, inseminated by the wind,
laid her silver egg
in the giant womb of the darkness.
Out of the egg came the son of the blowing winds:
a god with golden wings:
Eros, the god of love."

79. Ophion Hatches the World Egg

Image 79 shows the snake Ophion hatching the egg as the Eurynom myth describes it:

"At her behest Ophion coiled herself
around this egg seven times,
until it was incubated and it hatched."

The painter lays the light egg among the black-gray clouds of chaos letting the black snake surround it and lick it. Like a sentinel deputed by the goddess, the snake hisses against the chaos. She is an apotropaic animal, herself camouflaged in black against the black of her surroundings assigned to protect and defend that which is becoming. She is an important symbol for the artist, who had so often allowed what was becoming to get lost – she would just quit. Here the positive side of the mother complex appears, the side that knows how to defend an egg or a child against anything chaotic that wants to swallow it up.

80. The Hatched Egg

In Image 80 the time is now ripe – for the myth and for the artist – to let "all that is" emerge from the now incubated and hatching world egg. In many respects this painting resembles the second painting of the Sophia series (Image 68), but with noteworthy differences. Here everything is more open, lighter, with brighter colors. The silver egg lies exactly in the center of this painting allowing all things to issue forth from it: a waxing moon, stars and a dove in the upper realm, and everything in the earthly realm as well. The earthly realm here is more inhabited than in the Sophia series and also seems less cut off from the upper realm. Here everything originates from one single feminine source. The artist felt a need to express symbolically that the silver world egg is like a womb containing everything in itself and releasing everything from itself. She also felt that she had to include the heavenly bodies together along with the tree symbol in the painting. These symbols had become so important for her at the end of the last series, but as we saw, they were still somewhat premature and proved to be not yet completely ready to be painted. Though the painter was artistically capable of executing the motifs and symbols, the painting revealed unmistakably which motifs she had painted prematurely, and which ones she was able to live up to existentially at the time.

In the two paintings closing this series (Images 81 and 82), the tree symbol is now wonderfully, organically woven into the total picture of the myth.

81. The Egg in the World Tree I

In Image 81, painted on August 14, 1987, the silver world egg rests slightly above the exact center of the picture, but definitely within the dark vessel. The Tree of Life with its twisted trunk is growing up through the middle of the vessel like a cosmic axis. To the left, among the deep-reaching roots inside the dark vessel rests a dark celestial body – the dark pole of the cosmos. To the right of the axis, in the crown of the tree, nests the light pole, a yellow-red celestial body. A smaller, yellow "satellite" orbits around it, visible still further to the right. Likewise, left of the dark pole a bright spark flashes in the darkest region of the painting. The entire image is reminiscent of Yin and Yang, the ancient Chinese symbol of the opposites. At any given time the dark half contains a light point and the light half contains a dark point. This is constituent of the opposite poles of reality.

The same thing happened inside the artist while she was executing the painting: the "dark" side of her femininity, which until now had been split off, shared itself with the "light" side, which is to say the more conscious side. They reconciled with one another.

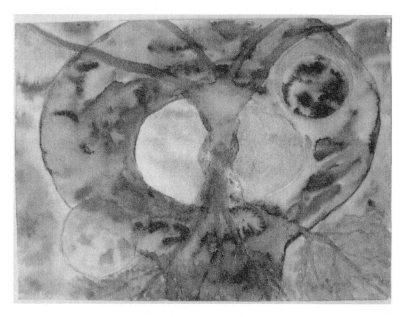

82. The Egg in the World Tree II

Three mountains complete the painting. They stand in the upper left, the zone of the fatherly. Their greenish shimmer is all but absorbed by the dominant stone gray of the mountains. Upon noticing this all-too-meager green, and recalling the lack of foliage on her Tree of Life, it apparently occurred to the artist that the painting still needed something in order to truly be a "picture of completion". Therefore she painted Image 82, whose twisting trunk is meant to express the tree's ability to dynamically adapt itself to the changing light. The tree appears much more elastic and softer than in the last painting. Such a twisted tree would be very inviting to a snake, and we could easily imagine one eventually winding itself up the trunk, or the figure of a woman leaning against it. Both would be echoes of the biblical story of the fall from paradise and original sin. Here, however, the story is turned positively: the snake that surrounded the egg at the beginning of creation, which in Uroboros form is again recognizable around the vessel here, has now hatched the cosmic egg. Out of it sprouts the Tree of Life, yet another image of the creator Eurynome, who contains everything within herself and brings everything into being. Finally the position of the world egg in Image 82 is even better balanced than in the previous picture. Now it comes to lie really in the center of both the picture and also of the dark vessel that protectively surrounds it.

Although Image 82 is without a doubt a better-rounded and more enclosed picture, it cannot completely replace Image 81, which still has something going for itself in its openness and its dynamic. Image 81 appears more permeable, allowing the collective unconscious to flow into and through it. In fact, it depicts a symbolic passage through the picture originating in the symbolic zone of the unconscious. A diagonal line is traceable from the dark lower left all the way through the small, bright satellite planet in the upper right. The planet, by the way, looks like Saturn with its rings and moons.

It is very easy to see in both of these series by Elisabeth Weth, that they no longer end in a "split in the feminine". That split, as we said, is a collective problem for her generation of women, and it had long impaired her personal experience and understanding of herself as a woman. Now she creates herself anew in that she has worked on overcoming the split in two impressive painting series. She started with Sophia, in whom she could be a playful, creative woman, at first still "beloved" of a most high creator, but with equal rights and the power to co-create. Finally in Eurynome she discovers a figure not derived from the masculine principle. Rather, this feminine being with its creative and fertile powers is non-derivative, an entity subsisting in itself. The series contains many paintings that illuminate tension between opposites. They culminate in two paintings that are true images of feminine completeness containing such archetypal motifs as the world egg, the Tree of Life, daystars and night stars. In them she overcame the split in the feminine.

From beginning to end the path of individuation for each of us is marked by a search for the symbols that point us toward our completeness, toward our self, which is always out ahead of us. Often these symbols of the self are at the same time religious symbols. The two series of pictures, which Elisabeth Weth spontaneously painted out of her inner necessity, impressively illustrate her process of self-discovery. That process extended far beyond the possibilities and time limits of a therapeutically led analysis. Although she had been strongly influenced by the patriarchal image of God from her parent's household, and that had long hindered her sense of self as woman, she went in search for ultra-new feminine self images and images of God.

C.G. Jung saw in active imagination, which included for him the creation of pictures, a way to make life-long contact with the inner figures and images, independent of therapy and extending far beyond it. Jung saw possibilities and opportunities in this creative relationship with the inner images. For Elisabeth Weth this process with her pictures meant redemption.

Summary

Putting all of this together, how do I recognize therapeutic effectiveness in a picture series?

In the first place, naturally, I ask the artist. By its nature of course the answer is not objective, but it reveals the subjectively-experienced transformation of the mood most directly. I also consider the perception and comments of the painting group, if there is one. These can be checked and verified. But generally, here is what I look at:

1. Are there changes in the individual's relationship to the therapist or to the painting group? Are such changes reflected in the pictures?

2. Are alterations in the individual's emotions noticeable in connection with the pictures?

3. Are there modifications in the corresponding symbols in the paintings?

4. Can the apparent steps from picture to picture in a series be verified and interpreted? This includes the clarification and significance of each individual picture in the context of the entire series and of the entire developmental and individuation process.

5. Have the ways and means of producing the artworks developed or changed in ways that make the therapeutic effects perceptible? Here I look for various indicators:

   - Is there a growing individualization of the artistic style? Often works produced early in the process appear less personal, clichéd or all too abstract.

- Is there an increasing differentiation regarding variety in color and form, differentiation of technique, and differentiation of symbols?
- Is diversification increasing? If so, are details unfolding with growing coherence? Does the content of the picture hold together? Ascertaining growing coherence is very important, because it indicates the stability of the painter's ego complex. The condition of the ego complex can be very easily read from the coherence or incoherence of the pictures.
- Are the paintings increasing in clarity and concentration? Often the pictures in a series exhibit a growing tendency toward order in the drawing space, sometimes also mandala-shaped centering.

Using an entire series of dreams that illustrate a natural individuation process, Jung describes the path upon which our unconscious takes us again and again. It is a path that develops itself spirally. This spiral form can be recognized just as clearly in the inner structure of a picture series as it can in a dream series, and so we can easily transfer what Jung wrote about dreams in *Psychology and Alchemy* onto pictures and picture series:

"The way to the goal seems chaotic and interminable at first, and only gradually do the signs increase that it is leading anywhere. The way is not straight but appears to go around in circles. More accurate knowledge has proved it to go in spirals: the dream motifs (read also "picture motifs", ed.) always return after certain intervals to definite forms, whose characteristic is to define a center. And as a matter-of-fact the whole process revolves about the central point or some arrangement round the center, which may in certain circumstances appear even in the initial dreams (pictures, ed.). As manifestations of unconscious processes the dreams (pictures, ed.) rotate or circumambulate round the center, drawing closer to it as the amplifications increase in distinctness and in scope. Owing to the diversity of the symbolic material it is difficult at first to perceive any kind of order at all. Nor should it be taken for granted that dream sequences (picture series, ed) are subject to any governing principle. But as I say, the process of development proves on closer inspection to be cyclic or spiral. We might draw a parallel between such spiral courses and the processes of growth in plants; in fact the plant motive (tree, flower, etc.) frequently recurs in these dreams and fantasies and is also spontaneously drawn or painted." [22]

22 Jung, Carl Gustav: *CW*, Vol. 12, *Psychology and Alchemy*, § 34.

Part III:

Painting in a Group

As an incarnation of the mother archetype
the group provides a relatively anxiety-free space,
creating good conditions for the emergence of
fantasies, images and symbols out of the unconscious
so that by painting out of the unconscious,
symbolic creations of greater expressive power
can succeed.

Introduction

Today, painting in groups has become the most common setting for the practice of painting therapy. Jolande Jacobi already held it in high esteem, especially for work in clinics.

In order for painting therapy to be Jungian, however, the focus must remain on individuals and their individuation processes, even when the therapy is carried out in a group. As therapists and in this case also as therapeutic group leaders, we must be clear about what we are doing, what is gained and lost when we choose a group as the context for therapy, which conditions to set up, which ways and means to use, which modalities of therapy, of active imagination, of painting, of discussing the works and of encountering each other.

Naturally we can let individuals paint within the group without following up afterwards with a group discussion. In such cases, we either discuss the pictures privately in individual meetings or quasi-alone in that only the group leader does the talking about each picture. However we are not then utilizing the therapeutic potential available in the group.

For painting in groups a common theme is typically found that can either be painted by each single member or by all together as a group composition. The Jungian methodology is better approximated when each person paints his or her own picture. Still I would not want to miss the lovely opportunity offered by the occasional group painting session where everyone paints something together on one big sheet as an expression of his or her common experience. However, I would not suggest such a group session right away for the first meeting, because I use this session to help everyone find their place in the group and document this also through their own individual painting.

Jung's Reservation about Groups

It is no secret that C.G. Jung had reservations regarding groups, but when we look at his concern more closely, we see that he was thinking more of the phenomenon of crowd psychology. For Jung, the group is in fact a constitutive element of the individual, and he based his understanding of the human person and his therapeutic concept upon: "working on the pairs of opposites, collective and individual, for the good of the individual"[1].

The concept of group therapy had not yet been developed in Jung's day and he could in no way have known the phenomenon of a group engaged in group therapy. Keeping this in mind, Jung's opinions regarding the collective and the consequences for therapy need to be reviewed and corrected[2]. Jung was especially critical of "the modern tendency to replace man's inner cohesion by outward community, as though anyone who had no communion with himself would be capable of any fellowship at all!"[3]. Jung feared that as individuals our autonomy and contact with ourselves, with our deeper Selves, might be more likely to be avoided than realized if we were too strongly embedded in a community. The interior would remain divided and simply be replaced by the external community.

---

1   Jung, C.G. *Psychologie und Alchemie* in Rascher (Editor): *Psychologische Abhandlungen*, Vol. 5, 2nd Edition. Zürich 1952, p. 64.
2   Seifert, Theodor: "Die Gruppentherapie im Rahmen der Analytischen Psychologie" in *Zeitschrift für Analytische Psychologie* 5.1, 1974; also Dorst, Brigitte: *Der Archetyp der Gruppe: Gruppen als Erfahrungsräume der Individuation.* (Diploma thesis for the C.G. Jung-Institut Zürich) 1990; and "Der Archetyp der Gruppe: Gruppen als Erfahrungsräume der Individuation und Ko-Individuation" in *Analytische Psychologie* 181,3/2015.
3   Jung, Carl Gustav: *The Collected Works of C.G. Jung (CW)*, vol. 14/1, *Mysterium Coniuntionis*. Translated by R.F.C. Hull. Princeton: Bollingen series XX, 2nd Edition 1970, § 9 footnote 45.

Even today it is often bemoaned that in group settings the individuals can be rolled over by group pressure and the group norm, so that a certain style of behavior and even of painting is pressed upon them, which does not necessarily correspond to their own essence.

A Jungian Concept of Group Therapy

Considering the above reservations, group therapy according to Jungian principles could be just the answer to the very problem that Jung formulated. Jungian group therapy makes conscious the collective as it is reflected in the individual, and "strives to differentiate and work through both poles – the personal and the collective – of this pair of opposites. Much of the practical work for members of an analytical group involves learning to see the internal parallels to outer events. By paying attention to the social interactions of the group, I as a member become more conscious of my own internal participation. For example, when an outsider to the group is aggressively spurned or rejected, he is at the same time the dark inner brother whom I cannot accept."[4] Everything would depend upon my learning to accept him, that means the side of me that he embodies, firstly interiorly within myself and also exteriorly within the group. "It is about recognizing the personal processes at play in the social event. As the processes within the group become conscious, I begin to see my own inner coherence or lack thereof. If I have a tendency to replace my coherence with external cohesion, I risk remaining infantile and unconscious. But it is possible to challenge this and work on it, and that is precisely what is worked on in the group process. Through the social interaction, interior completeness takes place, which Jung among others formulated to be the goal of analytical work."[5]

Jung's work on society and crowds is based upon an outdated mass-psychology in which group phenomena had not yet been studied. It is somewhat ironic that "Jung's critique of the masses and their dangerous influence on the individual can be overcome precisely by

---

4   Seifert, Theodor: *Die Gruppentherapie im Rahmen der Analytischen Psychologie*, p. 182.
5   Ibid, p. 180. Also Dorst, Brigitte: *Der Archetyp der Gruppe: Gruppen als Erfahrungsräume der Individuation und Ko-Individuation*, pp. 340-343.

including group phenomena directly in the therapeutic process."[6] We now understand that a group is fundamentally different from a crowd. In the crowd the individual gets lost, and that is how collective images can become so overwhelmingly potent. On the contrary, in a group the individual has to stand for himself and to answer for himself.

In this connection we should also distinguish an anonymous or spontaneously formed group from a therapeutic group. The former may get together, for example, under an unschooled group leader or a charismatic party politician or a zealous sect member set on converting them. A therapeutic group on the other hand, meets in the presence of a therapist or leader trained in group-dynamics who can meaningfully interject and introduce new concepts, perceptions, and styles of behavior.

Symbol Constellation in the Group

A Jungian therapy group practicing active imagination or painting differs from the kind of self-experience groups where the interaction between the participants forms the focus. Jungian groups focus upon symbolic material that has come up from the unconscious through active imagination, the creative process, or the painted image. For example, I give my groups nature symbols or fairy tale motifs to stimulate their imagination. The symbolic material enters as a third party forming the center of the Jungian group process between group members and therapist. In this way everyone has simultaneous contact to the unconscious material through a single content or symbol that has been accessed and extracted from the collective unconscious. The group thereby gathers together around a natural center. They share a common interest in digging deeply into the goldmine of the unconscious and further developing what they find there.

The setting of a painting therapy group itself is already symbolic. A session begins by sitting or lying in a circle ready for the active imagination. Later, the pictures that were painted are also shown around the circle and at the end are laid beside each other in a circle. This ensures

---

6   Seifert, Theodor: *Die Gruppentherapie im Rahmen der Analytischen Psychologie*, p. 181.

that the common material, the material from the unconscious, forms the center of the group.

The process of encounter and relationship within the therapy group occurs at a deeper level than in everyday consciousness. It is a level in which we are more related to each other, and where we find that we carry the images and symbols of humanity within us. Here every contact with ourselves becomes a discovery of that "inner cohesion" that Jung was speaking about. And when the contact achieves a high point of archetypal experience, it leads to a harmonizing; yes an "at-one-ment with oneself and at the same time with humanity"[7].

I have noticed that conflicts of power, position, and rivalry tend to diminish in this group process, even though they do not disappear completely. More energy is therefore available for the common effort of gaining access to the unconscious and its symbols. Manfred Krapp[8] reported this phenomenon in his groups even with psychotics, who otherwise are known for their great ambivalence when it comes to behaving socially. In the painting therapy group it was often observed that the person who painted what everyone acknowledged as "the most beautiful picture" was indeed placed in the alpha position, as the one who best incarnated the group norm of "creativity". However, this did not produce so much envy from the others as it did an identification with the painter vis-a-vis the picture. Painting groups are also considered to be good for psychotics since nobody remains too long in the outsider position. The group norm is "creativity", that does not allow an individual to remain for too long outside the happening of the group. The outsider position also makes other group members nervous, partly because they begin to identify with the outsider.

Again and again, painting groups have the following powerful experience. A symbolic-archetypal motif is assigned for everyone to paint, for example, a source or spring. It appears differently in the imagination of each individual, conditioned and impacted by his or her life history. And yet everyone also experiences and expresses trans-personal aspects of the symbol that become very obvious when the pictures are being

---

7   Jung, Carl Gustav: *CW*, vol. 16, *The Practice of Psychotherapy*, § 227.
8   Krapp, Manfred: *Die Gestaltungstherapie als Beitrag zur Psychotherapie der Psychosen.* (Diploma thesis for the C.G. Jung Institute Zürich) 1986, pp. 107-109.

shared in the group. Everyone who painted in that group experiences the meaningfulness of the symbol emotionally, and its complexity becomes visible.

In such an activity, the positive as well as the negative aspects of the symbol come to light. Staying with the symbol of the spring as an example, the way it is depicted usually suggests how positive or negative the mother complex is, since that complex is so often constellated in the symbol of the spring (but also in other symbols). When the complex arises, we can recognize how good our access is to the symbol, and to the emotions it awakens within us. We get an idea of how we relate to the generous and nourishing aspects of life, of how good our access is to the sources symbolized in the spring, and what significance we attach to this symbol and the area of life currently depicted by it.

Sometimes a single aspect of a symbol is particularly important for us, but we did not paint it, because it was not currently realizable. But comparing our painting with those of the other group members can make that aspect more conscious. Perhaps someone else did paint it, and so now we see it. The abundance of aspects contained in a given symbol always overtaxes the possibilities of realization for an individual artist, but appears in many and various ways when an entire group paints the same symbol. Often an individual's spring at the moment holds little water, meaning little libido is flowing. But by looking at the pictures of the others who have captured the aspect of vitality contained in the spring motif, the "dry" member will be swept up and carried away, so that personal libido once again begins to flow. Naturally the opposite can also happen: the experience of one's own barrenness and dissatisfaction in comparison to the richly streaming springs of the others can awaken feelings of deprivation and envy. But from that moment on, these are at least mentioned and made accessible and so they can be worked through.

Former sibling rivalries from our family's past can reappear, no matter whether we were the beloved child or the black sheep. This happens in all groups. We begin to experience the group as a matrix, as a symbol of the mother and of the family as a whole. It becomes the place where each of us experiences both a sense of belonging and the interest of others in our attempts to live and to create. This is one of the group's most important functions overall. Feelings of deprivation and of dissatisfaction that up until then were avoided can also be addressed and taken care of. Clearly the group itself represents an aspect of the spring that ultimately is the mother archetype.

In ancient times the group formed the matrix for initiations, transition rituals, and transformation experiences. Rituals were often carried out in a group and by a group. The reason why fairy tales and mythological material is so suited for this work is that they contain such transitions and the possibilities to survive them, and are especially useful when they are actively imagined, painted, and discussed[9] in the group. It has been shown again and again that fairy tales and myths are especially well suited in constituting painting therapy group meetings, including the beginning phase of group work with psychotics[10]. The stories offer a common vessel for everyone, and at the same time the individuals can clearly distinguish themselves from the others by identifying with and painting that part of the fairy tale or the myth that moved them. It is revealing to discover with which part of the fairy tale most of the participants identify – the presenting problem, the quest, or the discovery of an interior guide. This tips the therapist off to both the interior themes of each participant and where the group currently stands. If the same fairy tale is again selected in a later phase of the group process, everyone in the group can readily see the changes in the problematic and in the inner position of the group that become apparent.

Czerny, in discussing group dynamics in art therapy from the viewpoint of analytical psychology[11], notes this about group formation: often a newcomer at first experiences the group as more or less an unstructured mass, which causes anxiety. Against this, the group leader provides a protective counterweight by guaranteeing and embodying the group's future structure. By doing this however, the leader will be

9   Compare this with the ritualization of the Demeter myth in the Elysian mysteries in which the Greek people participated as a large group. See Riedel, Ingrid: *Demeters Suche: Mütter und Töchter*. Zürich 1986, pp. 145-160.
10 Krapp, Manfred: *Die Gestaltungstherapie als Beitrag zur Psychotherapie der Psychosen*, pp. 35-38, 62ff; Riedel, Ingrid: *Die weise Frau: Der Archetyp der alten Weisen in Märchen, Traum und Religionsgeschichte*. Ostfildern 2016, pp. 61-67, 89-95; Kast, Verena: *Folktales as Therapy*. Fromm International Publishing Corporation, New York 1995.
11 Czerny, Michael: *Gruppendynamik und Gestaltungstherapie* im Verständnis der analytischen Psychologie. Stuttgart 1983, pp. 34, 38/39.

raised by the group members to a position above them, a sort of hero in the battle against the workings of the group dragon, meaning the temporarily chaotic state of things. Being raised up to a leader-father though, could make him threatening to each individual, for each is now in danger of becoming dependent upon him. By embodying this danger, the leader thereby inherits something of the devouring tendency of the group dragon. Here the group member would finally be required to become an individual, to individuate. Symbolically that would mean taking on the role of a "son hero" and coming up against the "father monster" in order to claim for himself the powers which he wrests from the group monster. For Czerny the therapist's role must be to remain conscious as a helping-ego to each individual group member. The painters will want to heap their psychic energy upon the identification figure of the group leader, who in turn must repeatedly reject this and instead refer it on to the painted image and to the effort bound up in creating it. The therapist rejects the projection in order that the psychic energies are turned back onto the painter and the creative production: "In art therapy the goal is identification with the creative product, not with the group leader."[12]

The Mother Archetype as Group Matrix

Although Czerny's position does have something to teach us, it is derived from a group model that emphasizes conflict. Comparing the individual's encounter with the group to a mythological battle with the dragon describes if anything a masculine psychology.

In contrast it is also completely possible to understand a painting group as a matrix of the mother archetype and arrange things so that new members first experience the positive side of the mother archetype, with the group leader embodying the caring, protecting, loving, *Magna Mater* (Great Mother). Only after the membership has matured

12 Krapp, Manfred: *Die Gestaltungstherapie als Beitrag zur Psychotherapie der Psychosen*, pp. 34/35.

to a certain point should the group occasionally be experienced as the "smothering, devouring, evil" mother, against which we must defend ourselves and out of which we must define ourselves. What matters here is that patients experience the group in the initial phase, "as they originally experienced their mother with her conflicting comments"[13]. Naturally the experience of our family history, above all of our sibling group, is part of this matrix. There is plenty of potential for tension here, and everyone must learn to differentiate between what belongs to the past from what is happening in the present. If the group with its leader can achieve this differentiation, it can free itself of significant tensions, and its members can again come to trust each other. This depends on the stability of each individual's ego complex. It is upon my ego that I support myself as an individual but I may also be able to stabilize my ego complex through my encounter with the group. If nothing else, I become more stable through the care and attention that I receive from the group through my pictures, and once again experience the positive side of the mother archetype. Finally it is essential for me to experience the group as a type of "transitional object". It both accepts me, yet has its limitation. This is how the child experiences the mother. At first she is all encompassing but only in order that I can finally become a mother myself.

As an incarnation of the mother archetype, the group creates a relatively anxiety-free space or at least allows itself to be molded into such a space. This space in turn provides the right conditions for fantasies, images, and symbols to emerge from the unconscious. By painting out of the unconscious, works of even greater symbolic power can come to expression. Whether a relatively anxiety-free climate can arise naturally depends upon the group leader. Can the leader constellate the positive mother archetype by building up a trusting communication style?

Much also depends on how the group's pictures are handled. Will the necessary respect for their content be safeguarded or not? After all, they contain messages from the unconscious. Will the members give each other feedback with curiosity and empathy and make an effort to understand each other? Or will feedback tend to be critical and evaluating? A

13 Ibid, p. 100.

"loving intercourse with pictures"[14] can be achieved in such a way that the danger of devaluing some pictures while idealizing others is avoided.

Compared to other types of self-encounter groups, I always notice a relatively anxiety-free climate with painting groups. I believe this is because everyone in the painting group is on the same experiential level. All are seeking contact with the unconscious and are allowing it to confront them. In enduring this confrontation, people find that they are stronger when united than when they are separate – and that is how group painters endure it. Everyone is in the same boat, by doing active imagination, allowing something essential out of their unconscious to arise, painting it, showing it to each other, and talking about it. They are really sharing with each other.

The group discussion over the resulting paintings and how they came about is a pleasant experience. The members are pleased at how they cooperate, how they look at things together and make common discoveries, and above all how they share a common sense of being gripped by the expressiveness and feeling-content of the symbols. As discussion leader, my main task is to encourage people to "feel" themselves into each other's paintings and speak about their feelings, to ask each other questions, and to share their perceptions openly. My primary task is not to interpret. Discrimination, provocation and contention fall away, because this group approach is primarily concerned with understanding the paintings as self-expressions of each person. The paintings mean something for that person and should never be evaluated, neither from the aesthetic nor the psychological standpoint. It is the leader's place to interpret the works as expressions of a psychological situation, but only with the utmost empathy and competence. By being empathetic and very careful, the leader can soon create a climate and a discussion style in the group wherein the individual members become competent in discussing the paintings among themselves. They become able to really perceive the paintings and understand them as mental processes.

I have noticed that painters always look for some sort of echo or reaction to their painting from the group and the group leader. This expresses the group's interest, participation and empathy. In such an

14 Kast, Verena: Lecture manuscript about *"Imagination"* in WS 1981/1982 at the University of Zürich.

empathetic context one can then ask even critical questions such as, "Why is there so much black in this picture and not a bit of red?" But I always let the painter introduce the picture first, so that the group has a sense of the painter's condition, and can respond with the appropriate feeling tone. And at the beginning I only ask something like, "What was most important for you while painting? What touched you most while you were painting?" One can naturally begin by having the other participants sharing their feelings, questions and perceptions about the painting. In some cases that makes the discussion more exciting and surprising. But once in a while this can be frightening or hurtful for the painter who has not yet had a chance to explain what the picture means.

A Method of Perception and Interaction

I share Theodor Seifert's opinion that "the concepts of analytical psychology as a method of perceiving and interacting are applicable to groups"[15]. However, as I understand it, using this method to become aware of a group's insider rules and group dynamics is definitely not the primary theme and function of painting therapy according to Jungian principles. On the contrary, applying analytical psychology's "approach to perceiving" within painting therapy means to perceive a patient's personal psychological situation – as well the group situation – in the presence of the individual's paintings; and interpreting this situation in view of the symbolic material on both subjective and objective levels. With a series of paintings, this also includes recognizing the progressive steps toward individuation, or discovering their possible obstacles, whichever the case may be.

Analytical psychology's "method of interaction" can also be applied in a painting group. Everything that a group shares regarding the examination of a picture, the questions asked about the picture and the feelings that come up during the process, all reveal the underlying psychological situation and give access to the unconscious. As a result of this "perception and interaction method", participants who construct their paintings too consciously, and don't dare to contact their own

---

15 Seifert, Theodor: *Die Gruppentherapie im Rahmen der Analytischen Psychologie*, p. 183.

unconscious, easily fall into the shadow of the group. They become
the scapegoat, representing the group's dark side. In such situations it is
essential for the group leader to intervene carefully and consciously. The
leader must first make the group's impatience with the shadow member's inhibited manner conscious in order that the group's perceptions
and interactions can bear fruit. Sometimes the leader can intervene
with a pinch of humor, for example by suggesting paradoxically that if
the painter meant absolutely nothing symbolic by the painting, then
the group is also not allowed to interpret it symbolically. In this way
anxious painters, who do not yet want to let the unconscious flow
into their paintings, are protected from the pressure of the group, yet
still encouraged to one day allow more to flow into their painting,
thereby experiencing more about themselves during the discussion. This
is Franzke's advice: keep all afterthoughts and interpretations to yourself
if the painter is rationalizing too much about a picture.[16]

Even in cases where the Jungian perception and interaction method
was implemented well, my observation is that members will keep things
to themselves if subgroups have spontaneously formed and are acting
independently.

Now I shall try to apply the general principles of group therapy according to Jungian psychology to the specific conditions and circumstances
of a painting group. Jungian therapy is primarily an individual therapy.
If it is practiced in groups, including painting groups, it is important that
the individual learns to be carried by the group, yet not come up short as
an individual. I make sure that every picture in a group is discussed even
though this requires adequate time and sufficient energy from everyone
in the group. One requirement is that the ideal group size of eight
members should not be significantly overstepped. This counts above
all for a painting therapy group in the traditional sense, which endures
over a long period of time. In the case of a short-term group (say a week
or a weekend group), where this size limit is significantly exceeded,
the discussions of the paintings should take place in more phases with
adequate pauses in between. Even better is the formation of sub-groups
containing three or four participants that have their own group leader,
so that nobody comes up short.

16 Franzke, Erich: *Der Mensch und sein Gestaltungserleben.* Bern 1977, p. 187.

Theodor Seifert points out that one can more easily "become conscious of the collective consciousness" in groups. One becomes conscious "of the system in which we live with its self-evident assumptions, general principles, and truths. It is a system with which we are fully identified"[17].

This phenomenon is often easy to see in painting groups during the first meeting. Participants have an expectation from society regarding standards of performance. These standards tend toward a critical, judgmental, and competitive way of interacting with one another and with the pictures. Such an attitude has little confidence either in the unconscious or in the self-regulating and healing powers of the psyche. This mentality thinks that one must "do" everything and is constantly intervening and interpreting. Usually an individual is at first unaware of such "self evident assumptions of society", for example the ideal self-image where we always have to be good, or may never show aggressive or very tender feelings. In the beginning phase of a painting group with eight people, these assumptions are refracted eightfold and appear in at least eight forms. But during the subsequent group discussions, these assumptions are on the one hand acknowledged as a norm that was brought in from outside, but on the other hand are relativized in the face of the group's plan, namely paint together spontaneously. At this point a new group norm can come into being: creativity without pressure to perform. The group leader stimulates this norm by dealing with the paintings and their creators with gentle acceptance. The progress of the group process from meeting to meeting reveals itself in the members' increasing sensitivity to this apparently self-evident assumption, and their willingness to sensitize each other to it. They also begin asking each other questions in a more sensitive manner.

The collective consciousness will often appear in picture form, often as a symbolic scene, and often in a certain part of the painting. One looks first at the upper right quarter in the picture for the phenomenon of the collective consciousness, because it so often localizes and concretizes there. For symbols of the state (the word "patriotic" contains the Latin word for "father") the upper left quarter is often used, and for

---

17 Seifert, Theodor: *Die Gruppentherapie im Rahmen der Analytischen Psychologie*, p. 184.

the school or "mother church" the lower right quarter. Often symbols of new development appear in the lower left of a picture, which is the polar opposite corner of collective consciousness. These create energy in opposition to the conscious attitude that is so fixated on results.

Personality Types

In a group, people's various personality types and conscious functions reveal themselves all at once[18]. Jung described these in his book *Psychological Types*. The encounter with these varied and diverse personality types makes it possible for each of us to gain insight into our own type. Then we can discover just how limited and one-sided we really are, and how our point of view and our preferred ways of experiencing reality result in inner and outer conflicts. Personality types have their distinctive painting styles. Some prefer an exact graphic style and sketching with pencils for example, while others lean toward flowing and creating atmosphere with watercolors. Each type also has its preferences for certain colors and groupings of colors.

From the start we should realize that the differing personality types will have different expectations and attitudes toward active imagination, toward painting, and toward discussing the pictures. One could very simply say that those whose "thinking function" is dominant (every person is made up of a mixture of all four functions), have to be very convinced of the value of pictorial representations before they dare to paint one. Such types like to express themselves precisely through facts, content, words, logic and technical symbols rather than through pictures. On the other hand, it might be agreeable to them to search for appropriate, structured design ideas that bring together the opposites into one conclusive symbol. These types would rather execute blueprints than paintings. Therefore the challenge of experiencing the feeling-tone, atmosphere and mood of a painting would be most fruitful for them. Perhaps such a painting will just "appear on the page" for them. In any case, they'll be able to observe and experience the paintings of the other personality types.

18 Ibid, p. 185.

Those with a dominant "feeling function" readily accept the revelatory expressiveness that is a given in painting. They expect agreement or rejection of their work. Moreover they're familiar with how colorfulness and mood create atmosphere. They will be more painters than draftspersons. The necessity of observing structure and of structuring oneself that is a part of every pictorial creation will agree less with feeling types, but this in turn is their creative challenge.

On the other hand, "sensate types" as Jung describes them, like to work with material to produce something concrete, sensory, and aesthetic. They will sketch and paint at the same time: exactly, precisely and lovingly. Their challenge is to see the symbolic meaning behind the actual appearance of things, and to express this adequately through creativity.

The primarily "intuitive types" have an aptitude for synopsis and premonition of developmental processes. They will love the active imagination process and quickly see the symbolic connections between things. And they will have a spontaneous perception of their meaning. But they won't like as much the concretization of the individual parts, nor the rendering of free imagination into a concrete, material painting. They will sense that levels of freedom are lost as their ideas are pressed to the limits of their ability to realize them.

Each personality type has its strengths as well as its weaknesses, and all members of the group will be addressed and at the same time challenged to expand their possibilities through active imagination and painting. Above all they will learn to better recognize their own type by comparing it with the others in the group and their paintings. By comparing their own abilities with the gifts of the opposite type, they can let themselves be inspired, and in some cases even get to know their own typical limits and difficulties, in other words, their own shadow.

As Goethe pointed out in his teaching on color, extroverted and introverted types distinguish themselves mainly in their preference for either the yellow-orange-red scale or the blue-violet-green scale. The former, which has a warm effect toward the outside, is preferred by extroverts, while the cooler scale invites limited contact toward the outside, corresponding to introversion. In painting therapy however, the various types will not exclude the colors of the opposite type forever, otherwise an entire half of reality would remain locked off.

Shadows

The so-called "shadow" is that less-known, less-acknowledged side of each individual. In therapy groups, especially those that paint, it becomes more quickly and intensely experienced than in individual therapy, because so much mirroring takes place. The shadow becomes projected onto the other participants and their paintings. It is reflected in our own pictures too. Above all during the group discussions it is fed back to us from the group participants – making it conscious. Whether in paintings or in dreams, the so-called shadow often appears in par-ticular symbol formations such as "the black man", "the temptress", or "the persecutor". It most often appears in a certain color range, namely black, brown and violet. Its corresponding symbols often appear in the lower left corner of the painting, the quarter of the "unconscious". Often positive qualities can be hiding themselves in the shadow. According to the Jungian understanding of the shadow, these are unable to step into the light because of the conscious situation, and so remain devalued and suppressed. Painting groups are especially helpful in pointing out the positive in the formerly devalued shadow figure. This is very helpful, because the future developmental tendency of a person can be hiding precisely here. Jung emphasized again and again that the shadow is often "contaminated" with the potential for future developments. Whoever wants to help people discover their future potential must ask, "Where do you suspect that your shadow lies?"

Anima and Animus

Groups make possible a "nuanced encounter with the other gender"[19] as both an outer and an inner theme. Mirroring or projecting one's own anima or animus (also one's father or mother image) onto one's counter-part of the opposite sex becomes especially obvious when experienced in

19 Ibid, p. 187.

a therapy group. Sometimes it is as if I can almost physically recognize in my interlocutor either my own partner, or my father, brother, mother, sister, etc. along with all the invigorating and deadening experiences that I have experienced with them. Insofar as this becomes conscious, the expectations and disappointments connected with these figures become recognizable and can thereby be reconfigured.

Countless entanglements in outer life – caused by our inability to differentiate our own interior image from the person it was projected onto when they captured or touched our transference – can be avoided in the future. At the same time father, mother, anima, and animus figures constantly reflect themselves in the paintings produced in the group. Members get the chance to work through them during group examination and discussion. Spatial symbolism gives a strong clue to unlocking certain symbols. For instance, the experience with the motherly or the feminine is mainly found in the lower part of a painting, in the lower right quarter is more the personal mother, in the lower left more the impersonal mother or the unknown. Correspondingly, the fatherly is often reflected in the upper part of a picture, above all in the upper left corner. The group provides multiple chances for mirroring the animus and the anima, which are reflected in our discussion partners, in their pictures, and most importantly in our own pictures. Here we might also recognize our own current animus-anima pair[20]. All this is re-mirrored by the group, who gives feedback not just about our painting, but also about our presentation of our painting.

Archetypal Phenomena

A final comment by Seifert is perhaps the most important about group therapy, including painting group therapy: "Archetypical phenomena can be demonstrated in the group process."[21] First he justifiably considers the phenomenon of the group to be archetypal. Group experience touches on an archetypal-instinctual foundation of our life

---

20 Kast, Verena: *The Nature of Loving: patterns of human relationship*. Chiron Publications, Wilmette Illinois 1986, pp. 87-101.
21 Seifert, Theodor: *Die Gruppentherapie im Rahmen der Analytischen Psychologie*, p. 188.

that constitutes a necessary completion of our individual consciousness. As already mentioned, many primal experiences can be found in a group, experiences such as initiation, transformation mysteries, rebirth and religious experiences. Cultural and religious history documents this quite richly. An underlying archetypal pattern causes groups to respond especially strongly to themes such as death and rebirth, initiation and transformation. This is still the case today, even when the group has another function such as therapy.

This same archetypal pattern enables groups to create deeply gripping experiences from archetypal material such as myths and fairy tales. "The group conveys the experience of a firm foundation that one can stand on, a fertile ground that one can live on."[22] Primal desires for security, motherly protection, and of a paradise lost are stirred within a group, as well as insights into these desires. At the same time the group can enable a constructive handling of this desire. This is especially true for a painting group, which roots itself in the "ground of the mother", that is in the unconscious, through its activities with pictures. A painting therapy group is able to recognize itself as "a matrix" and symbol of completeness and its members can gather around this archetype of the self that they constellate together. This is not just homesickness for the great mother or a nostalgic quest for this grand symbol of "completeness". Neither is it simply infantile longing for basic security found by remaining in a group that replaces the father or mother or sister. Above all it is a sharing in expectation, in longing and in Utopia that is constellated in the symbol of completeness that the group represents. This is what matters most to the painting group that has committed itself to unlocking and painting material out of the unconscious.

Examples

I want to give two examples of how some pictures from a painting group were created and discussed. Jakob, a 50-year-old theologian,

---

22 Ibid.; See also remarks about "Das Mutterfeld (the mother field)" in Schlotten-loher, Gertraud: *Das therapeutische Potential spontanen bildnerischen Gestaltens.* Hartung-Gorre, Konstanz, pp. 110ff.

painted a very differentiated flower (Image 83) after participating in an active imagination around this theme. He introduced something of the anima quality into the motif: tender, floating, poised. The flower is yellow, which is a bright, extroverted, and goal-oriented color. Jakob's flower is very precisely painted. Its two leaves and four buds are distinctly recognizable. It is drawn toward a red sky, toward a red sun. Perhaps a relationship between this sky and the depths of the earth is established in that he also paints the roots of the flower red.

The painting depicts a lotus blossom, an exotic flower not found in our region, but with spiritual meaning in the eastern religions. Jakob tells the group to imagine the stem, leaf and root system as being "under water". We have a fine, tender construction of the image before us. The group makes many subtle observations about this picture. They notice, for example, that not only the sky, but also the roots are red and they wonder whether there might be a deeper relationship between the two. But the group grows frustrated and feels rejected by Jakob's rather intellectual and scientific elucidation of the meaning of lotus blossoms. They cannot experience what the lotus blossom means for him. Is he evading some very personal feelings about himself that this blossom symbolizes? Besides the lotus, what else might "break into blossom" in his life? Is he hiding behind something super-personal and tradition-bound? These were questions that a group member posed. I shall let them stand for the moment.

I choose as a second active imagination motif "the forest clearing" (Image 84). During the imagination a sort of totem pole appears to Jakob and he paints it in his picture. In the ensuing discussion some group participants thought the totem pole looked like a person who is tied up and lacking any freedom of movement. But the mask-like face looked as if it did belong to a totem pole, not to a living person. The group members automatically and perhaps over-hastily related the totem pole to the painter himself.

83. *Lotus Blossom*
84. *Totem Pole in the Clearing*
85. *Spring under Barren Trees*
86. *Structures*

Totally missing the group's point in their feedback, Jakob re-clarified with business-like objectivity that a totem pole has to do with ancestor worship, that it is pre-Christian; but that for the people who used it, it was none-the-less religiously effective. In any case, this tradition-bound theologian warmed up here to a pre-Christian cult. Although his conscious position was cast in a Christian mold, the painting process led him beyond it and back to more ancient, near-to-nature levels of experience. This is what one would hope that an active imagination called "forest clearing" would induce. The "forest" is a symbol of the unconscious, and a "clearing" or brightening or enlightenment appears in it.

Still, in the face of Jakob's second painting the group remained frustrated. Although they were interested in the totem pole and what it meant for Jakob himself and asked him about it, he only answered with a more expanded "lecture" over the meaning of totem poles in tribal cultures. Is all this not basically a question about Jakob's own "tribe", his family perhaps, or maybe his religion, or membership in his "order"?

At this stage it seemed clear to me that the symbolic meaning of Jakob's paintings was really not yet accessible to him, although the group was asking about it. I didn't pressure him. I trusted the inviting and challenging power of the group process that awakens and supports curiosity and insight.

A woman in the group pointed out to him the erect totem pole's phallic shape. She went on to point out that it is not organically alive; rather it stands in strong contrast to that tender flower that he first painted and which he depicted half hidden under water. Both the tender flower and the rigid totem pole apparently depict essential sides of Jakob. Both are self-portraits. But he did not yet want to see them as such.

When the third active imagination was experienced, this time to the motif "wellspring", and the painting work began, Jakob laid his sheet of paper, which up until then was always oriented in portrait format, for the first time in landscape format. He planned, as he later told us, so to paint his spring, that it could flow broadly through the whole picture. What he painted was a stream flowing toward the left, which usually means into the region of the unconscious (Image 85).

Up to this point the movement in his pictures had been upward. The movement suggests straightening oneself up or becoming conscious. Now in this painting the movement has changed itself to reveal a desire to flow through the painting space, to fathom and sound out the zone of the unconscious, to penetrate with a streaming energy that which is not yet conscious.

The wellspring poured itself out mightily, streaming from the base of a tree. This appealed to the group members, and they mentioned it several times. But they were also very concerned about the very black ground in the region of the tree's roots and the distinct bareness, in fact *barrenness* of the trees: they seemed dead. But Jakob didn't get these questions either. Rather he explained that he had only wanted to display the lower region of the trees, as one would see them from the spring. The whole thing was a mere question of perspective.

"But why had he chosen this perspective?" I asked myself. At least he could see "from the perspective of vitality" that the trees looked like they had died, over the newfound spring which was bubbling up. The trees in the background, painted in brown-red, have the effect of tree skeletons and speak for themselves. I did not express this at the time, because I didn't think Jakob could take it, but it appeared to me as if the region of vitality in Jakob, represented by the trees as his vegetative nature, had taken some damage in the past. At least his spring of life was flowing again. Its appearance at this point was perhaps made possible through the work in the painting group. Life energy again became available as this picture was created.

In the end Jakob was concerned about the number of pestering questions the group and even the group leader were throwing at him regarding the meaning of his paintings for himself. He sensed that he had not posed these questions to himself yet. Before the three-day painting weekend was over, he sought to bring himself back into equilibrium by painting an extra picture to hold in check the colors with their corresponding emotions. He executed it through a consciously structured division into fields (Image 86).

Lo and behold, a few months after that painting weekend Jakob showed up. He wanted to consult with me in order to discuss most consciously the meaning that the pictures he had painted back then could have for him. In this discussion he spontaneously brought up personal material from his life history that had become visible in the pictures, giving them a verifiable background. Naturally a private discussion about something so personal was more appropriate for Jakob in his shyness, than to speak thus about his pictures in the group. However, it was the group members with their perceptions and their questions, which had succeeded in making Jakob notice something that he had unconsciously concealed in his paintings. Also, the group asked everyone in the same way, not only Jakob, but everyone else who painted, about the possibility of symbolic interpretations. This too helped make Jakob aware that in pictures symbolic meanings are to be seen, also for himself in his own paintings.

87. Red Flower

A further participant in this group was Peter. At the time he was about 35 years old. After the active imagination to "the flower" he painted a similar flower. It was a simple red bloom with two green leaves. It stood in broad, brown soil in landscape format (Image 87). What really stood out were its white roots, which some members of the group immediately noticed. They asked what the painter wanted to express by that, but he could not answer immediately. He had not painted the roots that white consciously, rather it was automatic. Now he asked himself whether he really only wanted to indicate "objectively" the lack of light which such roots have under the earth causing them to remain white, or whether it betrayed a still unconscious "light deficiency" in his soul in the area of his own roots. Wondering what this could stand for, the group associated the root region with several things. If it had to do with the body, it might be the belly or sexual region. But it might also mean the region of home, or the family history, or the father, but especially the mother. Might there be something here that has simply been forgotten and become faded and pale, or is there something that was "deleted" or "painted over"? With "ceiling white" one can do both.

88. Clearing with Dwarf

Already in the active imagination, Peter experienced the way through the woods (Image 88) as especially long and narrow and dark, as he explained to us. It led him through a thicket or stand of trees that had grown so closely together that their tops touched. Up ahead the path opened into a clearing from which light streamed through its gate-like opening. In the clearing itself Peter spotted a dwarf. However, he had found it downright "kitschy" and wanted to really devalue it before the group.

The group strongly opposed this. To them the dwarf appeared to be important, and they wanted to take him seriously, because this painting, which had arisen from the active imagination, and the way it worked, was peculiarly different than Peter had consciously planned. Some group members thought the "path" looked like a penis with a bright head, over which the dwarf's blue-jacketed trunk arose together with his head and its red pointed cap.

89. Spring and a Small Human Figure

It was very clear to the group that out of the white root region of the first painting, a brown, phallic root power has shot up here in the second painting. And it continues upward until its incarnation as the blue man with the red cap. Some group members reminded everyone that this painting was supposed to be about "the way", and they pointed out a structural relationship between these first paintings and the painting that followed. The location of the flower's roots (Image 87) had become the way through the woods (Image 88), and so the group naturally looked to the corresponding localization in the following painting (Image 89). The group's questions and feedback about the white roots of Image 87 had incited Peter to reflect on his own "root energy". This in turn had summoned from his unconscious a helpful companion in the figure of a dwarf.

The painting of the wellspring (Image 89) also displays an erect penis, as Peter noticed later to his own surprise. The form appears in white, like the roots in the first painting. On its tip a small person can be seen holding up a golden ball – a symbol of the self. The fountainhead is housed by a vertically oriented stone wall, and a heavy black arrowhead juts into the painting from above, energetically pointing out the opposite direction to the gushing spring: downward! Further below, the spring water discharges into a pond, which in this painting has the form of an eye looking at the painter as well as the observer. Alternatively, as the group members noticed, one could also see the opening to a giant vagina which is gazing at Peter as if through a single eye.

It had indeed been Peter's conscious intention to have the energy of his well-stream flow downward to the ground, indeed also the feminine. He tried to almost "force" it down with the massive arrowhead. But at first the energy still pressed automatically upward, toward masculine self-assertion, probably also toward the intellectual.

The group members insistently asked why also in this case, the figure remained in white? Peter could not say. As group leader I once again pointed out that white, when it is the white of the drawing paper left bare, often means that something is left open, is still un-drawn. When, on the other hand, it is consciously painted, then it covers or hides or paints over something, as is the case with the "ceiling white" here.

When root and spring both appear in white, there could be a problem where the symbolic spring and root of life lies: the mother. It seems to be a problem that is touching on Peter's manliness, but one which he is keeping well-hidden from himself. At least the man with the golden orb is now pressing all the way to the mouth of the spring, that means all the way to the root of the problem. It is Peter's self symbol, the dwarf, who had been so embarrassing for Peter at first. As the group had learned during their associations to the theme, dwarfs appear again and again in fairy tales and myths as helpful, skillful figures who work in the earth and vital regions. This is the region of the "great mother", and they are sometimes also her skillful assistants. That association session enabled Peter to take on and accept his dwarf as an inner guide. Now he perceptibly helps assure Peter of his manliness, makes his wellspring and his libido flow, and connects him with the feminine.

Can painting therapy change the way one acts? Can it result in visible changes in behavior? The series with the marshy island (Images 11-13) that we already looked at in Part I of this book illustrate such a change in a mother who was clinging to her youngest child. The possibility that she could let go of the child first made its appearance in the painting process, where the mother's emotions and insight came together. These were highlighted and challenged during discussions in the painting group. In the weeks following, the mother succeeded in finding a suitable attitude toward the detachment process by realizing that the child will continue to be related to her. In the act of painting we play through various scenarios, making test runs as it were, until we can settle upon the concrete action to take in the real world; for example going to the boss to demand a raise or quitting a job. By painting we prepare and empower ourselves to action.

A further series impressed me as it made recognizable a certain child-ishness in the painter's stance vis-a-vis her partner regarding their sex life. This was quite obvious in the way that she unwittingly portrayed the couple with children's bodies. The shock of this realization produced some very strong emotions, which resulted in the painter becoming aware of some personal immaturity. This made possible a new relational pattern toward her partner that in turn changed their sex life. Because behavioral therapy aims to be an effective therapy for negotiating daily life in the external world, it might also consider utilizing this method of painting therapy.

By painting in a group, we are brought into contact primarily with our own interior images. But we are also exposed to those of the other group members, and therefore we compare our paintings directly with theirs. This makes us even more conscious of our own paintings since we notice the ways they differ from the others'. We take our own paintings even more seriously, because they have become the focus of comments and resonances from the others: our paintings are being discussed, which enhances them in our own eyes. They now take on a different quality than if we had just painted them for ourselves in the stillness of our rooms. Add to this the fact that for many people painting together in a group atmosphere has a stimulating and loosening effect that sets the emotions free. Looking at everyone's creations afterwards has a clear effect on our sense of self-worth. Emotion and insight come together and become liberated during the painting process, which makes the paintings themselves effective. An even clearer effect is made by the group discussion of the resulting paintings. However, the way we carry out these talks and interpretations of the pictures can also shut the emotions right down. Everything depends upon finding ways and means that open up the discussion.

In a case where much emotion is present and seeking expression, painting in a group can be an especially effective therapy. The very act of painting sets our hidden emotions free, and the forms we paint help us make sense of those emotions. As patients, if we can paint our emotions, the process itself diminishes our fear. Doing the same activity together along with others makes us less nervous about being in their presence. Our reduced anxiety level enables us to participate more easily in the group, and this in turn strengthens the coherence of our ego complex. We become more able to relate to others with appropriate boundaries, yet with more elasticity. As our ego complex becomes ever more coherent and complete, we experience ourselves as freer, no longer the constant victim of inner and outer powers and problems. From now on we experience ourselves rather as potential creators, and we first try out our newfound creativity by painting pictures.

Painting therapy groups are often sought by those with a deep desire and yearning for creativity. They often have an aptitude for it, and are frequently suffering from their gift. They may feel themselves blocked in their drive to create and so are frustrated by the excitement and stimulation present within them. I want to underscore once more that the creativity such people desire is not at all limited to painting and art. Painting just happens to require it in an exemplary way. The creativity I am talking about is the ability to take back life in one's own hands and to arrange it as one sees fit. Finally, it just requires regaining the courage and the competence that we all had as kids to express ourselves through painting.

The Wellspring

Painting Archetypal Motifs

The German word *Quelle* can mean basically two things: either a source generally, or specifically a natural water source. It could thereby be translated variously: on the one hand with words like "source" or "origin", and on the other hand words such as "wellspring", "well", "spring", or "fountain". The double meaning makes translation of this chapter tricky, because regarding the active imagination and paintings the images are usually "springs of water" whereas the archetypal meaning is more generally "origin" or "source" (Translator's note).

Using the natural image of a wellspring, I would like to demonstrate in this section just what archetypal images are able to activate. I have used this image as an active imagination with many groups and then asked the participants to paint it. The motif is closely bound up with a child's original dependence upon its own source – its mother – and therefore with bearing, birthing, nursing and completely taking care of the infant. The symbol further extends into all the possible "origin" experiences of adult life and can ultimately include the mystical experience of the spring of abundant life. Using this trans-personal symbolic image of a reality upon which we all depend, I want to illustrate just what such a major symbol contains and what it can evoke from every individual willing to engage with it.

On the one hand, trans-personal symbols contain distinctive contents that recur anytime someone encounters the symbol. Each of these contents characterizes exactly one theme and none other. The spring is a natural phenomenon whose distinctive symbolic content arises from our seeing and experiencing springs.

The individual's experience of the phenomenon and the symbol of the spring can naturally unfold itself in many variations. For instance, it can remind us of our own origins as children, perhaps even our birth. Or it can make us aware of where we stand in relation to resources in our present life. Or it may reveal our attitude toward our inner springs. Herein lie the individual variations of the theme, and these move completely uniquely within the inter-personal phenomenon and symbol "wellspring". Within a group where each person has painted this motif the individual differences are especially visible despite the trans-personal similarities.

What makes the spring a symbol? What raises it above the plane of simply being a natural phenomenon?

First, a symbol always bears significance: it carries meaning. We said earlier, a symbol is made up partly of memory, partly of expectation and desire. A wellspring, where water "originates", therefore reminds us of our "original" experiences – the things that took place in childhood. It also points out possible experiences of rebirth and new beginning in all phases of life. And it points ahead into the future's still-to-come experiences of spontaneous revival or inspiration. The meanings often tend to be figurative.

Second, all true symbols contain a unification of opposites which otherwise would diverge. They are always composed partly of memory and partly of expectation and desire[23]. Thus symbols point toward reconciliation and completeness. In experiencing a spring, the existential contradiction between spontaneity and continuity is bridged. The memory of a spontaneous, unrepeatable experience of constantly changing water is combined with the desire that I can always find it. The

23 Kast, Verna: *Die Dynamik der Symbole: Grundlagen der Jung'schen Psychotherapie.* New Edition Ostfildern 2016, pp. 28-29. English version: *The Dynamics of Symbols: Fundamentals of Jungian Psychotherapy.* Translated by Susan A. Schwarz. Fromm International Publishing Corp, 1992.

spontaneous experience of the spring symbolizes freedom, graciousness, constantly renewed bubbling, and surprise at discovering it. The desire for continuity is answered by the reliability that at this place I will always again find water: that I have found a place of springs. The survival of many people and animals in the desert depends on the reliability of this experience. Reliability and spontaneity: the two are combined inimitably in the symbol of the spring.

Third, a symbolic image can unlock undreamed-of powers in anyone for whom the image becomes meaningful. In the case of the spring, these are powers of hope and renewal. The image can become meaningful because of a dream, or we might just stumble upon the symbol at the right moment, or we might really have the experience of coming upon water in the desert.

Fourth, symbols contain the theme of inhibition vs. development[24]. With the spring, inhibition means being pulled backward and becoming entangled in a longing for the mother that cannot be fulfilled.

Fifth, a symbol contains a great plethora of meanings. Listing all the possible meanings of the spring would take forever. And trying to list them too exhaustively threatens to impoverish any symbol by relegating it to a sign.

Now, I want to present a method that we as therapists and group leaders can use to evoke a natural archetypal symbol either in individuals or in entire groups. The leader selects a symbolic image that will be the motif of an active imagination. I will use the image of the wellspring here. First, I explain to the participants that in our inner perception we are able to make things perceptible – audible, touchable, visible, etc. Then, I lead some introductory relaxation exercises ending with everyone comfortable and attentive. The active imagination with the wellspring goes something like this: "I hear a spring, a gurgling, a babbling, a rushing. I look around for it and can smell the damp leaves

24 Kast, Verena: *Imagination als Raum der Freiheit*. Walter-Verlag AG, Olten 1988, pp. 94/95. English version: *Imagination as space of freedom: dialogue between the ego and the unconscious*. Fromm International Publishing Corporation, 1993; see also Kast, Verena: "Die Bedeutung der Symbole im therapeutischen Prozeß" in Barz, Helmut / Kast, Verena / Nager, Frank: *Heilung und Wandlung: C.G. Jung und die Medizin*. Zürich/München 1986, pp. 68ff; and Dorst, Brigitte: *Therapeutisches Arbeiten mit Symbolen: Wege in die innere Bilderwelt*. 2nd Edition, Stuttgart 2015, p. 176.

and moss. Then I discover it in its surroundings. I can see the water coming spontaneously out of the ground (or from between the stones). It just flows and keeps on flowing like living water. I'm filled with a desire to lower my hands in, to submerge them, to feel the water on my hands, on my skin, and to feel its streaming movement. I want to cool my face with it, to feel this refreshing water on my forehead and my cheeks. Now I want to taste it. I slurp a mouthful of the spring-water, taste its minerals, its unique flavor. Now I want to experience the spring with my whole body. I jump in and feel myself completely surrounded by the flowing spring, and I experience myself as a spring."

90. Spring at a High Elevation

The image we had during the active imagination will, by painting it, take on more depth. Some things, which at first were unclear, will automatically become clearer and more visible. For those of us perhaps still unpracticed in painting, just trying to reproduce what had been before our inner eye will automatically clarify it, as it did for us when we were kids.

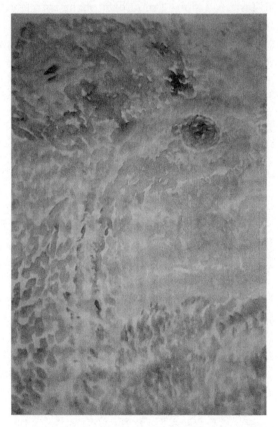

91. Tender Trickle

At the end I may invite the participants to share their inner image with the person next to them.

The exercise continues in that we now attempt to paint "our well-spring". We paint the colors, the movements, the impressions, and the feelings from the active imagination that most strongly impressed and touched us, the ones which became most perceptible to us.

As an illustration of what can come out of such an exercise, I will now present a series of pictures painted in one of my groups. It was a quite varied group, but all painted the same motif, the spring, which really is a symbol of our existential dependence upon the water of life.

Image 90: One young man found the approach to his spring only with difficulty. He first had to get out of the unconscious corner of the picture, the lower left, and from there, climb quite steeply until the spring and the small lake around it became conscious. At first he was far away from his source but has apparently rediscovered it, surrounded in yellow light as with a sun-like aura.

Image 91: Painted in the other direction, a spring in the upper right softly trickles and loses itself in the lower left of the picture. Localized clearly in the picture's region of consciousness, nestled high up in a quiet landscape surrounded by nothing but grass and moss, it shows that the painter knows what her wellspring is. But it is as if the wonderful energy welling up for this woman from her inner spring often gets lost in the unconscious, becoming unavailable for the vitalization and organization of her daily life in the outer world. The woman is a physician, and she often over-extends herself for her patients. Years before, she lost her only child. This loss robbed her of much vital energy, and sometimes it still threatens to suck her into a depression.

Image 92: One man's spring gushes up very energetically out of the depths. In the attempt to paint the energy that keeps spewing forth from the spring in ever-widening concentric rings of water, the spring unintentionally transforms into a breast emerging out of the earth to nourish him richly. His spring has become more compact, more earthy than watery. Toward the right, toward the outer world, steep cliffs shield his spring, while to the upper left, the region of the fatherly, it is protected but not blocked off by a plant's undulating fronds. His spring water collects itself in a motherly space, a space within Mother Earth, even when the energy channels itself from above, from a source not revealed in the picture.

92. Spring as Breast

Image 93: The next picture shows that for another man it is not easy to search for his energy in his depths and to expect it to be there, since it is usually focused outward and upward toward some far-off point on the horizon. Inserted like "a picture within a picture" into the upper left of the composition is a canopy road whose vanishing point directs the eye outward and upward. At the same time, the spring pours its energy like a penis into the depths of a small lake containing fish, sea grass, wonderful bright stones, and plants. This mysterious world is the depth of his own soul from which he has preferred to flee up until now toward some vanishing point outside and far away.

93. Spring and Boulevard

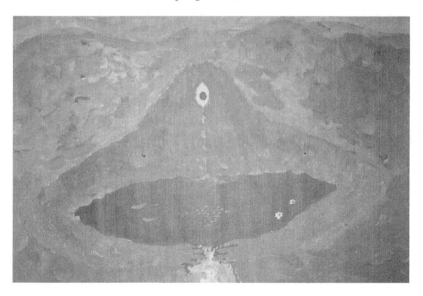

94. The Eye of the Troll

Image 94: The next painting was made by a Scandinavian woman now living in Switzerland. For her the spring means home with its native landscape. The moss surrounds this spring in a most curious way in this harsh, gray, northern landscape of moor and mountain. The spring basin could be the mouth of a Cyclops. The painter herself called the creature a troll. Out of its single eye (located where the mystical third eye of a medium belongs) flow the tears that feed the basin. This third eye is the actual spring. Upon the exceptionally dark water of the spring basin float tender traces of gold. Something precious appears to be hidden in this painter's dark, mysterious spring. She had not just experienced the lightness of her homeland, but also the deep access to nature and to the dark powers that lie hidden inside it. This is exactly what the trolls are, making them an access to myths and fairy tales. So her dark spring also produces gold! Only a personal discussion with the painter of the picture could ascertain whether there is a body related theme expressed through the shapes of the image.

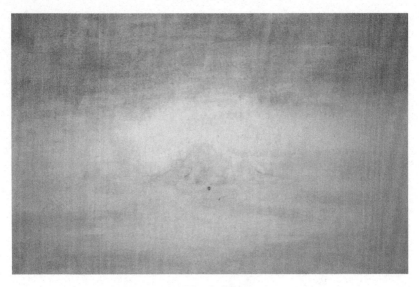

95. Island of Desire

Image 95: A painting by another Scandinavian woman fits here. She moved to central Europe from Finland because of her marriage, and her "wellspring" is a tiny Baltic island off the Finnish coast. She spent every summer there as a child and to this day returns annually. There she rediscovers her original vitality and is able to do the creative and artistic work which, as mother of four children, she would otherwise hardly get to do. Here she can connect with pristine nature in a way that speaks to her deepest soul. Out of her island she formed a mystical image of desire, a soul image that appears like an "isle of the blessed" at the end of the world. Borne by transparent blue where heaven and earth almost blend into each other, separated by nothing more than a zone of light, the island appears in softest turquoise with mere suggestions of trees and cliffs. It looks more like a gemstone than a natural island, and a gem would also be a symbol of the deepest self.

96. *"I am the Wellspring in You"*

That this island constitutes the exact middle of the painting forming a center, further indicates that for this woman it is a symbol of the self. A soft hint of rose expressing tenderness and desire, shimmers over the island. The original drawing paper is edged in black suggesting that the island will be painfully missed because it lies so far away. In any event, this island, this hard-to-reach treasure, has become the spring of life par excellence for the painter. Not everyone needs to draw a literal spring of water when the theme is "wellspring" because in a certain sense anything that gives the artist life can become a wellspring for that person.

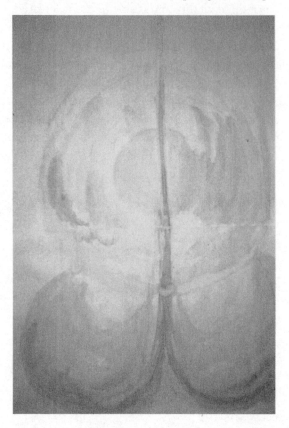

97. The Spring as Energy of Life

Image 96: A spring can appear troll-like in other ways. From it things can be released that are weird, goblin-like, naughty, toad-like or elfish. This happened with the next painter while painting the wellspring motif. Anima-like, natural powers came up for him, which on one hand are fascinating and on the other hand a little bit scary. Even the stones between which the spring issues appear to be alive in this painting, and they have eyes. It's always a little eerie with so many eyes around. The painter had such an astonishing and multifaceted experience at his spring that he needed to assure himself and us that the spring is inside him. With its eyes it is looking at him, so that it is he who becomes the one observed, the one seen. The spring in him begins to speak, addressing him: *"I am the spring in you."* He needs to write this sentence into the picture. When such lines and pieces of text are written into a picture, they give verbal clarification of what is being pictured. The painter is assuring himself of what was really meant, apparently not yet trusting the power of the painting itself to express it. But his own deeper nature with its elements and energies, which formerly lay in shadow, reveal themselves here as a spring.

Image 97: Sometimes we can feel the spring deep within our bodies, like the painter of the next picture, who felt a soft, warm surge in her solar plexus as she heard the catchword "wellspring". She could feel a sanguine flush spreading out through her belly, to her sex organs, and all the way into her buttocks. So she painted a flux field like the sun or a stream of energy pouring itself into two water bowls in which two moons are floating. These collected energies are drawn upward by a long cannula which brings them into consciousness and from there sends them back down into the depths of the body. This woman experiences her spring tangibly in the Hara chakra as a streamingfeeling in her body, a lively exchange of energy, a wellspring of life.

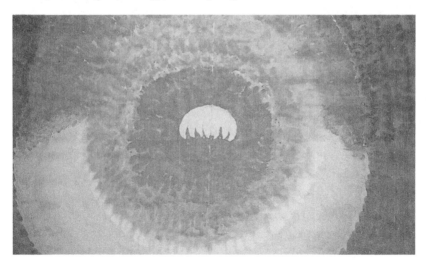

98. The Eye as Spring

Image 98: Another saw the spring welling up within the image of an eye. For him the wellspring is a "thou". His fountain surges up from the center of a chromatic circle whose lower half is the rainbow spectrum with red-orange surrounding yellow, then green, turquoise all the way to blue. The entire iris is surrounded by deep purple. The picture forms a sort of mandala, making it a meditative image of completeness. With it the observer penetrates through the various color frequencies with their corresponding emotions all the way to the spring. Conversely, one can begin in the middle with the spring and move outward, experiencing its outpouring as emanations into ever new color variations. The colors unfurl like concentric waves with each circle always oriented to the center. The heart of this picture is pure white, that pristine, un-fractured fullness of light. It spreads itself out like an umbrella over the spring.

99. The Father as Spring

Image 99: Another painting utilizing the full color spectrum, along with the rainbow symbol, was done by a woman who, interiorly, sank herself into the spring. As she did so, the face of her long-dead father appeared in the water. In the painting she cradles his masculine countenance in a bowl of femininity – the moon – which is also a symbol of transformation. The moon reminds us that everything has its time: its beginning and its end. It is therefore a sign in which one can reconcile oneself with death. Fittingly, that ancient sign of reconciliation, the rainbow, appears over her father's face. The spring has become more of an ocean here. It lies in three colored layers: light blue, turquoise and light blue again. The brown earth grounds the lowest layer. For the painter it was important to acknowledge the layers that have made up her life all the way down to the load-bearing ground. The sky with its rainbow, the three-layered water with the moon and her father's head, and under it all the motherly earth – this all ends up forming a symbol of completeness wherein the painter can be reconciled with her father and with his death.

100. The Spring Gate

Image 100: Another man's spring originates very high up in rugged mountains. It is hard to get to, and it seems almost as if the painter himself had to work his way up in order to find the source. The nearest mountains could almost be a black gate crowned with six spikes. Behind them rises an enormously high three-peaked summit (or are there four?) that towers over the gate. Behind these loftiest peaks appears the orange-red sun. Is it a sunrise or a sunset? The painter experienced his spring as lying very high up, difficult to get to, and very challenging, and the spring's mouth is also jagged. Might this be a reminder of the mouth of the uterus, therefore reflecting his birth? What prompted him to stylize his origins or self-portrait as high as it appears here? Would not a prince portray his high ancestry with such towering mountains? Out of the jagged hole gushes a torrent of turbulent water. It is a virtual waterfall pouring itself with great energy into the left, the inner world, and thereby into the painter's unconscious region. The question is whether it gets lost down there or whether it flows back under subterranean channels to the person's consciousness. A hopeful sign is the jets of water, drawn like roots, as if the painter seeks new anchoring, anchoring in the depths.

Image 101: As with the previous painting, the spring here originates at a similar altitude. It was executed by a woman who had been fasting for a long time. A spring arises on a bright height of almost cosmic space. The space is painted like a grotto flooded through by white light. In the light a swelling figuration is recognizable, which is supposed to represent the geyser-like spring and at the same time a female figure. Is it a spring goddess, or Mary? The spring is located in the spiritual region (upper left) and for this painter it condenses into a goddess of the well, since the painter is also consciously very close to feminine spirituality. Out of the region of collective consciousness, the upper right, sparkling green-golden light falls onto this goddess of the cosmic well. Doubtless, the painting sets free enormous energy and touches on spiritual experience, but it could appear as too aloof if the lower part of the painting did not exhibit such great plasticity and realism. This is especially thanks to the rounded, three-dimensional, body-like earth-toned stones being carried along by the water as it flows into the lower right and recollects itself in the symbolic zone of the mother.

101. The Spring Grotto

Images 102 and 103 will close out this series of wellsprings painted by my group. Both images were painted by the same woman and illustrate an outstanding experience of energy renewal brought about by the spring. Before she painted the spring, she painted a river that she was unable to cross. In it she is looking from the right bank, the side of consciousness, across the stream. She sees a woman on the other side standing in a frozen position, looking confused, powerless, and unable to do anything. That woman stares at a white figure on a broken piece of boat that has washed onto shore. The accident must have occurred much further upstream, symbolically much earlier in her life history. A dark spot in the river still marks the spot. While painting the scene, the artist realized that both the drowned woman and the woman standing powerless and frozen on the shore are parts of herself. This accident was about her. She was greatly shaken, but at a loss about how she should handle this crashed, dead, frozen part of herself.

102. The Drowned Woman

The next day she began again to paint a spring (Image 103). This time she climbs into the spring completely, bathes in it, lets it whirl her around until its centrifugal force slings her out upon a green meadow, where she lies with outspread arms and legs as if freshly born. She lies spread-eagled over the part of the painting space where powerless woman in the previous painting stood frozen before the drowned one. The outspread arms and legs may mean that the woman has been renewed by the spring and will now be able to function and move again. She has gotten hold of the frozen part of herself, has gotten it moving again, and thereby been transformed. As the coloring of this painting reveals by juxtaposing blue and red, this woman has gone through water and fire, through her unconscious and through passionately melting emotions. The right shore of the first painting becomes a yellow zone here, which stretches like a sandbar across the former river now reaching to the place where the drowned woman earlier lay. Now she lies transformed in a green meadow.

103. The Bath in the Spring

To conclude this section, I would like to compare my painting group's wellspring series with a work by the Italian painter Giotto in which he painted St. Francis of Assisi's miracle of the spring.

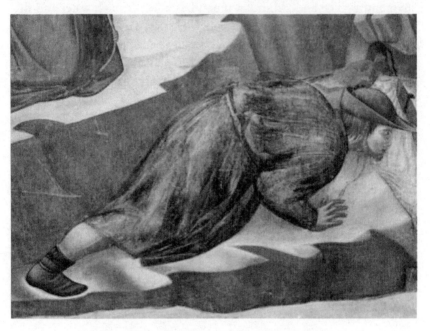

104. The Spring Miracle of Saint Francis, Detail (Giotto)

Image 104 is a detail from Giotto's larger fresco, showing only the miraculously arising spring from the Francis legend. Notice that the water is really springing from the earth, not from the sky, and not from the high mountains. And the man who wants to scoop and drink from it must bend down low to the earth, must be humble. Giotto cloths his figure in earth tones, the color of humus, which underscores his bodily position: *humilitas (*humility). So close to the ground, the man's posture suggests a farmer or a shepherd. The tension created by his supporting hand and stretched out leg emphasizes that the man's whole body, from the foot all the way to the head is stretching forward, reaching out for the water. This painting depicts what thirst really is, and how utterly dependent we humans are – body and soul – on the living water of the wellspring. Giotto lets us experience the appearance of a spring expressly as miracle. But isn't it always so? Isn't "the spring" always something ungraspable? Whether we stumble upon a spring in the woods, or the spring within ourself, or upon that, which for our life is a wellspring in the trans-personal sense, it is something special. This painting by Giotto juxtaposes the creation of an artist of enormous expressive power with personal experiences and illustrations of several individuals in a painting group. By now the fullness of meaning, the "overflowing of meaning", to be found in the symbol of the spring should be very clear.

Mother Earth

Further Development of Pre-selected Motifs in Active Imagination

A group requires a common theme with which each and every member can resonate individually and which, at the same time, binds all the members together. To this end archetypal symbols taken from the natural surroundings are particularly well suited. I offered a weekend group which was open to the public called "Painting Inner Images" where I selected the motifs "forest lake", "well", and "cave". What follows are paintings by Mrs. E., who after the weekend continued to paint by herself, further developing the figure of Mother Earth that she had discovered to her own amazement through the motifs I had selected.

Up until that weekend, Mrs. E. had had a very negative mother image. After the active imagination to the theme "forest lake" came the first painting of the weekend. She used pastel crayons, which have a generally earthy, subdued tone, rather than strongly radiating colors. But she didn't rub these pastels lightly. Rather she pressed hard on them producing a thick color surface. In her first paintings she left no space on the paper blank.

A dark purple lake appeared with an indigo-blue boarder. This lake was at the same time the interior of a circle of pale beige flower petals, giving the whole thing the character of a water lily or lotus blossom. The flower rested on an almost black background that could have been taken for the dark water of the lake were it not for the barely visible silhouettes of black firs. That is how the motif "forest lake" was rendered. (Image 105).

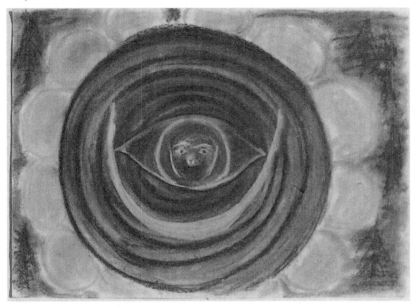

105. Lake in the Woods

What most astonished both painter and painting group was the interior of this lake. A face appeared there, inside an eye-shaped structure. With two eyes, two clearly visible nostrils but no visible mouth, it looked much more like the face of an animal than a human. The group thought perhaps a dog or a pig. What is it? What came up? Since it is in the dark, could it possibly be something instinctual and animal-like that so far has been suppressed and is now coming up from the dark forest lake? The active imagination motif of a "forest lake" does touch on what lies hidden. It entices things that were previously unknown to consciousness because they were unbearable, to come out of the dark depths of the unconscious. They're allowed to climb up a bit. The theme lake also speaks to the origins, being inside the mother's body or in her environment.

The dark circle could symbolize a mother complex which has until now protected something which had been spurned. Finally it emerges out of the depths as a swine. The group discovered that the swine is the symbolic animal of the goddess of mothers, Demeter. Naturally it portrays a very bodily aspect of Demeter – her fertile aspect. And when we look more exactly, we could say that the lake is actually gazing at the artist like an eye.

The painter readily accepted the suggestion that this swine symbolism may have something to do with the feminine. Understanding that made her realize why a crescent moon just popped up spontaneously under the eye while she was painting.

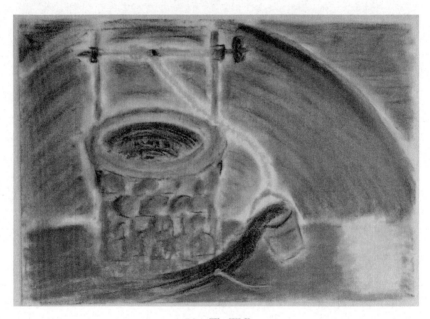

106. The Well

The next active imagination motif I selected was the "well". It is a motif that invites participants not just to peek into the depths, as does the lake, but also to draw out of it. Like the previous painting, this well (Image 106) is painted very thickly covering the paper completely and leaving no blank space. It is done in landscape format using predominantly dark colors: black, brown, ocher, and olive. The well appears to stand not outdoors, but rather within a vault, and in the lower left quarter of the painting, where the unconscious often appears.

The well is lovingly painted, as if the artist had laid each stone upon the other. Several members of the group mentioned this and were in awe of the sculpted presentation of the well. They also noticed that no person is there to draw the water out of this crank-well. Yet somebody had drawn water. The dark water, which had been drawn up, is running out of the tipped bucket and back into the corner of the collective unconscious. The symbolism is that life energy is being dumped out and poured back into the unconscious in streams. At most the green plants at the foot of the well will be watered, and probably also something in the unconscious itself. Perpendicular to the streaming water lies an up-rooted sprout. The light-colored soil out of which it was pulled is the same color as the lotus blossom petals of the previous painting. Here however, the color only emphasizes the hole out of which the deep stretching root was ripped and how hard it had clung on. It is a picture revealing spilled life energy and the tender shoots of life having been ripped out. It reveals this in combination with the negative aspects of the mother complex. Everything that puts down roots will be ripped out again here. The group posed a most insinuating question: Does the painter have to defend herself so much against Demeter's bodily earthiness, which incarnates itself as the swine, that she is constantly tempted to rip it and its sprouts out by the roots?

Even the painter herself found the picture of the well dissatisfying and torturing as she recalled how lovingly she first executed it, but then poured its water out again. So she started painting afresh in order to get a closer look at this destructive side of herself. She felt she would have to go deeper than in the pictures so far. Two days later she imagined a subterranean cavern and painted it (Image 107). As this third painting shows, she was in a hole under the earth beneath roots whose deepest tips protruded partially into the cavern. Against its walls leaned large stone plates with graffiti in the form of spirals, concentric circles and rings: images common in earlier megalithic cultures. During a stay in Brittany, she had been very much touched by such symbols as witnesses to matriarchal megalithic cultures.

During the active imagination, the painter was startled when the earth mother herself stepped into view from between the stones. She stood there bodily, alive, heavy, monumental, and in the colors of the earth. In her hands she held a round object, something made of gold. The encounter both moved and frightened the painter. Afterwards in the group she tried to dismiss her imagination and its resulting painting as not completely genuine, as partially forced and constructed. Quite a few women in the painting group strongly disagreed with her, expressing just how strong and real this earth mother appeared to them. By expressing their feelings, they made Mrs. E. more reflective but did not completely eliminate her ambivalence regarding this painting. She could not yet allocate this mighty appearance of the mother archetype in its positive aspect. She could not yet own this experience, even though it was exactly what she needed. This archetypal image had the power to counter the negative effects of experiencing her personal mother. Like nothing else, it was the appropriate and capable means. This earthiness of the great motherly struck her as too earthy and compact, almost back-breaking. The way the picture portrays it, it looks almost like the black-brown arch of the cave vault is settling heavily upon the figure and weighing it down. At first Mrs. E. did not let herself get any nearer to the earthiness of the great mother because she found it too oppressive. But after this encounter the earth mother wouldn't leave her in peace.

107. Cave with Earth Mother

108. Frau Holle

So almost a month later Mrs. E. decided to try approaching the earth mother again using active imagination. This time the earth mother appeared to her, no longer in megalithic and archaic form, but rather in the familiar-unfamiliar figure of Frau Holle. This fairy tale character made the encounter easier for the painter to bear. Now she could have the experience and even paint it with joyful excitement (Image 108). Frau Holle appeared at the bottom of a well, under roots of verdant growth, and in an earth-brown garb that surrounded her head like a scarf. But the figure has really developed! It has become more human and no longer looks like an archaic block of earth. The facial features are now painted in white, revealing themselves more prominently. The figure's body has become three-dimensional, no longer appearing like a two-dimensional sketch. Above all, this figure is no longer surrounded with stone tablets resembling menhirs, but with vines bearing red blossoms or fruit. Are they grape vines? It is as if the six stone tablets have morphed into six living plants with red blossoms and berries. Six is the number of the eros principle.

This painting is the first to use red in the series. It is wine red, in fact: a somewhat muted shade, but in any case, part of that spectrum of vitality. Red can be blossoms or fruit, feelings, love, or sexuality. Another sign of change in the artist is the vines. Compared to the stone tablets, they are painted much more freely, loosely, breezily. Also some free space was left around them: there is no more compulsion to fill up the entire space.

Measuring this series against the criteria for therapeutic affectivity that we earlier compiled, we can clearly see here a changing world-view and from picture to picture – a developing self image.

It is illuminating to pay attention to the changes in Mrs. E.'s painting technique and use of artistic means. From painting to painting we can observe a widening band-breadth and expressiveness, a brightening, and a greater clarity of colors. For example, she brings in green in Image 106, and finally that red in Image 108 that was so important. Also, that somewhat compulsive need to fill every inch of the drawing space with color was finally broken in the last painting by holding the pastels more loosely and freely. It appears as if the dry pastel sticks themselves were moistened or at least smeared in painting the blossoms, and so they literally came into flow a bit.

What about the development of coherence with increasing differentiation?

The coherence of all the pictures is unambiguously clear, showing that the painter's ego complex is stable. With one picture element in Image 106 it was hard to understand what was happening. It was supposed to be a ripped-out plant and the piece of earth where it had been removed. But the plant appeared rather inorganic and showed no connection to that light patch in the right corner. However, the artist's attempt caused an imbalance in the picture, tipping its weight toward the left. Psychologically seen, this gave special accent to the unconscious. Image 107 has regained the balance, although it is somewhat too compact and shut in. The paintings contain a relatively large variety of elements, which are well related to one another.

Is there a change in symbols?

The mother symbolism was almost a given in the pre-selected motif of the forest lake. It appeared for our artist in the form of Demeter's swine (Image 105). With the wellspring motif, the negative mother was revealed. In Image 106 the water is poured out and the plant ripped out by the roots. In Image 107 the earth mother first appears. She is not in the form of a symbol, but rather appears in her own form, although very archaic and at first also threatening. Finally in Image 108 an archetype of a good-evil mother is found in "Frau Holle". Using this figure Mrs. E. can further work on her mother problem and perhaps finally solve it.

In the next weeks it became ever more important for Mrs. E. to stay with the theme of "Mother Earth". So she began to work in clay. That meant working with earth itself in order to create. In her creations she utilized real earth, sand, and natural objects such as leaves, twigs, and roots. At the same time, she started becoming a "good mother" to herself. She lovingly cooked for herself and invited guests. She took relaxing hikes. She would sit out on her own balcony the whole weekend and enjoy herself. Most importantly, she now took time for herself after half a lifetime of giving her time up for others. People conditioned by the negative aspect of the mother archetype believe they are of little value and may not indulge themselves. They must devalue and retract all positive developments, as Mrs. E. was still doing when she portrayed it as the freshly drawn well water and the plant that had begun to take root (Image 106).

Painting in a group was important for Mrs. E. It provided a safe space where she was able to endure her anxiety, given that some of the motifs were at first scary for her. No less important was the nudge she got from group members through their spontaneous comments, their shared feelings about the paintings, their amplifications, and their questions. Also important was the experience of admitting her true feelings about the oppressive earth mother before the group. Finally it was important that she didn't let go of this theme until she could get it into a form she could work with. She was able to develop her inner image into a form which was fitting for her, a figure she could relate to and come into deeper contact.

Four Colors

Painting to Color Motifs

Another exciting option with painting groups is to select colors themselves as the motif to paint. Already every color is a symbol that can
activate an entire symbolic-archetypal field all by itself[25]. We can be certain of this, because when we compare traditional symbolic-archetypal
shapes, again and again they are portrayed using the same color and the
same color attributes. They are bound together. Thus the Virgin Mary
wears a blue mantle, by which she is presented as the Queen of Heaven
(*Regina Coeli*) and Star of the Sea (*Stella maris*). Or again the color green
is frequently attributed to the figure of Wisdom. Hildegard von Bingen
often does this, because for her green so plainly expresses the energy of
growth and life. Whoever plays around with blue or with green comes
immediately under the spell of that respective color and experiences
something of the growth potential of the green Sophia or the protection
of the blue Mary. Every single color has a certain character of expression,
a certain symbolism, which naturally fans out in many nuances.

Moreover, a color combines its power with the impact of its complementary color. The two heighten each other in brilliance. The use of
a complementary color can provide the polar complement to a mood

---

25 Riedel, Ingrid: *Farben in Religion, Gesellschaft, Kunst und Psychotherapie.* Stuttgart
    1983.

or experience that has colored things up till that point. An example is a painting series (Images 22-30) which I have already presented: there an alcoholic went through a long blue phase of painting his drunkenness, addiction, uncertainty, and nearness to the suction power of the unconscious. Then one day he was struck by the need to paint in yellow-orange, the color symbolizing going out to the "thou" and to the external world. It is important for our psychological balance and mental health that we are able to realize all colors and to find our particular stance toward each of them, otherwise the corresponding emotional and symbolic area for which they stand is lacking in us.

I began two of my painting groups, which met regularly during the summer semester, by having the participants paint color motifs. I told them, "First, each of you choose a color that really speaks to you, a color that does you good. Now, imagine it." When given this free choice, each and every person can begin with something personally relevant and comfortable. Thus, I consciously choose a pleasant beginning, but more importantly a personal beginning, exactly because everyone is painting in a group. Such a way of beginning gives all the group members a chance to present themselves to each other, to share by means of their color a first impression of themselves. They reveal not only the color they chose, but also naturally, how they have formed it into a picture.

A woman in her early twenties, Mrs. K., surprised her group by choosing black[26]. The others asked whether black wasn't hiding something depressing. She fiercely defended the color. She had painted it with relish (Image 109) and said that it had shone even more beautifully while the paint was still wet. Black is a color that we can certainly have fun with. It can express protest, rebuff, distinctive detachment, or the rejection of all other colors because they do not fit our current mood or condition. Mrs. K. spread her black diagonally across the entire paper with exceptionally powerful strokes. We can take it that she was freeing herself from something and that she had finally shed some sort of pain or remonstrance. She didn't just stay with black, however. After a manifest lightening of the black, she then applied yellow. Although

---

26 Ibid, pp. 156-173 (concerning black).

it was darkened with a little black, some streaks of pure yellow shone clearly. One sees how the psyche seeks balance and completion.

Mrs. K.'s attachment to black was elicited here as a contrast to the lighter color yellow. It resulted in an extraordinarily rich, tension-filled, dynamic picture. To include both that which is threatening and that which is full of light at the same time speaks for Mrs. K.'s strong character. We later learned from her that, directly before the painting group began, she had gone through a difficult time which she was now energetically seeking to overcome, but only after first acknowledging its difficulty, precisely in the black that she painted first.

109. Black

For the group's second color motif I chose red, the most vital of all colors. It derives its symbolism from blood and from fire, and is capable of expressing the intense feelings of love as well as of hate and aggression. Usually I begin groups with blue as the color motif because it is able to unlock and develop the deep layers of the soul, the unconscious. It derives its symbolism from the waters and the heavens. But this time

I decided to go with red[27] because it promised to further unfold the dynamic that the favorite color motif had brought to expression.

110. Spiral in Red

Red drives things on and heats things up. It can be well used near the beginning of a long group process in order to discover which feelings get stirred up. These can then be worked through again later in the process. I would not use the color red as the very first motif at the beginning of a group process since it can also produce fear, including fear that strong feelings and aggression might break out. First trust needs to be built up as the basis of the group process. Applied too early, the red motif can also lead to blockages, because the group members are not yet familiar enough with each other and with the leader. In this case, however, I dared to introduce this motif as the second in the series, and it released in Mrs. K. an energy-rich maelstrom of red and black rotating to the left from a red center approximately in the middle of the painting. The energy turns itself inward, into the past. Charged with the power contained in red, this vortex brings into movement the black that had

27 Ibid, pp. 16-49 (concerning red).

lain in a wide band across Image 109, symbolizing the artist's experience of pain and disappointment. The black with its vital energy is brought back into action in the wheel of life.

The red and the black simultaneously intensify each other, keeping the wheel turning. In the same way, the painter managed to reintegrate even her pain and disappointment as sources of her vitality. The red here is dark and luscious, almost the color of blood. This suggests the energy of the body that is coming back into action after a grieving phase.

111. Flags in Red

Another participant painted a group of red flags (Image 111) gripped by a stiff wind. The wind is blowing from the left, the region of the unconscious, and the flags flutter toward a red sun. There is a good chance that protest and a desire for liberation underlie this scene, since she has "nailed her colors to the mast", and the flags stretch out toward a huge source of energy, the sun. In talking about this painting, the artist told us that she has worn herself out many times in protests and in her desire for more freedom. This was especially the case in the context of her job, where she could not express her views satisfactorily. Indeed her workplace appears as the rather barren landscape in this picture. It is however touched with traces of tender red. The piece of land where the flags are standing is sticking out into the landscape like the prow of a ship.

112. Woman with Flower

The red motif awakened in another participant a tender, warm feeling. In nuanced red tones she painted a woman rising up out of the region of the unconscious, the lower left, and turning toward a flower of the same tender red. The flower is somewhat larger than the woman herself (Image 112), suggesting that her desire is great. This painting, by a woman in heavy demand in her career, speaks of a desire to turn her attention to the tender blossoming things in her life.

Green[28] has to follow red, according to that law of complementary colors that I'm constantly referring to. This rather peaceful and reconciling color is found in gentle, natural growth.

Mrs. K., who had painted the black-red maelstrom in such strong movements, begins again, as she had with the red, with an energy center only now it is green. It is somewhat in the middle of the picture, but definitely a little higher than the center had been in the red painting

28 Ibid, pp. 100-123 (concerning green).

(Image 113). Bold green stripes swirl out from this center toward the left. It is almost as if she wants to repeat the red tornado, this time in green. But she cannot stick with green alone. She adds some of the red from Image 110, but primarily broad stripes of the yellow that had appeared already in Image 109 as a contrast to her black.

113. Spiral in Green with red-yellow Traces

This image has a couple of important differences from Mrs. K.'s previous whirl. First, the arms swirl out of a rather coy green in contrast to red. Secondly, the arches going out from the center do not close themselves around the vortex, but rather remain "standing" like a carefully bound together bundle of grain, quietly and almost humbly bowing its head. Under the sign of green Mrs. K.'s powers have been gathered, gleaned and bound together; under the sign of green she has become able to let her destiny unfold and to a certain extent become fruitful. There is still black in this picture. It lies as if upon the back of the sheaf's neck, pressing down on it from the zone of the fatherly-patriarchal. But the entire right side of the picture, the future side, the "thou" side, is here left open. This side is not weighed down at all.

Mrs. B.'s green motif (Image 114) has two greens. On the right stand two blue-green fir trees in the region of consciousness. Consciousness is further emphasized by their upright position as if in a standing posture.

These trees may also indicate a relationship. Further to the left in the picture an almost poison green sweater jumps out at the viewer. It is as if it has been set free and has escaped into the zone of the unconscious. A rather uncomfortable association is connected with it for the painter. The sweater raises itself up almost garishly from the tender red ground that the artist has carried over from her previous painting (Image 112). With such ground as her basis, she is able to confront the affair of the green sweater. The way it "sits" in the picture, the sweater's shape reminds her of a frog, which she connects to a childhood wish, which has remained rather thwarted up until now.

114. Green Sweater

On the other hand, the green motif inspired Mrs. V. to paint with extreme tenderness a tree standing in a broad landscape (Image 115). The cool, fresh color atmosphere is achieved by combining blue with green. It is able to express desire for expanse and freedom. A further expression of this desire is the person placed in the landscape. Tiny because of the distant perspective, the figure stands on one of the soft hills. Still further in the distance, to the left on the horizon, Mrs V. takes up the soft red from her last picture.

115. *Desire for Expanse*

116. *Wing in blue-gray*

My next color motif with this group was blue[29]. It appeared in wonderful luminosity in the fatherly zone of Mrs. K.'s painting (Image 116). This is where that oppressive black had been in her previous work (Image 113). In recent days she had begun seeing a trustworthy male therapist. Had the good experience with this new relationship positively reset her father image and her image of men and now appears in her painting? The soft bending that we recall from the sheaf of grain in Image 113 has thickened here into a black feather, or perhaps it has developed its own backbone. It throws out fiery red and yellow sparks, then colorful lines of mainly red and black, which arch themselves over to the right edge of the picture. The intervals between these arcs are filled in with a light gray-blue. The image looks like a huge wing.

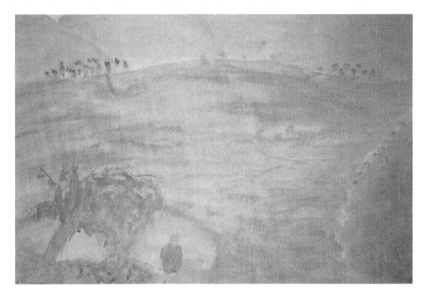

117. Lake with Swimmer

For Mrs B. the blue formed a river flowing into the picture from the lower right quarter and broadening into a wide lake surrounded by mountains and large settlements (Image 117). Two people are swimming

---

29 Ibid, pp. 48-79 (concerning blue).

toward one of the settlements, and a third remains alone on a tongue of land to the left.

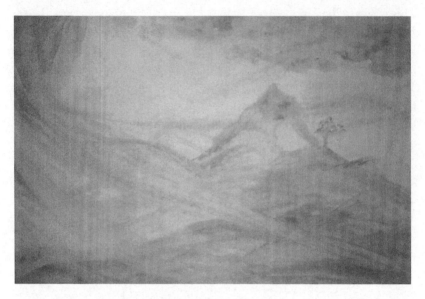

118. Desire Landscape in Blue

The landscape of desire, which Mrs V. had painted in Image 115, opens up even further under the influence of blue. In Image 118 it stretches into a pulsating distance. The tree has moved deeper into the scene and stands approximately where the person in Image 115 had stood. It appears tiny from this distant perspective. Lilac-colored veils breeze through the blue landscape providing the sole color nuance. These give the effect of wind or fragrance wafting across the open territory. Looked at differently, these billowing veils may be the waving hair of a figure in whom land and sky meet. Structurally they recall the woman's figure from Mrs. V.'s painting in red (Image 112). In both paintings the head would be in about the same place, but here it has become much larger. An entire mountain ridge makes up her right shoulder and a mighty cloud her head. Lost in thought, she gazes upon the expanse of landscape that at the same time is her body, as if floating in the color of desire, blue.

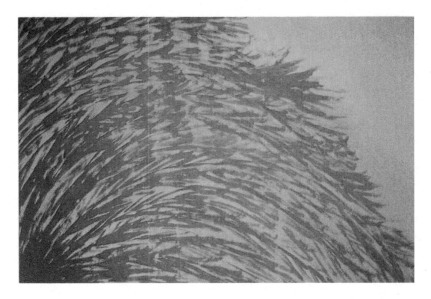

119. Ripe Sheath

According to the law of complementary of colors, yellow-orange[30] must follow blue. Yellow is a goal-oriented color representing light and awareness. It symbolically possesses the same traits as light, dissolving boarders and going out indefinitely.

Mrs. K.'s yellow took up the entire ground of her painting (Image 119) so that it wallows in corn yellow, the color of ripe grain. The sheaf motif has been appearing in her pictures since Image 113 and here is consciously being taken up yet again. The wing shape of Image 116 is repeated in soft arches resembling stalks of grain that bend across the page toward the right. Mrs. K. chose violet, the complementary color to yellow, to color the fronds of grain. Indeed, she used violets that very specifically complement her corn yellow. Violet is the color of transition, and it has very often been purposefully selected to represent women and the women's movement[31]. This painting reveals that Mrs. K. has experienced a ripening process, or in any case stands in the middle of one. She has undergone a transformation of her femininity in these summer

30 Ibid, pp. 70-99 (concerning yellow).
31 Ibid, pp. 156-173 (concerning violet).

months, just like the corn outside in the fields. The painful experience she had before the class began will grow over. She can therefore dare anew to let herself trust a man again, first her therapist, but soon also a new relationship partner.

The paintings in this chapter should be enough to illustrate some of the possibilities that can arise when we imagine and paint color motifs. They have much to offer. The method makes it possible to discover the colors as such and to experience their luminosity together with the emotions and the symbolism that they evoke. When we are painting in order to discover our personal problems, we do it with exactly the colors connected to them. And as we work them out, we do so with the aid of the corresponding complementary colors, because these contain precisely the possibilities that unlock what is still lacking in the previously experienced dominant color, even when it is our own favorite color.

House, River and Tree

Two Picture Series from an Introductory Seminar on Painting Therapy

by Christa Henzler

Preliminary Information

The two picture series that I have chosen were produced in a seminar called "Introduction to Painting Therapy" led by Ingrid Riedel. She utilized a combination of active imagination and painting, offering the students three motifs:

- the house, in which I would like to live,

- water or a river,

- the tree.

Each segment included an exercise to relax the body; then an active imagination followed by the painting of an image we had "seen"; and finally discussion. In the first active imagination, we were led through our dream house (a desire motif) and could also encounter an animal in one of the rooms. With the water motif we experienced the flowing of a river through various landscapes until it emptied into the sea. And lastly, we observed our interior tree from its roots all the way to its crown.

Because they exemplify just how very different the painting process can be after hearing the same active imagination and then working under the same external painting conditions, I chose two series, both painted by women, and both characteristic of how individuals paint in a group. Carmen was a 27-year-old student teacher at the time, and Ira a 21-year-old student. I interviewed them three weeks after the seminar. Their personal comments provide very important points of reference for describing and interpreting the pictures.

To understand the relationship between an imagined picture and a painted picture we will be demonstrating how the processes of imagining, painting, discussing, and encountering all affect each other. For each series, I will first recount each woman's active imagination experience, then go on to describe and interpret the resulting pictures, keeping as a general guideline, the actual painting process described by each woman during our later discussions.

The Active Imagination Motifs of House-River-Tree

Before interpreting the individual paintings, some points regarding the general symbolism of our chosen motifs may be in order. All three – the house, the river, and the tree – have very strong symbolic character. They are "carriers of meaning" which speak very personally to every single person.

The house is an image par excellence of the very person. Our self-worth and self-image express themselves in the ways and means in which we form our house in the active imagination. How it stands in the environment reveals how we see ourselves from the outside. What kind of foundation does it stand upon? How do we get into the house (how accessible are we)? Can we see inside the house? If so, which rooms are revealed? What kind of house is it – a high-rise, a farmhouse, an igloo, a castle?

The house also alludes symbolically to the body. The facade can correspond to external appearance. The roof could be the head. The upstairs is sometimes the mind (we say, he has nothing upstairs). The basement might be related to the lower body or to sexuality, thereby to the drives, the instincts, and the unconscious. The kitchen is often in the middle of the house and is a place of transformation[32]. On the other hand, we usually hang out in the living room, which reveals how comfortable we're able to feel in our house.

Erich Neumann considered the house to be a variation on the container: this great symbol, often called "the vessel" is an elementary characteristic of the feminine[33].

In contrast to the static motif of the house, water (in this case the river) moves, and so it is clear that it can express our vital energy. "Symbolically the stream expresses the unfolding development of our soul: the unhindered flowing of spiritual energy. And we must not forget that a stream is water, which is very closely related to the unconscious. As one of the four classical elements, water expresses vital energy. It refreshes and enlivens. Life without water is unthinkable. Therefore, it also includes the notion of fertility."[34] A discussion following an active imagination about water lends itself to certain questions: How strong was the current? Was the flow in any way hindered? If so, by what? How much water did the river transport? Such questions can clarify for us just how strong or weak our "life river" currently feels to us, and how we deal with its possible hindrances. Moreover, the river motif generally stimulates the flow of inner images.

In contrast again, the tree is a motif that recollects us, and like the house, it has much to say about how we experience our bodies. In painting a tree, sicknesses and psychological wounds are often indicated as lesions on the tree. For example, a cut on the tree can often point to a surgical operation; a broken-off limb might be a sign of a serious loss such as a divorce or a death. The tree is also a symbol of the personality, which depicts our self-perception. Its trunk often represents our "standing" or position in the world. The crown displays the spiritual/mental condition. The position of the trunk in relation to the crown, and of both in relation to the root system can tell whether the state of our

---

32 Oesterreicher-Mollwo, Marianne: *Herder-Lexikon Symbole*, Freiburg im Breisgau 1993, p. 71. Also available as French edition: Oesterreicher-Mollwo, Marianne: *Petit Dictionnaire des Symboles*, 1992.
33 Neumann, Erich: *The Great Mother*. Bollingen Foundation Inc. Pantheon Books, New York 1955, p. 282.
34 Leuner, Hanscarl: *Lehrbuch des Katathymen Bilderlebens*. Bern 1985, p. 34.

physical and psychological health is currently in balance. If something is very distinctively painted, for example only the root system, this indicates that an aspect of the personality or a problem is pressing into the foreground. It wants to be worked on or at least be looked at. Often one's own life is depicted, but frequently it is one's entire family tree and its history along with it. We use the word "stem", in relation to our family history and origins. By comparing the age of the tree with that of the painter, we can usually tell whether it symbolizes more the artist's own life history, or the family history. When a 20-year-old paints an eight-hundred-year-old oak, we can be pretty sure that the family history is meant. Judith's tree (Image 14) is an impressive example of how both types of tree can be unhappily connected.

Carmen's Active Imagination and Painting Series

Active Imagination and Painting Interpretation to the motif "House"

As already mentioned, the first motif that the participants of the seminar imagined was "the house I would like to live in". Regarding the active imagination Carmen recounted, *"I first saw the house from an airplane, from above. It was a little similar to a church with various levels to it, domes, big windows – very multifaceted."* After her bird's eye view, Carmen entered the house through a long entrance hall. Several staircases led from it in various directions. Carmen took a winding flight of stairs up into her tower room. She said this was her favorite room, from which she had a broad view over the landscape. She continued, *"And it was very bright with a cozy corner. And I saw a cat. It was like a meditation room: the carpet was white, the walls were white, and there was nothing in it except that I saw a hammock, which stretched diagonally across the room. It was a beautiful, white hammock. It was simply a room to "be" in."* At some point Carmen was briefly far below in the house: in the kitchen containing an antique stove. After the active imagination it was clear to her that she would paint the tower room, because that is where she would most want to spend time.

120. Plant, Cat, Cozy Corner

Carmen chose a large, heavy, sheet of drawing paper and tempura paints. She laid the paper in landscape format for a wide and roomy spatial perspective (Image 120).

The room is accessed from the darkened lower left corner of the painting. Because of the gray shadowing here, the room is no longer as light and bright as Carmen experienced it in her active imagination. Also, the hammock is not stretched diagonally across the room, but rather finds its place in this darkened entrance corner. Furthermore, it is painted a subdued wine red, making the white hammock of her imagination warmer, but duller. Before she painted, Carmen first divided the room. In doing so it was very important for her to have a convoluted room with rather oblique walls. She began by painting the cozy nook at the left side of the painting, using an intense wine red. From there, she painted two walls, dampening the colors with gray. One she made yellow-greenish and the other violet. An almost door-like arched window and a smaller one of the same shape, allow a broad view of the landscape. These windows are not sub-divided nor hung with curtains or blinds, and looking out one has a broad overview. However, because of the height, nobody can see in.

Next the black stove appeared, standing near the cozy nook. Then came the cat in front, and next to her the hammock. *"Actually, I wanted to paint the cat white, but then I realized that a white cat on the white floor wouldn't do, so it became gray. And then the floor became gray, too. Why? I don't know."* The elements of the picture associated with the cozy nook – the cat, the stove, and the red-speckled wall – were painted with a great deal of care and effort.

But in painting further, Carmen had big problems with the sloping ceiling surfaces she had placed over the cozy nook and the entrance. When I asked what had given her difficulties, she said that it was mainly the form and the color that disturbed her and made her dissatisfied. Finally, this peculiar "plant figure" appeared in the lower right corner. In painting it she had become very emotionally engaged. This picture element takes over lower right quarter of the painting. It stands in color relationship to the picture's upper left corner, but with an antithetical shape in comparison. While the upper left corner hems it's colors in, the lower right corner "licks" and "shoots forth" the same colors creating a "flame plant". Its form speckled with the splashes of red remind us of a fire, while the blue-gray actually stands in contrast to fire. Noticeable on this "plant" are the red and yellow fruits. These awoke associations in the other seminar participants with a "baby" or "bear cub".

Another color correspondence occurs between the stove and the plant. The visible fire and embers in and around the stove match the red speckles and the fruit on the plant.

With its pointed windows, the room gives the general impression of a church, and Carmen herself referred to it as a *"sacred or occult room"*. She felt that the bowl-like form in which the fruits lay was a sacrificial bowl.

In a later discussion with Carmen even more insights into the meaning of the picture came up. As already mentioned, the upper left corner was rather difficult for her. She found the colors drab and the slanting walls oppressive and constricting. She recognized that this was the same feeling she experienced as a student teacher in the daily grind of school. To my question of whether she knew such constriction from earlier in life, she said, *"Yes, my father had placed heavy restrictions on me, sometimes very heavy. Afterwards my mother would loosen them up."*

Then we discovered that the colors of the "plant" in the lower right corner are related to those of the ceiling in the upper left, but their shapes are in opposition. The meaning then became clear: in opposition to the constriction of the upper left corner, Carmen found in the "plant" something lively and aggressive that did her good. She experienced it as something primordial and vital, yet also as somewhat dead – somewhere between dead and alive. The "fruit basket" looks a bit like a baby in the cradle, and may well be expressing her wish for a child. If so, then the blue-gray color could mean that the father's restrictiveness still casts its shadow over any decision on her part to allow herself to be with a man.

Carmen discovers her femininity in the cat, the stove, and the cozy red nook. Here is her space where she can relax and discover herself. It is noteworthy that this "cozy feminine space" is to be found directly underneath that part of the picture which Carmen finds so constricting and which she identifies with experiences that limit her personality – earlier her father and today the "masculine" expectations and demands of student teaching.

Is it possible that she is documenting a rapprochement with the masculine by placing her bed here? Is she psychically integrating the masculine side of her personality? The red dabs of color in the "plant" along with the stove embers could be a further indication of such a rapprochement.

On one hand this picture suggests a rapprochement in the broad sense of the masculine and feminine poles coming together. On the other hand, it strongly expresses the tension that is inherent in such a rapprochement: tension between the "cozy feminine niche" on the left where she retreats into herself, and the aggressive "flame plant" on the right. Based on its color relationship with the upper left region of picture, one could say that the plant contains a significant amount of masculinity.

A further hint as to how we might interpret this "plant" is found in Carmen's strong emotional engagement while she was painting it. She said she tried to express that it was somewhat aggressive, but the way the colors worked out, she actually dulled it. This is how Carmen experienced her own aggression: dampened, held back, but perceptible as vital energy. Perhaps this blue-gray "fire tree" is blazing out against her father and against the masculine in her current situation as student teacher. After all, she experiences the school system as masculine, especially in its representatives, such as the subject director. She cannot yet completely live out the full strength of this feeling.

Very closely connected to this feeling is another one. As she herself worded it, a feeling that she must *"sacrifice"*. When I her asked about her "sacrifice" she mused: *"I had the feeling that something feminine was being sacrificed. Or maybe even that it was a feminine occult room. I couldn't figure it out."* Could this sense of victimization be mitigated if she were able to marshal her full aggressive energy for herself and for the unfolding of her femininity? Might her feeling of being offered up then peter out? This is worth considering. At the very least Carmen felt stronger after she had painted. This indicates that by painting the picture, especially the "flame plant", she had experienced something of her vital aggressive energy and could give it expression.

Active Imagination and Picture Interpretation to the Motif "River"

As part of the guidance into the second active imagination, the participants were led to a river whose course they could follow all the way to the sea. They were also to imagine the obstructions, constrictions and thresholds, anything that hindered the water's free flow.

Carmen found this active imagination harder than the first one. She began again from a birds-eye view somewhat above a river that was almost always in the forest: *"It was dismal. At some point I saw in the forest a house in the background. The stream was small, approximately two meters wide."* In connection with obstacles, Carmen saw a waterfall, and at its mouth, the river crossed a flat landscape before emptying into the sea. There Carmen's active imagination experience was not very impressive. The liveliest part of her experience was at the waterfall.

Again with this painting Carmen chose a landscape format on heavy drawing paper (Image 121), and again she painted primarily with tempura, although she also achieved a differentiated image effect by indicating the small trickles of water in the "rocky" part of the picture and among the tree roots with wax crayons. Because she had experienced the water-fall most vividly during the active imagination, this is what she began to paint. This waterfall and its right bank made up pretty well the center of the painting. At this point the bank is a stone ridge with two trees anchored on a river that flows from the upper right corner. It then pours itself as the waterfall into a dizzying depth while dividing the painting into two halves. The perspective makes this a very interesting picture in that the upper half of the painting provides a broad view of the landscape, while the waterfall in the lower half invites a close-up look. The dynamism of the thundering water inevitably draws the attention down and to the left, toward itself. Then the water gathers at the lower right side of the picture into a deep pool. Carmen has a tree growing to the right of this pool that was originally intended to be on a cliff. Completely at the foreground of the picture, it stretches into the upper limits of the drawing space, and two of its limbs reach all the way into the middle. The tree is painted in strong dark red with only about a quarter of its full circumference pictured, and across from it, in complementary green, a snake can be seen at the base of the waterfall.

121. Waterfall

According to Carmen, the waterfall had to come "crashing down" between two boulders, which would cause the left side to appear utterly gray, she emphasized. But then painting anything green on it would not have fit. What impressed her most while she was painting had been how hard it was for her to use light colors. It was a mighty effort. To my question of why that should be particularly difficult in this painting, she said, *"You know, I kept thinking: Does that make sense? I was simply wary in the sense of: is that right for me?"* The light colors appear only in the background and are not as differentiated as the colors in the foreground. When I asked with what she associated bright colors in a painting, she thought: *"With a rather joyful and optimistic attitude toward life, or that kind of feeling."* Given the requirements of student teaching, this optimistic attitude toward life had been pushed into the background for Carmen. Through her color selection and placement, she expressed her current situation rather well.

I kept asking where she might picture herself in the painting. It was down on the roots of the two trees. This is the spot where most is happening in the picture, but also a location containing something scary for Carmen. It is in the middle of those picture elements that were most important for her as she painted them: the trees, the waterfall, the snake, and the peaceful lake.

Does the shape of the two trees not resemble the "plant" in the last picture? It seems that Carmen has left her protective cozy nook and gotten nearer to this aggressive and vital "plant". Staying with the interpretation of the last painting (Image 120), Carmen must then be getting closer to her aggressive and vital side, although it is still subdued. An indication for this is the nearness of the waterfall with its enormous dynamic. This would also be her masculine side. As our discussion progressed, she thought about this and said, *"As I looked at this painting, I had a pretty strong hunch that it had something to do with sexuality and the theme of man and woman, because there are these two trees with apples on them and this snake, too."* Carmen's hunch is confirmed by the different ways the water is depicted. On one side the water is "shooting", but in the so-called "mother corner" it is an oval-shaped peaceful lake. Interesting in this connection is the snake, whose shape combines masculine and feminine elements, thus playing a multifaceted role. On one hand the snake is a primeval feminine symbol associated, for example, with Eve. On the other hand, because of its phallic shape it also stands for masculinity, and manly potency.[35] Because it played such an important role in Carmen's feelings, we know that the snake in her painting serves the function of bringing the opposites of masculine and feminine closer together.

Now let's go back and compare the two pictures according to color. It is very noticeable that the wine red of the cozy nook (Image 120) has moved itself to the right in Image 121. Now it is in the tree trunk that is only partially seen in the picture. Her "tree of life" is growing here – large, spread out, and strong, if we could see the whole thing. But here in the picture it can only claim a relatively small space. This again corresponds to Carmen's life situation at that point. She had very little time for herself and her interests. She had to constantly put these on hold for the sake of the internship. This often unleashed a feeling of helpless rage in her, leading to partial resignation. Carmen gives this tree a feminine character in the lower half with the trickling that issues from a root hole and trunk hole. It gives this part of the picture a very lively expression. With the thick, red-orange colored "tree arteries" Carmen wanted to show energy currents, and it is clear that her energy is grounded in the feminine. But this energy, like the tree that is only partially in the picture, is not completely accessible at this time. As Carmen put it, *"Lately I keep noticing that my life energy feels locked out."* Nevertheless, there stands this tree assuming an important role. It inspires the secure feeling, as if it is holding its protective limbs out over Carmen's "inner" landscape. It stands for the possibility of refuge within herself when life gets to be "too much". To an extent she can evoke the image to protect herself.

How blue developed in these paintings is also striking, and obviously important for Carmen. In Image 120 it appears only as the sober color toning for the slanted walls and the "plant". In Image 121 it gains the quality of a definite color and becomes a river. For Carmen the blue brought relief. No longer pressed into a frozen form, now it can flow. Her life energy can also flow now. The tension expressed in Image 120

---

35 Osterreicher-Mollwo, Marianne: *Herder-Lexikon Symbole*, p. 143.

between the lower right plant and the upper left ceiling can loosen up a bit.

In this second discussion of Carmen's pictures we have been alternating constantly between two interpretation levels thus switching the discussion between two themes. On the one hand is the examination of the male-female theme and Carmen's growing awareness of her own feminine and masculine sides. On the other hand, her real-life situation of currently being very heavily challenged as a student teacher and having to fight to keep up with its so-called masculine expectations.

122. Moon, Tree and Embryo

Active Imagination and Picture Interpretation to the Motif "Tree"

Because the seminar was full of participants eager to discuss their paintings, it was exhausting for Carmen. So she decided to paint the third picture at home. Because of this, she would not be able to take part in the common active imagination, but she still chose the active imagination motif of the group: "The tree". She did so because she felt so drawn to the two "exhausted" trees of Image 121 and the bizarre "tree plant" of Image 120.

In the center of Image 122 stands a sturdy-looking blue tree, and behind it diagonally to the right a second one in violet. The trees stand so close that both their limbs and their roots could come into contact with each other. In the root system of the blue tree lies a curled up "embryonic image" in glowing orange. The same glowing orange adorns the orb lying in the fork of the blue tree's trunk and the crescent moon rising out of the black background from the picture's lower right side, across the middle and into the upper left corner. Carmen begins the moon's background in black, gradually lightening it until the darkness runs out in the upper limits of the painting. This brightening is shaded with red and blue. The centered composition of this painting invites the observer to ponder it in a collected, concentrated, meditative fashion.

In our discussion of this painting we started discussing the blue tree right away. It was the first thing she had painted, and it harbors the orange-colored *"embryo-shaped image"* in its root system with the matching *"moon"* behind it. Carmen saw in the embryonic image a corresponding part of herself – a part full of energy and ready to development. Of course, we both also made the association with a real child, which led directly to Carmen's desire to have children. Indeed, she had been wrestling with this theme over and over in the recent past. The picture speaks for itself to this topic: feminine symbolism is inherent in all three orange objects: not just the embryonic image in the roots of the tree, but also the ball between the three-forked limbs and the glowing moon. Above all, the moon, since it is a goddess for many peoples. The Greeks called her Selene and the Romans worshiped her as Luna. The waxing and waning of the moon symbolize the female organism[36]. This moon

36 Ibid, p. 113.

not only stands in color correspondence with the "embryo" and the orb, it also takes up a great deal of the space in Carmen's painting.

I also noticed a lot of "threes" in Carmen's painting. Both trees fork into three sturdy limbs, and the color orange occurs noticeably only in the three images of circle, moon, and embryo. Carmen had a real wish to have children, but I had a hunch that hidden behind this wish also lay the desire for a relationship. Carmen confirmed this. Three is the dynamic number pointing toward development. It easily lends itself to the constellation woman-man-child. This painting may well indicate this in the form of the two trees depicting the "couple". However, the spatial ordering of the two trees makes it clear that for the moment the blue one, the symbol of herself, has the central and more important meaning.

A further level of symbolic meaning could be the three phases of life reflected in the feminine goddesses handed down in Greek mythology. The child is the beginning, the orb is the consummation, and the waning moon the fleeting. The goddesses of spring, of love, and of death, appear namely as Persephone, Demeter, and Hecate. They represent the three phases of life: beginning, consummation, and death. By coming up with these three symbols and painting them together in a single picture, Carmen is discovering a major interrelationship, one that she currently finds herself in as a woman. She is experiencing a phase in which she needs to let go of something. It is not the end, but rather a transition to a new beginning. Concerning what was said about her waning moon, she added that for her it symbolizes dying and therefore letting go, but also new beginning: *"It reminds me also of the school where I am often running along exactly in this stupid performance race. I am afraid of not being good enough and of failing. I think I have to learn to let my anxiety die, to let it go. I have to do this for me. It makes me mad, too, when I realize that it has so much control over me."* Does the painting's dark background express this anxiety?

Perhaps it is not just her fear of ineptitude in the school context that must die. Underlying this anxiety is an over-arching pressure that she puts upon herself that forms a partial aspect of her self-image. She burdens herself with "false" expectations and demands. This is what really has to die. I think it was very important that Carmen could experience what it is like to let go. She experienced it by painting this picture. At least during the painting process and for a while thereafter, she forgot the fear of not being mature enough to meet particular demands, and she could embrace the values that really belong to her essence. This expressed itself primarily in that after the painting process, she had a very good feeling and felt herself very much strengthened, even for her school day. She also felt a certain confidence in herself after painting this picture. Carmen sensed that it would be important in the future to plug herself more frequently in to the source of energy represented by this embryo. Then she wouldn't so easily become the victim of such anxieties. In a broader sense, this embryo stands for everything in Carmen capable of or in need of development. Now it actually constitutes in Carmen a power to develop. It can help her to find and to claim her completely personal values and norms, even in the school.

Carmen's developmental process in this series of paintings is primarily expressed through the color presentation – especially the complementary colors of blue and orange – and through the tree's development. Carmen puts it this way: *"What was most important in the whole series is that in the beginning I was painting very intensely gray, but became ever more capable of painting with colors. It was like an act of liberation."* What was Carmen able to free herself from? In Image 120 she had the feeling that she was sacrificing something about her femininity. She saw the sacrifice expressed as the fruit placed in the offering bowl of that bizarre "tree plant". That sacrificial fruit's orange color returns in Image 122 appearing even more brightly and radiantly, and again it is in a tree. This time the tree stands in the center and is painted intensive blue – everything gray and bizarre about it is gone. The middle point of the painting now becomes the orb, a symbol of completeness. This orb no longer awakens in the observer the feeling that something has been sacrificed here, but instead stands in direct relationship to the embryo and to the waning moon, revealing the great connection of life – of becoming and of decaying, of birthing and of letting go. Painting these three pictures was for Carmen an act of liberation, because she could express herself in their symbolism. The liberation expresses itself in Image 122 as the concentrated presentation of the symbolic images, and the use of clear, unadulterated colors which achieve a glowing intensity by standing out in contrast to the partially dark background.

The Relationship Between Active Imagination and Painting in Carmen's Series

With the example of Carmen's series I would now like to take a closer look at the relationship between an imagined and a painted picture by comparing the experience of imagining with that of painting, and tracing the conspicuous features and peculiarities that we can pick up.

In the first active imagination to the motif "house" Carmen had seen a bright, sun-drenched room -her tower room – and already in her imagination she felt primarily associated with it. The active imagination had guided her in a walk through the house where she soon found the room and saw it from the inside. "The house in which I would like to live" had been the description in the guided imagery. This was her dream house, the house of her desires, that Carmen imagined for herself. Now in reality as well as in fantasy, our desires often get stuck on obstacles and blockades. In her active imagination Carmen was able to maintain a bright, light, peaceful room and could own and enjoy her desire. But obstacles presented themselves during the painting process. Her house didn't become bright, it took on a gray layer. Design problems popped up during the concretization of her room. Carmen's problem with the upper left corner was not its "technical" execution, but rather that the color and form led to a constricted feeling (Image 120). We can see here how the principle of compensation can underlie the relationship between imagining and painting a picture. In this case the principle of compensation caused exactly the feeling that had been repressed during the active imagination (perhaps because it lay deeper) to push into the foreground during the painting process. Indeed, it can often happen that a positive experience dominates an active imagination, but when the ensuing painting gets underway, the underlying, oppressive layers of feeling then come, pressing themselves to the fore. The opposite can happen as well when a negatively experienced active imagination calls forth positive layers during the painting process. When Carmen began to paint, certain hindrances placed themselves in the way of how she wanted to concretize her image, and she had to come to terms with these. Her hindrances had mainly to do with so-called "masculine" norms and values. She was then able to discover that they were actually her own introjected contents.

Carmen did not experience the second active imagination as intensely as the first. She felt most alive at the waterfall. There was her strongest emotional participation. Therefore, the waterfall was the first picture element that she painted (Image 121), and from there the picture developed itself further. The active imagination motif possessing the most libido is often the first one taken up in a painting, because it is the element most wanting to be concretized. It wants to become conscious. In many cases this becomes the starting point of a psychic and creative process. When we realize this, it becomes clear that painting can't just be about merely copying the picture we imagined, but rather is a continuation of a process that has already begun.

Another student reported a similar experience. At first it had been impossible for her to give herself over completely to the active imagination because the images were rushing so quickly past her inner eye "like in the cinema". As she entered her imagined dream house, she looked around without excitement, and went into a room where she saw a book lying there. In her imagination she determined that she had imagined this all before, especially the book, but with much more excitement. Only when she had finished the picture did she realize that the imagined book must have continued working inside her, because at some point during the painting process it just suddenly appeared on the paper, as if by itself and stood as if in close-up in the middle of the painting. It was the book that had first attracted the painter's emotional involvement and which had led to a very intense painting session.

Carmen didn't participate in the third guided active imagination. Rather, she let herself be inspired by the picture element in Image 121 that appeared most important to her, doing her own independent active imagination at home. This is one of the possible variations available when using active imagination and painting. She selected this possibility because she needed to look more closely at something she had already painted. According to this technique, one selects one picture element or a part of a picture that had been painted from an active imagination and paints that part further – like a detail or a blow-up. Naturally imagination continues to play an active role. By mindfully contemplating the original painting, new images arise which then find their way onto the drawing paper.

Ira's Active Imagination and Painting Series

Active Imagination and Picture Interpretation to the motif "House"

As with Carmen, the house motif was the first active imagination. Ira recalled: *"For me it was clear from the beginning that it wouldn't be any normal house. Rather it would be a castle."* In Ira's imagination this castle was very large. It stood in a lush, green, hilly landscape. Following the guidance of the active imagination, she stepped into her castle. But before she could go into the room on her left, she took a quick glance into a dark, underground dungeon that made her shudder. The room on the left was very white, and in it she came upon a blue bird of paradise.

Ira found it very odd while painting that she was not reproducing what she had planned – the great castle that had so impressed her in the active imagination. Rather she began to "pile up" the most brilliant colors (Image 123). *"I suddenly got this hankering for color,"* she said. *"The castle only appeared up there in the picture during the last three minutes"*. Now it is really interesting that the castle, which she had experienced so vividly in the active imagination, moved as far back as possible and all the way to the upper limit of the picture, albeit agleam with yellow. Ira painted bright mounds of color, which span the painting's entire foreground. However, this could also be interpreted as a colorful road leading from the front edge of the picture straight back to the castle. Ira left both upper corners blank and open, and so the glowing yellow castle immediately catches the observer's eye. Almost all of the group members thought that the colorful hills were a colorful road. Some did see it as a road going up a mountain and leading to the castle. Ira protested against this saying: "*From the beginning it was something that I could not get to, regardless if others can see a road to it. For me it's more like a condition.*" I asked whether she could describe this condition precisely. She replied very reflectively: "*Somehow it's something that can't be described. But it's something unbelievably beautiful in itself: rich in color, iridescent, fascinating and appealing, and also exciting. But it's just there, and I can't get to it, at least not yet. I have somehow walled it up from myself. I can imagine someday being able to paint a road to it, beginning below and slowly painting something.*"

123. Castle upon the Mountain out of Colors

It was difficult for Ira to capture this castle in words or to say what it might mean for her psychologically. But she was intensely interested in fairy tales, so she could easily relate to her castle from that perspective. Indeed, her painting is reminiscent of a fairy tale illustration. Often in fairy tales the castle stands in the middle of an enchanted forest or upon an enchanted mountain. A castle "usually symbolizes the totality and completion of all positively oriented wishes. This is especially the case when it is light colored and gleaming"[37]. Iridescent, magnetic, fascinating, colorful, those are the attributes which Ira gives her castle. Naturally these are the same attributes she would wish for herself – to appear iridescent, attractive, and fascinating. Now Ira is certainly no "plain Jane", and she herself saw the castle expressing something very valuable and ideal about her own person. Nevertheless, I did not find this subjective-level explanation of the castle exhaustive.

Because of the perspective and distance in which it was painted, we also associated the castle with a golden key. But only the bit of the key is drawn, without a handle. That is how the interpretation discussion went with us: we could not "un-lock" the meaning content of the castle, our key did not have a handle.

I was primarily aware of how the painting at first glance left me with the impression of being very colorful, friendly and extremely bright. For her "many-colored way" Ira selected primarily bright, unadulterated colors and applied them partly in intensive lusciousness, partly in lighter transparence. This fits with her strongly pronounced emotionality and intensity.

At second glance it occurred to me that there is hardly any shading with dark colors, and that black and brown are completely lacking. I thought this cast the painting in an "unreal light" like something lost in reverie beyond this world. This caused me to wonder whether something dark might not be hidden under the magnificence of colors. Was something being suppressed by the bright-colored hills, as if under a spell? Perhaps here an enchanted mountain or an enchanted castle needed to be disenchanted just like in the fairy tales. And what could this "disenchantment" mean for Ira?

37 Ibid, p. 145.

But the glowing yellow castle and the bright mounds of color were not just expressions of Ira's un-dulled happiness. This became apparent after the painting process. Immediately after painting, it went very well for Ira. But during the course of the evening, and especially the next morning, her happy mood yielded to an ever-growing depression, which Ira could not explain at the time.

Active Imagination and Picture Interpretation to the Motif "River"

Ira resisted the second active imagination from the start. She said that for her the river motif was simply uncomfortable. It was an active imagination full of resistance. Firstly, the river could not spring up anywhere in her fantasy. Then it didn't want to flow. And when it finally did, it was with much difficulty, carrying silt and dirt with it. All of Ira's efforts to get the river to flow with more dynamism and a stronger current failed. She couldn't really see the landscape either, except for a little bit of green. The weather was gray: an overcast, rainy, foggy day. She found the rainy landscape threatening. The only "nice" feeling she connected to the scene was that it was also somehow peaceful. *"The landscape itself is so drab, but also locked shut."* By the end of the active imagination her river had picked up a little more speed. *"But it kept getting smaller and narrower, and then suddenly this mountain came down like a clap of thunder and stood there blocking the way like a hatch door"* Ira could no longer see the flowing water; she could only see this mountain.

After the active imagination Ira was absolutely mesmerized. She was under the spell of this mountain, which had positioned itself against the stream of water with, as she put it, "a clap of thunder". The appearance of the mountain had internally stopped her in her tracks. It was therefore important for her to start by painting it (Image 124). She made it tall, sharp, and jagged, placing it in the upper left corner. And she etched it in black, coloring its entire surface black and dark gray. The dark, narrow, little opening at the bottom makes the mountain by comparison tall and massive.

Ira's river enters the picture from the lower right and runs parallel to the lower edge of the painting for a long time before turning right and heading directly into the black opening in the mountain. Although the water is still clear and blue in the lower part of the painting, with increasing sand-colored shading it becomes ever darker and narrower until finally it becomes completely black as it disappears into the mountain. This gives the jagged, black mountain an even more sinister character. With outstretched arms, Ira herself can be seen in the current where the water is still blue. The stream is dragging her inexorably toward the dark hole in the mountain. Her body is red, her hair and arms black, and her hands again red.

124. River which Disappears into the Mountain

The picture's cement-colored center and its upper right corner are painted with heavy brush strokes and merely suggest a hilly landscape. In it a barren tree in exactly the same cement color appears to be open, as if one could let oneself down through its trunk into the depths of the earth. Behind this tree in the hilly landscape, a glowing red sun is going down. This red sun and the blood red of the woman's body provide an energetic counter-accent to the threatening dreariness otherwise expressed by this painting.

At the end of the active imagination Ira sat there stunned by the thundering appearance of the mountain. Under its spell she began to paint it. That the mountain touched her so emotionally, enchanted her and at the same time shocked her so deeply, suggested a large, unresolved inner problem. This much was also clear to Ira while she was having the experience, but still she could not name it. Whatever un-nameable problem the mountain symbolized seemed so huge to her, so mighty and unconquerable, that she first had to get some distance from it. This expressed itself in the painting process in that she had to take a half hour break after painting the mountain. She simply could no longer paint. Afterward however, she resumed contact with the mountain anew. At first she painted the river. However, she made it flow in the opposite direction, against the current that had been so clear in the active imagination. Now she made it flow away from the mountain into the lower right corner. Even in her art she first had to get away from that mountain before she could attempt a new rapprochement. The distance provided her a certain relief, which allowed her (as the painting shows) to lay herself in the river's current, which would carry her again to the mountain. This painting process reflected Ira's emotional movement – her psychodynamics.

If we, as observers, allow ourselves to sink into the feeling of this picture, we must admit that it produces an increasing feeling of constriction. Just imagine the consequences for that person in the river who is giving herself over to the current! Inevitably she will be sucked into the interior of the mountain. Ira identifies herself specifically with this figure. She pointed to it saying, *"I'm here."* What awaits her in this eerie mountain?

Analyzing the spatial symbolism in this painting helped us further. The river current carries Ira into a jagged mountain in the upper left corner. Symbolically it pulls her into the so-called "father corner"[38]. If the meaning of this "frightful mountain" is indeed Ira's relationship to her real father, it suggests that the relationship stands under great pressure. The combination of characteristics forming the mountain,

---

38 Riedel, Ingrid: *Bilder in Religion, Kunst, und Psychotherapie: Wege zur Interpretation.* Stuttgart 1989, p. 38. Reworked and newly formatted under the title *Bilder in Psychotherapie, Kunst und Religion: Ein Schlüssel zur Interpretation.* Stuttgart 2005.

namely threatening, dangerous looking, black, jagged, upward-thrusting, tapering to a point speak for themselves. When her father was invoked, Ira was quite shocked but immediately saw a direct correlation between her father and this *"projectile of a mountain"*. At the same time this painting confirms her readiness to grapple with this mountain, to confront her father problematic. By lying down in the water, she is symbolically letting herself be carried by her river, by her life energy, to this mountain[39]. This will inevitably precipitate an intensive encounter with the mountain, indeed with the interior of this mountain.

The discussion with Ira had made the direct relationship between the mountain and her father clear. Since I knew a bit about her life history, it also became clear to me why the mountain was so black and had such a "shrouded" character, and why the river led into its interior. Ira's father had died when she was fourteen. At the time she was hardly capable of emotion. She wasn't able to grieve. Therefore, her father had "enshrouded" himself inside her. Ira had never worked through this existential death experience. In therapy sessions this thematic had indeed come up, but as recently as two weeks before the seminar she herself had said that her father was a "blind spot" in her. That suggested that at the time she was "stuck" in her grieving process, as if frozen and unable to experience emotions like pain, sadness, anger, and rage. She had anesthetized herself against her feelings for her dead father[40]. Ira had been unable to work through her loss. In fact she had repressed her father, her experiences connected with him, and ultimately his death. Thus he became a "blind spot" in her, which transformed him into a threatening interior entity.

By imagining the symbolic motifs actively and thereafter painting them, Ira was directly confronted with her "repressed" father. This internalized father was impeding the life energy, which wanted to flow freely

39 Kast, Verena: *Imagination als Raum der Freiheit*. Walter-Verlag AG, Olten 1988, pp. 55ff. English version: *Imagination as space of freedom: dialogue between the ego and the unconscious*. Fromm International Publishing Corporation 1993. See also Anderten, Karin: *Traumbild Wasser*. Olten / Freiburg im Breisgau 1986.

40 Kast, Verena: *A Time to Mourn: Growing through the Grief Process*. Daimon Verlag, Einsiedeln *1988*. (Second edition 1993), esp. Chapter 2 "Death and Mourning Mirrored in a Series of Dreams". Using a dream series, Verena Kast demonstrates in her book the phases of the grieving process and the problems that can appear due to a repressed and protracted grieving process.

in her again. So she was compelled to confront the situation anew. This interior confrontation is strongly indicated by the direction of the river. In picture symbolism movement from right to left indicates movement from the outside to the inside. In other words, a confrontation inside herself was imminent. Although she could no longer struggle externally with her living father, he had become a part of her through their 14-year-long lived relationship and through her memory of his idiosyncrasies.

It is plausible that the open tree is a further indication that she will attempt this interior confrontation. As already mentioned, the tree is a self-symbol. The way this one stands open, it facilitates a "descent" to its own deep roots. For Ira that may mean that she will be pushed to the roots of this problem. She said that she needed an energy source in order to swim to this dark mountain. Therefore, she painted the red sun from which she can draw the required energy.

Active Imagination and Picture Interpretation to the Motif "Tree"

The third active imagination was the "tree" motif. Ira said she felt "totally exhausted". She was washed out and thought she couldn't paint anymore. Concerning the active imagination she said, *"It's true that I saw a normal green tree in the beginning, but it said absolutely nothing to me and didn't mean anything. At the time, I felt that this green tree was inappropriate and not right."* Nothing more occurred to her in the active imagination. Important is what happened afterwards as she painted the tree.

Ira had begun by painting the roots, which were very important to her (Image 125). She painted them strong and deep in thick blue and violet. The ones furthest to the left she partially darkened with black. The tree as a whole looks like some sort of vessel because the upper part, where the branches and crown should be, is left mostly unpainted.

Apparently the branches and the crown were completely insignificant for Ira. The most important and essential element of this picture is found in the center – a black "tree creature". Given the direction of its tail, it has come up from below and settled itself upon the base of the trunk above the root system with its head bent toward the roots. As I looked at this third painting, my first thought was, "Has Ira let herself down into the roots of the open tree from Image 124? Has she swum further along her dark river, all the way to the scary tunnel entrance in the mountain?"

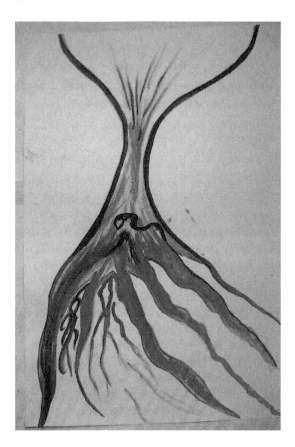

125. Tree Creature

She said she had "smeared" the painting onto the paper in less than ten minutes, then didn't feel well afterwards. I asked whether she had not actually felt a little relieved by painting the picture. She said, *"Just the opposite. It was a terrible burden. In the end I had painted myself dry.* (Ira identified herself with the tree creature.) *I somehow had the feeling, my God, you're stuck there in the middle, and it's eating you up, somehow killing you, destroying you. I had the feeling that I lay down there so small and hunkered up."*

After she had painted, Ira was gone – in a daze. And she felt a strong pressure within herself. She only felt some relief when the group began to discuss the picture. There she could fashion into words that she had indeed gotten emotionally close to her problem. She had approached the "father mountain". *"It was strange,"* she said during the interpretation discussion. *"For a year now my therapy has been about my father* (Ira had been in therapy for some time) *but I had somehow never had an access. It's true that I have always known he was once there, and he died when I was fourteen, and there were a bunch of problems, but I never had a real relationship to it, it hadn't touched me at all."*

Ira's third painting and the emotional experience that came with it make clear that by painting, a problem lying under the surface can be discovered and captured. Then its intense energy can be set free precisely in the group. She had not solved her father problematic by a long shot. But by painting this picture, she finally succeeded in gaining an emotional access to it, which mere verbalization of the problematic had not achieved. Emotionally reliving her father thematic was, of course, combined with pain and fear. This was all the more so because her dead father reactivated strong negative emotions. But mostly, the confrontation with him, because of his early death, was also a confrontation with death itself.

It is also interesting to notice how Ira created a compensatory counter-balance for herself in the painting. In the face of so difficult a problem, she painted a strong root system with six large roots. In number symbolism six very often expresses balance, adjusting inequality among things including masculine and feminine. It is therefore considered to be an expression of wholeness[41].

After the seminar Ira painted further. Following an inner logic, she created an entire series which reflected her confrontation with her dead father, with death itself, and last but not least with her own femininity. In one of these paintings I was very impressed with how Ira dared to paint the interior of the mountain. There she encountered a dead,

---

41 Jacobi, Jolande: *Vom Bilderreich der Seele: Wege und Umwege zu sich selbst.* Olten/ Freiburg im Breisgau 1969, pp. 97/98. (Available as Italian translation: *Dal regno delle immagini dell'anima percorsi diretti e vie traverse per giungere a se stessi*, translated by Murrau, Marina Pia. Edizioni Magi, Roma 2003.

faceless man in a coffin with blood-red hands. In this painting, she was dead herself, and lay on the coffin. This painting induced in Ira a psychic process whereby she consciously confronted her own femininity and her sexuality.

She involved herself intensively with the fairy tale "The Three Little Men in the Woods" after the seminar, and in the earliest paintings was confronted with the manhood of her father. *"It was like scales falling from my eyes as I realized that my father was not just my father, but also a man,"* she said of these paintings. In the course of these paintings it became ever clearer that her dead father still held her "in check" as a woman, so she felt threatened by him. Underlying this threatening feeling was the fact that internally Ira had never let her father die. Therefore in certain areas he was still dictating her feelings and thoughts from within. Ira herself expressed it this way: *"If I can ever make him small, and not see him as so huge, then I can grow. In other words, when he is actually dead – truly dead – only then will I really be able to live."* This would be paramount to a completed grieving process. Verena Kast describes this in her book *A Time to Mourn*[42] as being marked by a new self-reference and world reference. One's loss is finally accepted and those "life patterns" in relation to the deceased person, which we have gotten so used to, can be "unlearned". Then new life patterns appear in their place, without the deceased being simply forgotten.

As Ira and I looked over the first three paintings (Images 123, 124, 125) once more, considering their relationship with each other, we both had the impression that Ira had really been able to "tank up" through that first colorful painting (Image 123) as if she already had an inkling of the difficult material she would soon be encountering. Water very often symbolizes the unconscious, and the water motif indeed carried Ira away, directly into the great underlying father problematic in her unconscious. The further painting of this series demonstrates exactly how a process, once begun, follows an inner logic. Its development takes place as both the painter's inner experience and the external painting process. Ira's second painting (Image 124) gave the problem a name and revealed where the process was heading. In the third painting (Image 125) the

---

42 Kast, Verena: *A Time to Mourn, Growing through the Grief Process.* Daimon Verlag, Einsiedeln 1988 (Second edition 1993), p. 63.

problem has moved significantly nearer, especially on the emotional level where Ira experienced strong anxiety and even panic. In further paintings she plunged herself emotionally into the problem, confronting her deceased father, who lay at the core. She grappled intensively and constructively in those paintings.

The Relationship between the Imagined and the Painted Image

What is really noticeable and astounding about the relationship between Ira's first active imagination (her dream house) and the picture she painted (Image 123) is the difference between the two. Her imagined castle had been very close and real, but then it slipped further away during the painting. In the process, however, it became very bright, as if dipped in gold. It underwent a "change in levels". The realistically experienced castle standing in its green landscape became a fantastic one. It became a symbol.

In the active imagination Ira had walked through her castle, passed a dark dungeon in the cellar, then entered a room bathed in white where she encountered a blue bird of paradise. The reason why the castle could no longer be painted on the realistic level may lie with this bird. One could theorize that the blue bird of paradise stands for the "heavenly condition" for which we all are always longing. This could provoke a "change in levels" whereby the castle shifts to a symbol. Ira herself said that the castle stood for a "*Condition*".

How does the relationship between the envisioned and the painted image reveal itself in this example? In the active imagination, the image had been experienced very realistically, but as the artist painted it, it became a symbolic image eluding realistic depiction.

It remains to be seen under what conditions this "change of levels" took place from realistic to symbolic and also whether this was dependent upon the given active imagination motif. In this regard the dungeon, above all, cannot be overlooked. It had already appeared in the cellar before Ira's encounter with the blue bird. Only by deliberately hurrying past it in her imagination was she able to remain "above" in the castle. The problem of the dead father that has been "locked up" so long is unequivocally presented with this "dungeon".

In the second active imagination Ira built up a great deal of resistance. Firstly the water didn't want to flow properly. And when it finally did, it carried mud and debris with it. Unconsciously Ira suspected or perhaps even knew that the river motif stood for her "emotional flow" and for her unconscious. It would surely carry her to her problem. Naturally she resisted this at first, but she could not maintain the resistance for long. Nor did she want to. The river's current got stronger and stronger until with a thundering crash something unexpected happened that at first blocked everything: the mountain. Ira was dazed by the scene and became fixated on the mountain. Everything else receded. Completely under its spell, she painted the mountain, but then needed to give herself some distance from it (Image 124).

This was not simply an emotional preoccupation. Ira was nearly possessed – fixated upon a picture element whose sudden emergence called up strong affect. The intensity of the shock suggested a deeply-rooted problem. *"I was so blown away after the active imagination, and so I painted the mountain,"* she said. She had to paint the mountain. She was as if under a spell. It had to be made visible.

The relationship between the imagined and the painted image in light of this example could perhaps be characterized in the following way: The active imagination led pictorially to the problem. Because of its tremendous energetic charge, it had to be fixated first. Ira experienced herself as if paralyzed when facing this mountain. By painting it first, she could then begin an active confrontation with the problem.

Each subsequent active imagination and resulting painting then became implicated in this confrontation, a step-by-step moving toward a solution. Each contributed to the process of overcoming the problem. It was therefore very understandable that Ira could not imagine a "green tree" in the third active imagination. Instead, she first had to let herself down into the deep dark roots of her tree so that she could grab hold of her problem "by the roots" (Image 125).

If an active imagination and painting exercise happens to set such a problem-solving process in motion, it becomes important to help this process along through a careful selection of the subsequent motifs.

To this end the motifs in these pages are especially recommended: the house, the river, the tree, the flower, the clearing in the forest, and the well-spring, because they already contain within themselves potential solution possibilities. It helps to alternate between dynamic motifs that bring things into flow such as the river, the beach upon which something washes ashore, or a fire in which something burns up; and motifs by which the energies that have been set free can again collect and congeal such as the flower, the tree, or the garden.

A Comparison of the Process in the two Picture Series

Comparing these two series (Images 120-125) makes clear how one and the same symbolic motif can produce very different painting experiences, and just how varied the psychic processes can be that show up in such series.

Carmen's painting experience was that from picture to picture she came away from her "grayness" more and more until in the third painting she had achieved the free use of pure colors (Images 120, 121, 122). Describing her painting experience she said, *"It was an act of liberation"*. Through it she was able to overcome the "grayness" of her everyday life and rediscover her own true colors. Further, it made her realize that despite all external expectations and pressures, she could always come back to herself and recognize her own intrinsic value. The psychic process furnished Carmen with a concentrated, color-intensive symbolic image, her "embryo". Its primal growth-energy really became a source power for her to tap into.

Ira, on the contrary, had the opposite experience while painting. For her there was a deep, inner father problem. She had been throwing her entire opposition against it throughout a full year of therapy. In the active imagination she opposed this problem again with all her might. We discovered this by the way the second active imagination went. By staying with the active imagination, Ira was able to surrender herself to the inner images that appeared and was thereby able to overcome her opposition. Only then was she able to creatively approach her problem by painting Images 123, 124, and 125. Ira's psychic process was naturally full of anxiety, and sometimes panic, but she had to "go through it now" as she herself said.

These two picture series illustrate some important points. First, very deep-seated problems can be unraveled by activating unconscious contents (Ira). Second, inner power and self-certitude can be unleashed (Carmen) when these unconscious contents are rediscovered. Through the painting of pictures from the unconscious everyone can take the necessary steps for self-development and self-creation.

Part IV:

Painting in the Therapeutic Practice

Through painting, the natural individuation process gains momentum by coming into contact with the inner images. This keeps it flowing.

Indications and Contraindications for using Painting Therapy in the Therapeutic Practice

1. Painting works prophylactically to maintain mental health because painting out of the unconscious satisfies the natural human need for self-expression. Because it can also be applied therapeutically, we should be clear about which goal we are pursuing when considering whether to recommend painting to our patients.

The prophylactic application has practically no counter-indications, and is highly recommended simply because painting out of the unconscious makes people creative. This can be especially helpful for people who did not do so well in art class and therefore developed hang-ups regarding painting. Painting out of the unconscious can open up a spontaneous and utterly new access to a person's expressivity, melting away old criticisms, including those we level against ourselves, and thereby overriding the interior message of "I can't paint". As Schottenloher puts it: "Even in a non-therapeutic context the creative act serves to unfold and develop the person and thereby functions as a prophylaxis. Psychological splitting, repression, anxiety, and feelings of powerlessness are minimized and integral processes encouraged."[1]

---

1   Schottenloher, Gertraud: *Das therapeutische Potential spontanen bildnerischen Gestaltens*, p. 106.

Painting brings us into contact with our interior images. This can set the natural individuation process in motion and keep it flowing. It can overcome one-sidedness and psychological splitting. For those with a desire to paint because they are naturally haptic and aesthetic, painting is usually the therapeutic method of choice.

2. Painting combined with active imagination and discussion of the pictures recommends itself as a therapeutic method anytime that new constellations and psychological developments are just becoming recognizable. At first one notices only a mood. Something is emotionally afoot, but without a picture of it, it cannot yet be glimpsed or grasped by consciousness. Early on the new constellation or mood might be noticeable only in the body. If so, a picture might make it visible. Often a picture even reveals whether the mood has a physical basis. Headaches as well as other organ pains often show up in pictures as burning red places on the corresponding areas of the body.

3. Painting therapy is most strongly recommended when anxiety is at play, because the painter's own anxiety level sets the pace of therapy, which therefore unfolds in very regulated doses. Anxiety is always related to unconscious contents, and so the question is how we can best approach these contents. Creatively working with painting follows a patient's own rhythm more closely than some other therapeutic methods, because it takes place in several steps, making several attempts at creating several paintings. It is a very gradual process where the patient rather than the therapist establishes the tempo. Any forcing of the process through stimuli likely to stir patients up, for instance asking them to paint the color red or the element fire, is to be avoided until the anxiety-producing content becomes visible as a symbol and is thereby able to be integrated. Often it takes a long series of paintings before the anxiety-producing content becomes entirely apparent, but this has the advantage of embedding it in a context with other images and contents and of framing it.

Often the beginning of a therapy sees few paintings that are really individual. Rather they are general and harmonizing. It is only later, when an increasing feeling of security with the therapist and/or the painting group is established, that the fear-producing themes and creations dare to come forward and take on a face. As these later pictures appear, the painting style becomes visibly more powerful and more individual.

An important step is depiction of the negative image. When it finally appears, it can then be contemplated and ultimately confronted with counter-energies from the "mother field" of either the group or the therapist. This transforms the negative image so that it can be integrated. The energy that had been bound up in suppressing these demons and keeping them down is then freed up and becomes available for the painter to use once again. Thus even today – in our contemporary society the picture still fulfills one of its oldest functions: the banning of fear.

4. Likewise, painting therapy is strongly advisable for functional or psychosomatic illnesses. Sometimes the only image that can be found for someone's suffering is the symptom itself. In such a case it is very important to understand the symptom as a symbol, recognizing that there is something behind it. The popular idea that people with psychosomatic disorders are unable to symbolize does not correspond with my experience. It is just that the paintings of psychosomatic patients are often very realistic and very concrete in the beginning. Therefore, the patient's symbolizing imagination first needs to be awakened. Symbolizing can be learned through painting, looking at the paintings symbolically, and discussing them with a therapist or the painting group,

In exactly this way, a man afflicted with chronic back pain came to understand the symbolic language of his body. First he painted a picture of his back pain. In it a small man placed the entire globe upon his shoulders. In other words he took on excessive responsibility and it threatened to crush him. The symptom was based upon a failed attempt to work through a stressful separation experience. It was very liberating to turn the symptom back into a creative act, and soon the man in the pictures straightened himself up and threw off his exaggerated responsibility for the whole world.

5. It can be considered a stroke of luck when people afflicted with a depressive structure or currently suffering from a depressive mood begin to create something. Unfortunately, their basic problem is still standing in the way of this action – Fritz Riemann[2] describes it as a difficulty

2 Riemann, Fritz: *Anxiety: Using Depth Psychology to Find a Balance in Your Life*, translated by Greta Dunn. Barbara Budrich 2009. See chapter "The Depressive Personalities".

in bringing themselves to bear and in being true to themselves. Also, depressed people will all too quickly experience a request to paint as pressure; they may experience performance stress and right away react with feelings of guilt and anxiety that they will not be good enough. But, when they start to paint anything, a special chance offers itself to depressed people. In so far as they experience themselves as creative, as artists, they lift themselves above the feeling of helplessness that had been holding them down. They begin to take their destiny and their mood in hand, even if it is only by giving their depression a face. Through their pictures, they can finally look at their depression and thereby confront it. And because they produce something of their own and eventually even show it to the group and discuss it, they lift themselves above the basic problem of depression: they have brought something of their own to bear. This elevates their feeling of self-worth. And the lack of self-worth is generally what causes suffering in depressive people.

6. As already mentioned, in individual cases I have even had good experiences with painting therapy in suicidal crises. If someone in a suicidal crisis begins to paint, this is a very good sign. Even when the suicidal crisis itself is taken up as the theme, the creative act of self-portrayal can produce much libido in the artist. If I am the artist, it is exactly then that I am taking myself seriously in my situation, and in my doubt. This "taking myself seriously" produces a strong counter-movement to my self-destructiveness.

Also forgetting oneself in the good sense, can overcome someone working on a picture. An example is the subtle branch system of a tree like the one in Image 14. One suicidal painter described such painting as "a liberating experience in the middle of the crisis". For a few hours she forgot her suicidal fantasies, because painting the leaves of the tree in an exact and ordered way was more important for her during those hours. This ability to forget oneself by painting, even during a difficult crisis, is the experience Marion Milner describes as follows: "When I reached this level of concentration, I was no longer conscious of anything else I was doing. I was no longer acting upon a distant object from some center. Rather something very strange overcame my self-awareness."[3] This

---

3   Milner, Marion: The Hands of the Living God. New York 1969, p. 185.

condition of self-forgetfulness leads directly to an attitude of openness, of surrender to the unconscious, in which the deep forces of salvation, yes "the gods" themselves, can constellate. The experience can be so meaningful as to rescue someone in danger of suicide.

7. Hysterically-structured people (I still follow Riemann's character-ization, even though today we usually speak of "histrionic") will gladly paint as a medium of self-expression and then eagerly show the product to the group, taking advantage of the opportunity to talk about them-selves. But even here their basic fear[4] of regulation and being regulated will be a problem. On the other hand, painting challenges them to express themselves more clearly, and can provide an experience of conti-nuity and exactitude. But painting can also lead them into a hypomanic defense of a deeper-lying depression. Then, if the conditions are right, they will paint a great deal. They may create a huge series of pictures but use them as a defense against going to the roots of their problem or into its specifics. Indeed, a "hefty, expressive, colorful painting" can "hinder the surfacing of the deeper emotions"[5].

8. People with obsessive-compulsive structures[6] on the other hand, are likely to place themselves under performance pressure with their self-imposed high level of expectation. Their over-exactness will itself stand in the way when they begin to paint. "A stringent painting style occupied with details, as if copying something, can hinder the appear-ance of uncomfortable affects or contents while painting."[7]

Still, painting could give such people direct contact with matter, which they could then "smear around" using a wide brush or even finger-paints. Herein lies the possibility of re-contacting the anal phase of early childhood, where they likely developed their obsessive-com-pulsiveness. They may then be able to liberate themselves from the cleanliness compulsion that had been so excessively internalized back

---

4 Riemann, Fritz: *Anxiety: Using Depth Psychology to Find a Balance in Your Life*, translated by Greta Dunn. Barbara Budrich 2009. See chapter "The Compulsive Personalities"

5 Schottenloher, Gertraud: *Das therapeutische Potential spontanen bildnerischen Gestaltens*, p. 107.

6 Riemann, Fritz: *Anxiety: Using Depth Psychology to Find a Balance in Your Life*, translat-ed by Greta Dunn. Barbara Budrich 2009. See chapter "The Schizoid Personalities".

7 Schottenloher, Gertraud: *Das therapeutische Potential spontanen bildnerischen Gestaltens*, p. 103.

then. They might also rediscover the lustful and creative possibilities that were present before this phase and reconnect with them, thus developing them further.

Finally, the liberating "mother field" that can constellate itself in painting therapy can provide such people the necessary safe space to relax and dismantle their old behaviors.

9. People with various schizoid structures may also have problems with painting[8]. Schizophrenics require an especially cautious introduction to painting. They will welcome an invitation to paint and be creative with a "Sure, … if I can". They will indeed recognize the chance to portray their split-off sides in the painting process and thereby come nearer to themselves and likewise allow others to come nearer to them. But they will fear this process at the same time, since splitting off certain sides of themselves had been a fear-deflecting necessity for them. A basic fear of commitment also impedes them from trusting their unconscious. This fear of the unconscious leads them to rationalize a great deal. When applied to painting, this means extremely thought-out and constructed pictures. In other words, they take flight. Here the constellation of a supportive "mother field" seems especially important, since it makes it possible for patients to relax and forget themselves in the creative activity. Then transformation can occur.

With schizoid-structured patients however, because they are unaccustomed to relaxation, active imagination and painting, it can suddenly happen that they become flooded by unconscious contents. The walls holding back their split-off parts may suddenly become porous if they do not yet feel completely supported by the surrounding mother field of the therapy. These processes are so unfamiliar that at first they can be unnerving. But ultimately, therein lies the chance for the splitting to be overcome.

10. Our observations regarding schizoid patients naturally lead us into early disorders, where the split plays a special role. Here the law applies: "If an emancipated person, who has a negative inner mother imago, does not land in a carrying and holding field, the emancipation can become

8   Riemann, Fritz: *Anxiety: Using Depth Psychology to Find a Balance in Your Life*, translated by Greta Dunn. Barbara Budrich 2009. See chapter "The Schizoid Personalities".

a horror trip."[9] Balint suggests in such a case that the therapist must become like a "friendly base substance" for the patient. The therapist must become like the water in which the patient, like a fish, can swim around. Once this is guaranteed, then one can expect especially good experiences with painting therapy even with early disordered patients. This is also true where the first objective is merely structuring of the ego-complex. To create a picture always means to work *on* giving structure and to work *with* giving structure. Otherwise, a composition wouldn't let itself be created in the predetermined parameters of a sketching pad.

Patients with early disturbances are among those who regularly like to paint in a therapeutic practice. The reason for this includes the set-up. The setting for both the painting and for the painting therapy is designed to build up the so-called positive "mother field", from which new experiences with oneself can arise. Above all, it is from this "mother field" that bodily sensation and the physical self can be further shaped and worked on, which is tantamount to shaping and working on the basis of a coherent ego complex.

Ego disorders generally arise from a negative "mother field" wherein the patient was unable to build a coherent ego (i.e. a coherent ego complex) because of negative mirroring by the mother in early childhood. The condition of the ego complex can be readily diagnosed from the way a picture is painted. In painting activity we basically work on creation, structure, and coherence. In discussion about a picture, the therapist or the group can mirror the painter positively and thereby help to stabilize the ego complex.

If the ego complex has dissociated into a deranged condition or is undeveloped, like scattered islands, then the painting therapy aims at connecting these islands together, networking them with each other. This happens first on the pictorial level and later, based upon this, on the level of the total psychic experience. Painted pictures depicting such a networked, new self-image work upon their artist's inner self-image. More and more such painters begin to understand themselves as whole

---

9   Schottenloher, Gertraud: *Das therapeutische Potential spontanen bildnerischen Gestaltens*, esp. p. 143; See also Gabriel, Holgrid: "Die Behandlung früher Störungen mit kunsttherapeutischen Mitteln aus der Sicht von C.G. Jung" in *Integrative Therapie* 2-3, 1987.

persons who are outgrowing the splits that had been present to this point. "The pictorial process is able to draw things up from the unconscious dimension of psychic ordering, so that people with early ego disorders, (under-developed structures causing fragmentation and splitting among other things), experience integrative and structure-building moments."[10] From this we can assume that the creative portion of the ego has remained intact and is therefore able to counterbalance the experience of splitting and ego disintegration.

11. Creative activity is also a structuring activity. In painting and creating, the material/physical self gives structure to other materials. Positive experiences based upon such structuring activity are described by the physicians Manfred Krapp[11] und Margitta Giera-Krapp[12] in their use of painting therapy with psychotic patients having schizophrenic disorders, and with affective psychoses and psychotic episodes connected with borderline syndrome. Agreeing with Bader/Navratil, Manfred Krapp is of the opinion that "the creativity, the symbolic content, and the expressivity are greatest as an acute psychotic phase is fading away. By painting at this time, it becomes possible to capture and to structure the inner experience and images still influenced by the psychosis."[13]

Naturally the entire setting works together to foster this painting therapy work: the protective parameters of the clinic, the continuity of the painting therapy group, the trust relationship with the therapist. The group dynamic, the creative activity, and the charisma of the therapist – all these doubtlessly work together to enable the constellation of the positive mother archetype or "mother field". In addition, painting and creative arts therapy has advantages over other methods in the treatment of people with an incoherent ego and splitting tendencies. Coherence, structuring, and unification of opposites can be taught and practiced

---

10 Schottenloher, Gertraud: *Das therapeutische Potential spontanen bildnerischen Gestaltens*, p. 77.
11 Krapp, Manfred: *Die Gestaltungstherapie als Beitrag zur Psychotherapie der Psychosen.* (Diploma thesis for the C.G. Jung Institute Zürich) 1986.
12 Giera-Krapp, Margitta: *Ein Beitrag zur Therapie der frühen Störungen.* (Diploma thesis for the C.G. Jung Institute Zürich) 1985.
13 Krapp, Manfred: *Die Gestaltungstherapie als Beitrag zur Psychotherapie der Psychosen*, p. 21.

through picture creation, since they are constitutive of every picture composition.

I once took on a patient after one of her periods in the clinic caused by psychotic episodes. She called me one evening, unsettled because the familiar signs of an approaching psychotic episode were beginning to appear. I suggested that she come to me for a therapy session that same evening, and we both sat and painted together on the same paper–something we had never done before. We started by painting her fear and her feeling of being threatened. We sought colors and shapes in order to create a picture of these anxieties, painting in succession with one another. In this encounter we succeeded in giving the threat a face. And in looking at this face together, we could share the fear and thereby perceptibly diminish it.

Patients with whom one can hardly work therapeutically during their acute psychotic episodes will sometimes paint spontaneously even during the episode. Mary Barnes reports in her moving book *My Journey Through Craziness*[14] how she began to paint with finger-paints during her episodes, and in her deepest regressions, even with feces. She describes how she discovered her creativity, which helped her overcome the psychotic crisis and finally allowed her to become a renowned artist. Benedetti once said in reference to schizophrenic painting that "...the artistic will achieves a superior position in the ego because it creatively paints itself, thereby attaining a higher degree of organization in the midst of the disorder."[15] Apparently an ordering and structuring power is at work in creative activity such as painting, which remains independent of the illness. Despite fragmentation, the ego's creative ability remains intact, enabling this situation to be expressed[16]. According to Jung, creative ability belongs to an autonomous part of the psyche and forms an autonomous "partial soul" which can promote healing and remains functional even when other autonomous regions of the psyche

14 Barnes, Mary: *Two Accounts of a Journey Through Madness*. Other Press, New York 2002.
15 Benedetti, Gaetano: *Psychotherapie als existentielle Herausforderung*. Göttingen 1992, p. 117. (Available in French translation: *La Psychothérapie Des Psychoses Comme Défi Existentiel*, translated by Patrick Faugeras. Erès, Toulouse 2002.)
16 Reiter, Alfons: *Bildnerischer Ausdruck als methodischer, diagnostischer und therapeutischer Zugang zur Depression*. (Habilitation treatise for the University of Salzburg) 1985.

are disordered. Jung considered this creativeness in people as an autonomous complex, an independent organism that is, so-to-say, implanted
in the human soul, "a split off portion of the psyche, which leads a life
of its own outside the hierarchy of consciousness. Depending on its
energy charge, it may appear either as a mere disturbance of conscious
activities or as a supra-ordinate authority which can harness the ego to
its purpose"[17].

Accordingly, even when other areas of our personality manifest
pathological mutations, we might still engage the creative process to
foster development and healing. Painting therapy, when working with
psychotics, should, of course, "always aim toward strengthening the ego,
whether this is promoting the restitution of the ego after a psychosis
subsides, or strengthening the ego when psychosis is not underway.
Painting therapy can be of great assistance to the integration and partial working-through of a psychotic experience. One can perform and
even expand reality testing in a playful and symbolic manner. Social
contact and communication can be practiced in a way that improves
the relationship to the psycho-social environment."[18] With psychotics
it is especially important that the playful act doesn't lead to a mere regression, but rather to a "regression in the service of the ego", ultimately
to an ego strengthening. The basic point is that "art therapy is strongly
indicated with chronically psychotic patients because rigid psychotic
defense mechanisms are least threateningly called into question through
symbolic, creative depiction,"[19].

12. Except when the client has certain problematic conditions, some
situations in therapy are especially suitable for the inclusion of painting
therapy. These include:

 - when anxiety appears;
 - when dreams are absent or access to the unconscious is completely
   blocked or impeded;
 - when moods are present which may even be noticed from the outside
   but cannot yet be expressed in emotions or images.Here a painting

17 Jung, Carl Gustav: *CW*, vol. 15, *Spirit in Man, Art and Literature*. § 115.
18 Krapp, Manfred: *Die Gestaltungstherapie als Beitrag zur Psychotherapie der Psychosen*,
    p. 21.
19 19 Ibid, pp. 19ff.

therapist could, for example, make the suggestion to find a color or a color combination that precisely expresses this annoyance – and to paint it. We all have something like an emotional identity, and can find ourselves upset when we no longer feel in synch with our own general emotionality. Then we're in a mood that doesn't fit us. The bandwidth of the mood remains mostly unconscious to us as long as no annoyance points to it, showing that something is in fact no longer in tune or in synch;

- when the tendency to intellectualization is present with manifest avoidance of the unconscious and of emotionality;
- when the left-brain activities of logical thinking etc. are over-valued. This is at the same time an under-valuing of the imaginative, symbolically-thinking and creative activities which are at home in the right brain. More specifically, the relaxing, self-forgetting experience of painting can open up new vistas in the mind, bringing new ideas into play which can then be integrated. Sometimes it happens that we go through a phase in which we paint only abstractly and concretely. Then, finally, our emotion breaks through and seeks artistic expression. At last the unexposed side of our personality can step into the light.
- when we become stagnant. In such cases we must somehow get back into the flow of life. What can free us from this stagnation is a "regression in service of the ego": a submersion into the "mother field", which is at first de-structuring. But when a creative process begins, a new structuring can grow out of this "mother field". In another vein, an experience of loss, whether due to separation or death, can shake someone's psychic fabric to the point of threatening fragmentation. This threat can be intercepted through painting and creativity. The loss is brought to expression and symbolically "abated".
- The following situations seem to me to be especially promising for yielding results by painting therapy:
- where something new begins, when a new constellation has made itself emotionally noticeable, but is still not tangible and not yet coalesced into an image (such opportunities can reveal themselves as moods or also as bodily states);

- where symbols are being born, when a new archetype is being constellated (be it in the psyche, in the body, or even in the environment);
- where transference and counter-transference in the therapeutic relationship are intense and yet diffuse, unclear and collusive. In other words, they cannot yet be captured in imaginable fantasies, dreams, or imaginations. In the transference and counter-transference situation one can always catch a glimpse of what is playing out between analyst and analysand. Painting provides a special opportunity for this to happen. It can be through painting by the client (compare the chapter in Part II "Relationship and Dependence – Pictures from a Mother Complex Case"), or also combined painting by the client and therapist, whereby either both paint their own pictures during the therapeutic hour, or they paint together on one and the same sheet of paper. Painting together can liberate, clarify, permit aggressions and anxieties, and only occasionally does it give rise to fear. Of course, the general therapeutic situation must in every case be taken into consideration. Very often the painted picture makes it possible to steer negative and destructive transferences away from the therapist and onto the picture. The negativity will then be projected into the picture rather than onto the therapist. There it stands as a third party between therapist and client and can be constructively pondered and worked through by both parties. "The therapist and client don't look each other in the eye, but rather look together at the picture."[20]

This leads us to consider the use of painting for training and supervision. For example, it would be possible for the supervisor to encourage painting between therapist and client so that their relationship becomes visible, and the pictures can then be brought to the supervision session.

Jung's goal in therapy is well known. He wanted to help people become creative and motivate them "to experiment with their essence"[21]. Whenever one's goal is this creative process of becoming, painting therapy is indicated, whether someone is especially lacking in creativity, or perhaps has stagnated for lack of access to the interior images.

20 See Gertraud Schottenloher concerning transference onto a picture as a third party.
21 Jung, Carl Gustav: *CW*, vol. 16, *The Practice of Psychotherapy*, § 99.

Intuition in Painting Therapy

or

The Art of Questioning a Painting

According to Jung, the creative process is the principle at work in the entire creation, bringing forth ever-new forms and designs, in evolution for example. Being connected with this creative process makes us whole, and allows us to become whole again and again.[22] The creative principle becomes living and conscious through ideas, inspiration and imagination, but especially through "painting out of the unconscious" as Jungians call it, and as it is practiced in painting therapy based on C.G. Jung's analytical psychology. Jung once said in one of his English seminars, "In creation you are created"[23].

Jung based his theory upon his own experience of stormy emotions during a critical phase in which they downright threatened to break him. In *Memories, Dreams, Reflections* he says: "To the extent that I managed to translate the emotions into images – that is to say, to find the images which were concealed in the emotions – I was inwardly calmed and reassured. Had I left those images hidden in the emotions, I might have

22 Henzler, Christa / Riedel, Ingrid: *Malen um zu überleben: Ein kreativer Weg durch die Trauer.* Stuttgart 2003.
23 Jung, Carl Gustav: *"Nietzsche's Zarathustra".* Notes from the seminar given in 1934-1939. 2nd volume edited by J. L. Jarrett, Princeton, NJ 1989, p. 653.

been torn to pieces by them."[24]. Jung knew to paint his emotions and imaginings at that time, which we can see in the impressive pictures of the *Red Book*[25], for example. Thus his own experience became the basis of a therapeutic concept that he also applied in his therapeutic practice with his own patients. It is a concept that grants images in every form – dream images, fantasy images, and especially painted images – a decisive role in the healing process. It rests upon the experience that when we succeed in capturing a strong or even a too strong emotion in a picture, a positive change in personality can happen.

The "creative instinct", as Jung called it, is, as it were, a biological resource, initially in the unconscious. But when consciously selected, it becomes an intuitive, creative act beginning with a work of art. When we are creating, conscious and unconscious contents come into contact and struggle with each other until they produce a symbol or a sign whose meaning contains something of both and connects them with each other. Jung considered this to be especially healing in the painting process. Things that were previously unconscious or even split off in the painter's psyche can now become integrated.

By painting out of the unconscious, we remain open to the unconscious during the painting process, so that a constant exchange between conscious and unconscious impulses takes place. We could also call it "intuitive painting", by which a symbol formation occurs during the encounter between unconscious and conscious impulses. The symbol in the painted picture can, for example, be a bridge crossing over water that was hitherto pictured as unbridgeable. This works with the actual connection between the conscious and unconsciousness of the painter and makes the connection visible. We can observe and thereby discuss this connection using the symbol of the bridge. By reviewing and reflecting in discussions with the therapist, the meaning which the picture has for the artist can now come to speak and be understood in the context of the actual life situation.

24 Jaffé, Aniela, *Memories, Dreams, Reflections by C.G. Jung*, Pantheon, New York, 1962, p. 177.
25 Jung, Carl Gustav: *The Red Book, Liber Novus*, edited and introduced by Sonu Shamdasani. Preface by Ulrich Hoerni. Translated by Mark Kyburz, John Peck, Sonu Shamdasani. W.W. Norton & Company, Philemon Series, 1st Edition 2009.

What exactly is the water? What are the two banks that in both the picture and the psychic reality now seem really bridgeable, and have become bridged? Here Jung's concept of a depth-psychological therapy comes into play by painting and discussing pictures, as he himself did in his own psychiatric practice, even with severely disturbed patients.

Jung's close collaborator, Jolande Jacobi, who was the first to utilize this form of painting and discussing pictures in the clinical setting, first used the phrase "painting out of the unconscious". Naturally, we cannot paint directly out of the unconscious, but we can certainly be open to impulses out of the unconscious, so that we already anticipate that the first occurrence in the painting process, the inspiration, will come from the unconscious. Perhaps the first impulse to come up is simply that we begin with blue. But then, as we paint, the blue randomly takes on shape and concretizes itself as, for example, an ocean. This gives it a definite symbolism. The color blue has already opened up a certain emotional and symbolic field. Maybe the broad, horizontal surface of the sea now elicits from the artist the impulse to create a contrast, for example, to introduce the tall, vertical mast of a sailboat, in order to suddenly see – the reason for it cannot be completely grasped in the moment – a lightening bolt from the heavens driving down upon it. Now a previously hidden but not harmless conflict flares up. We can work on this conflict both by painting further and by discussing the painting with the therapist. In the discussion the therapist can start to speak about that stress in the patient's life-situation that has already been discharged into the painting.

In the Jungian school the phrase "painting out of the unconscious" has become a standard term referring not only to the above-described painting process itself, but including the entire method in which painting and discussing the paintings takes place in the context of an analytical therapy. It is an on-going process taking place in phases wherein a painting is created and discussed, and this creation and discussion give rise to subsequent paintings. This painting and discussing can be either introduced into an analysis already in progress, or it can accompany an entire therapy from beginning to end. Either way, such "painting out of the unconscious" is really an art therapy based upon depth psychology.

During a therapy already in progress, this way of painting may be instigated either by the therapist or spontaneously suggested by the patient, then taken into the therapeutic process by the therapist. In either instance, the pictures that appear become so-called material and messages out of the unconscious, and take on the same value that dreams have always had in a Jungian analysis, where they will be emotionally re-lived, contemplated, and discussed with the patient.

Using Intuition to Understand and Discuss Pictures

The patient is, of course, the creator of the paintings, while the therapist participates as an empathetic, resonating beholder and dialog partner with the picture and about the picture. In depth-psychological painting therapy, both parties are working together in an especially active and at the same time intuitive manner resonating with each other. The picture the patient brings is something complete in itself. But when patient and therapist relate to it in dialogue – it simultaneously becomes a third party to which the two people turn their combined attention. This makes a triangulation possible in the therapeutic relationship. By relating together to the picture, the patient and therapist are on a more equal footing and can communicate with each other on a more eye-to-eye level, thus avoiding entanglement in transference. The picture functions as a third member of a group, turning the dyad into a triad, thus reducing the risk of the analysand and therapist forming a symbiosis that could complicate matters. A helpful distance is established that enables some patients to immediately allow a certain closeness and trust.

In a Jungian analysis adequate time and space is reserved for discussion of the pictures, just as it is for dreams or fantasies. This guarantees a high therapeutic impact and significance in the discussions, even when not every individual picture is discussed. Sometimes the discussion makes more sense when a small series of pictures has already been painted. The artist is often not yet ready to talk directly after the creative process, when everything is still too fresh, whereas some days later a discussion may be very much desired by the painter. Such a discussion is an echo from the picture.

Obviously a high degree of intuition is required by therapists in this dialog both with the painting and about the painting. As therapists we have to be connected with our own unconscious as well as that of the patient. We require empathy for the artist while at the same time noticing our own resonance with the picture.We must study the entire picture, including its mood and its coherence.

Intuition is primarily pre-verbal, but it is what helps me as a therapist find the right words in the presence of a completed picture, to make the artist feel resonance. The artist tried to express something in the picture, and the therapist must empathetically express what the artist tried to say in such a way that he or she feels understood. In the presence of the painting, intuition is the art of asking the artist the right questions about the picture. One could almost define intuition as the art of asking the right question in every case.

With these hallmarks in mind, let us see how intuition works in the following excerpt from an analysis. It illustrates how important intuition can be when looking at paintings out of the unconscious.

A forty-two-year-old woman kept talking about her problematic father during the course of a therapy, but the original complex episode had not yet become explicit. From the beginning of the analysis, this woman preferred to express herself in painting rather than in words.

When her therapist, a colleague of mine[26], asked her how she would feel if her father were there right now, she couldn't answer. So the therapist encouraged her to paint a picture about it. In other words, the therapist encouraged her to paint out of the unconscious. A picture series came into being partially in water-colors and partially in crayon. The father was first portrayed as a rooster, which would already have said enough if the patient had experienced her father as intrusive and vainly dominant.

By her painting out of the unconscious, the vague perception clarified itself now in the strongly expressive symbols of a painting. This painting was discussed, and out of the discussion arose the impulse to paint the next picture. The series became ever more imaginative. Because of the contact between the conscious and unconscious, the latter released ever more symbols of the father's attributes. One picture includes a crow and

26 Kast, Verena: *The dynamics of symbols: fundamentals of Jungian psychotherapy.* Fromm International Publishing Corporation, New York 1992, pp. 40-48. Here my colleague thoroughly describes the painting process of this patient.

a snake, while she herself lacks arms and legs in the encounter with her father. She cannot act and cannot move. This picture series revealed to her a connection which had until then been unconscious to her. It had been completely inaccessible.

In order to illustrate how intuition comes into play with understanding pictures, I will interpret three of her pictures in more detail.

126. The Father as Rooster

127. The Father has Harm on his Mind

The father is first portrayed as a rooster with a red cockscomb rais-ing his arms boisterously (Image 126). He wears a dark violet suit, a color indicating heavy tension. This, combined with the aggressive red of the comb and the flames in the background creates an extremely tension-filled and disharmonious color scheme. The painter, herself dressed in a white outer garment, stands before him. It is as if she is blank, empty, without contour, and pale. She stands before him on extremely indistinct, unsure legs and without arms or hands that could do something. She has virtually no standpoint. Is he waving his claws in her face, or slapping her directly? That is how she experienced him, prompting her to paint herself and them both just so and not differently.

In the second painting (Image 127) she emphasizes the disparity between herself and her father even more blatantly to her disadvantage. Now his face appears before her in violet like a giant monument. A snake is coming out of his mouth, suggesting that he is speaking seductively here, as he so often does. The patient agreed with this, admitting that she experienced him as invasive. She said, "When he speaks, he is seductive." A raven sits above his eyes. This is a bird which proverbially foretells harm. Here the father has mischief on his mind and in his gaze, in those raging, wrathful, red eyes. For her, the father exudes harm and sadness. The worst thing is that she feels like he isn't looking at her at all, does not see her. To her he seems to be preoccupied, completely wrapped up in himself, while she depicts herself as tiny and in the background without a face. It is as if she is wrapped up – with twine? Entwined, shackled, without hands or arms. Somehow she experiences herself as always fascinated by him, in some way he is unalterably attractive to her. She experiences herself as powerless in his presence. This became very clear to her during the discussion over the picture, and so she painted further.

Then it happened, that she unintentionally transferred her father image upon other men. The dragon coming out of the upper left, out of the so-called "father corner" was absolutely not intended to represent her father, but rather her husband (Image 128). She used crayons here, which can be more precisely controlled than watercolors. This enabled, for example, the sharpness of the dragon's teeth. She said of this dragon, "He swallows up anything alive." At that, the therapist asked, "But could one not also look at it and say that he blows a lot of lively energy out from himself?" He somehow seemed to the therapist to be something very vital, even a little refreshing; and the colorful balls around him added to this feeling. The therapist sensed that the husband brought something invigorating to the relationship. But his wife, the painter of this picture, could not see this as long as she viewed her husband only through the lens of her father complex. She mixed up her father with him and mistook him for the father.

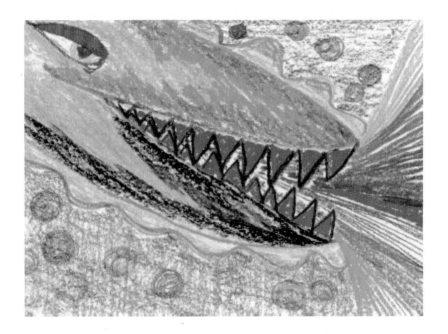

128. The Amusing-Aggressive Dragon

Another interesting thing is that the dragon comes from left of the picture where she herself stood in the previous picture. Is it possible that she herself can sometimes be such a dragon, with all its vitality and aggression? Might she possibly be this for her husband sometimes? After all, did she not up until now focus all her energy upon him and project upon him in discussing this painting? And wasn't this dragon undeniably painted with relish?

Very fruitful questions came to mind concerning the picture, which the therapist might ask the painter. But how should they be posed? Here again intuition was required. Such intuition rests upon a therapist's resonance and empathy with the patient. At first the therapist was only able to say that she could see something almost amusing about the dragon, but in the direction of amusing-aggressive. Naturally the patient could not accept this right away. However, it gave rise to an argument with the therapist over the picture in which the painter revealed an aggressive side of herself which made her more lively than she had been until then…

This example is just a small excerpt of a process where the therapist suggested that the patient paint out of the unconscious. The dialogic discussion led from picture to picture until an entire problematic life situation was revealed. During the analytical discussion of the pictures it was really the therapist's intuition which brought about the turnaround, as she posed the question of whether the dragon could not just as easily be seen as one that exudes liveliness, and not only as one that swallows it up. This made it possible for the patient to change her perspective in relation to her own picture. It caused her to reflect anew about her husband, about her projection upon him, and about herself as a wife. This turned the entire therapeutic process around. First she realized she was projecting her father upon her husband. Gradually she could pose to herself the question of whether she was also projecting onto her father. As she withdrew some of these projections, her father lost his dominating power over her and she won back for herself self-determination over and against him, and more importantly in relation to her husband. Most importantly, she won herself back.

These observations prompt us to return to the introductory question: what is intuition actually? What underlies it? How does it function precisely in view of painting therapy?

To intuit means to look at, to look into, to recognize. We must begin with a good look at the picture – a look inside the picture – if we are to arrive at an intuitive understanding and thereby the possibility of an intuitive intervention. Otherwise we therapists will be unable to intuitively ask the right question.

I believe that intuition is based upon a sensorium for coherence generally. We sense the degree of coherence in the painting and in the therapeutic situation even before we have all the information about the case. For me intuition is a delicate power of perception which notices the entirety of the picture, and also the entirety of the life situation. It notices how this patient's life both underlies the painting and opens itself to the future. Intuition also notices the entirety of the therapeutic process in which the painting was produced, and which is fostered by the painting.

Although intuition is above and beyond therapeutic knowledge, it includes that knowledge. It is the impulse to feel into the things that are still unconscious to the patient and get a hint of how this unconscious material appears in the picture – how it symbolizes itself there. In order to feel this, we need to be in contact with our own unconscious, which begins to vibrate and resonate when we examine a patient's picture. Both of our unconsciouses begin to resonate with each other through the picture. Intuition grows out of being touched unconsciously by another. Both parties become tuned-in to the same frequency. Intuition is a phenomenon of resonance.

C.G. Jung used the term "intuitive" to denote a person in whom intuition is the predominant attitude. Such people approach others primarily using their intuition. This holds true for their approach to pictures and to therapeutic situations. Intuitives are people who trust their intuition over rational observation and sensation alone, and also over an evaluation arrived at out of a mere subjective feeling. To possess intuition also meant for Jung registering the feelings coming up in regard to previously unconscious parts of himself and of his patients.

We can combine Jung's considerations on intuition with the concept of intuition as a "gut instinct" whereby the belly actually functions as a somatic measuring device. It sends an alarm as soon as we make a bad decision via a nauseous feeling "in the pit of the stomach". Consequently, we can understand intuition as a decision-making intelligence which can be at work even without conscious thinking. This gut feeling increases with experience, as psychotherapists using painting therapy have come to know. It grows as much out of experience with therapy *per se* as it does from experience in connection with pictures springing "out of the unconscious". It is always important to be open on both the creative level and the therapeutic level at the same time. We require openness to the unconscious, because the unconscious, as Damasio puts it "has a larger vocabulary than consciousness at its disposal at any given time"[27]. But even this so-called vocabulary of the unconscious rests upon earlier emotional experience.

27 Damasio, Antonio R: *Ich fühle, also bin ich: Die Entschlüsselung des Bewusstseins.* München 2000, p. 188. English original: *The Feeling of What Happens: Body, Emotion and the Making of Consciousness.* Vintage, Berkshire UK 2000.
See also Damasio, Antonio R: *Self Comes to Mind: Constructing the Conscious Brain.* Pantheon, 2010, p. 275. "I like very much the notion that our cognitive unconscious is capable of reasoning and has a larger 'space' for operations than the conscious counterpart."

The therapist depends above all on intuition to come up with fitting and adequate questions that enable a successful dialog with the pictures (that is, a successful interpretation process). The right questions will not be found unless we pay attention beforehand to our own intuition about the entire therapeutic situation at hand, and especially our intuition about the message of the pictures.

The interpretation phase, as I earlier called it – the phase in which therapist and artist dialog about the picture, with the picture and with the symbolism of the picture – is the actual therapeutic activity in painting therapy based upon the analytical psychology of C.G. Jung. However, the preceding painting process is no less relevant. By painting the pictures, the patient independently introduces something to the therapy. Painting brings creativity to bear and liberates the symbol-creating function. Jungian analysts and psychotherapists understand something about this.

The act of painting also occurs within the therapeutic relationship when using this depth-psychological therapy method. Alongside their contact on the conscious level runs the resonance on the unconscious level. The more or less intuitive discussion with the therapist about the last picture painted (or about the finished pictures in the series up to that point) will work consciously and unconsciously upon the next picture to be painted. And in discussing that next one in turn, the therapist begins with the partially conscious, partially unconscious resonance with the new picture. It is the contact with the therapist's own unconscious that intuitively discovers the questions which will access the symbolism and unlock the message of the picture. What is it pointing back to, and where is it pointing forward to?

Painting Therapy in Training and Practice

Art therapy seems to me a very intuitive matter, and all the more so when practiced in the context of depth psychology. Already the word itself, not to mention the practice, brings together two realms – art and therapy, and without intuition, neither of these realms is even accessible. I want to talk here primarily about therapy, but therapy that takes place through art, through creative activity, through so-called "painting out of the unconscious". In all the methods of art therapy that I know, it is of little importance that patients create aesthetically valuable pictures, but rather that they find ways to express themselves creatively, as they already did in childhood. The expression of their sensitivities, problems, and conflicts is very important, yet often they simply cannot find an expression for them at first, because they lie mostly in the unconscious. There they cannot be emotionally expressed, let alone verbally expressed.

Stefan Reichelt[28] uses art therapy in his work with traumatized children and suggests that through creativity an access to the trauma can be found for both the patient and the therapist, even before it is possible to verbalize it. Using a picture or picture series, the trauma can be unlocked step by step, making it then possible to talk about it and ultimately to overcome it.

Painting involves the whole body and with it the corresponding regions of the brain. Luckily, the painting regions work differently than the speech region, which has often been inhibited through the trauma. Painting involves the processes of movement, of seeing, of touching, and even of smelling (when paints, glue and wet paper are involved). This is how painting brings the whole person into contact with the area that was traumatized. It is an area that both should be and wants to be noticed and worked with. Of course, what comes up during the painting process will automatically resonate with that which the sovereign unconscious wishes to express. Some of this will be suppressed material, but there will also be resources and creative possibilities. When the unconscious sets itself in motion, it deploys the intuition, which is related to the imagination. All at once the painter vaguely imagines things like a threatening animal, or a dwarf, or a monster or some saving creature.

Deciding whether art or painting therapy is indicated requires itself intuition sometimes. This is less the case where, as in clinics, art or painting therapy is simply available and made accessible for anyone who

---

28 Reichelt, Stefan: *Kindertherapie nach sexueller Mißhandlung: Malen als Heilmethode.* Stuttgart 1994.
Also *Prozessorientiertes Malen als traumatherapeutische Intervention.* Regensburg 2008.
And also Gruber, Harald / Reichelt, Stefan (Editors): *Kunsttherapie in der Palliativmedizin.* Berlin 2016.

wants it. Also, when people freely seek out a psychotherapy practice in order to receive art therapy, they have already chosen this form of therapy themselves. But in all such cases, deciding what direction to take and which method to use does require intuition. Where the indication requires serious consideration and intuition above all else, is when painting therapy is being considered as a creative psychotherapy to be applied in conjunction with a verbal psychotherapy. In the practice of psychotherapy according to C.G. Jung, such a combination often belongs to the treatment plan. At this point it is perhaps worth mentioning that in the C.G. Jung Institutes of Stuttgart or Zürich every psychotherapist is taught how to work with pictures so that in the course of the therapy "painting out of the unconscious" is encouraged. The students learn to unlock the symbolism of the pictures that are produced in order to decipher their message to the painter as well as to the therapist. Part of the final examination at Jungian institutions is to test whether the graduate is able to intuitively understand patients' pictures and work with them.

Painting out of the unconscious has been practiced in analytical psychology ever since the time of C.G. Jung and his early colleagues such as Jolande Jacobi. It has always been a constitutive component of the training. Today there are various modes of working with painting out of the unconscious. What is and remains classic is that the patient paints the picture at home. The impulse to do so can come either spontaneously from the patient or be suggested by the therapist, but after that there is no further technical support. The patient brings the picture to the therapy session where it will be discussed in the context of the analysis that is underway and upon whose themes and process it is related.

Intuition is already necessary regarding the suggestion to paint. The therapist should be thinking, "When and how do I suggest it to my patient? And how do I handle the reaction?" One of my early patients was a leading nurse. Her last working year was overburdening, and out of exhaustion she fell into a depression. When I suggested that she paint a picture of her interior condition, she was quite offended. She found such a suggestion so ridiculous that in the next session she brought a picture, alright, but it was painted on sandwich paper! Luckily she struck a virtual gold seam of painting talent right away, and later came to enjoy unthinkable treasures from painting out of the unconscious.

Anytime we think we have to convince our patients to perhaps try it just once, we had better intuitively reflect. Would this patient really enjoy it? Does the patient have a relatively good aptitude for painting? Has the patient produced any art before? Perhaps the patient, like many, hasn't painted anything since high school. Patients should not experience their therapists' request as a burden, otherwise it works counter-productively. To repeat, even the suggestion to paint requires intuition. And yet, I will make this observation: with very strong interior pressure caused by things like trauma, suicidal tendencies, separation or grief, a need arises spontaneously in many people to bring the overflowing feelings into a creative process, just as we saw earlier regarding Jung's own experience.

When an analysis is in progress, intuition (i.e. comprehension of unconscious perceptions) is what can give the impulse for artistic creation. For example, when a dream or fantasy has not yet been understood, painting might provide a fresh approach to it. Other patients (often those with sleep disorders) worry that the absence of dreams is a hindrance to their analysis. The suggestion to create pictures can often bring the stagnated therapy process back in motion. Painting can also be recommended to combat an intense and almost overwhelming influx out of the unconscious, or even to encourage the unconscious simply to reveal some of its images. The suggestion to paint can be especially helpful during a depressive episode so that the patient can have at least some sense of self-efficacy by being able to create something. Flora von Spreti once suggested that therapeutically the most effective thing about painting is that as a patient I can experience myself as creator and have a certain pride about it, realizing that I have painted this very picture. With obsessivecompulsion the playful element of painting can have a loosening-up effect, and in the differential diagnosis it can also reveal the specifics of the obsession that has come to expression in the picture.

All this, however, is not a manual one can call up. Rather the individual situation must be intuitively weighed in order to notice with empathy and resonance what is going on in the transference and counter-transference. When posed at the wrong moment or when the personal situation is inappropriate, a suggestion to paint only creates blockage in the patient or a tortured acquiescence to the wish of the therapist.

With guided painting, intuition is needed even more. Although this method is more often used by therapists influenced by humanistic or psychoanalytic theories, it can be (and is) also practiced in the context of Jungian painting therapy. In such guided painting, self-creative technical or therapeutic interventions are applied during the painting process. For example: "You paint yourself so tiny in that big space. Is that OK for you?" Incidentally, this intervention gave the painter an important developmental kick which she also utilized in her painting. I myself started to seriously consider the value of guided painting when I began to pursue an early trauma with a patient. She brought in a picture and remarked: "It would have been good for me, if you had been there as a ghost suddenly climbed through the window while I was painting. I tried to paint it here. I know it has to do with that trauma which I cannot exactly remember but which causes me so much anxiety. I was able to capture it in a way in this picture, but your guidance would have been really valuable for me. I have the feeling now that this picture I've brought with me is just the visible outer shell of the course I have run through alone."

When doing painting therapy with groups, I like to give the participants a common theme. Where possible I give a symbolic theme, for example "the four elements" or "the three primary colors". We begin with an active imagination so that a common symbolic field is established in the group. The individuals can thereby find their place within that field throughout their individual painting process. I leave it to my intuition to select the right symbol for the group at each point in the therapy. The order in which the group paints the elements or the colors makes a difference. Red at the beginning awakens vitality, but also aggression in the group. However, one can usually get away with it when it can be followed by green in the next session. Red at the end of a group process, at the end of a weekend for example, is a bit dangerous, since the loud and agitating power of red can no longer be contained by the therapy, and the individuals go unaccompanied home with it. Blue at the beginning makes possible a good dip into the unconscious, into the depths, into stillness. Yellow can make possible a light winding up session, and green a reconciling and hopeful ending.

Already when planning a painting therapy group, intuition is needed. Simply establishing the group requires a sense of how many participants should be admitted, where to meet, and at what times. Here again intuition is always a combination of conscious experience and fresh contact with the unconscious. The conscious experience is about the method of painting to be used, the already-established relationship with the participants, and a combination of empathy, transference, and counter-transference. The fresh contact is with both the therapist's own unconscious and that of the group.

We cannot create a manual for such a method, because ultimately intuition is what makes this work possible. But that intuition rests upon experience – experience with both aspects of painting therapy, namely the painting processes and the therapeutic processes. Both are valuable experiences providing points of view which should not be overlooked. This is how the depth psychology made possible by "painting out of the unconscious" gave rise to the method of painting therapy developed by C.G. Jung. It is a method in which intuition plays an essential role.

Supervising Therapists Using Patients' Pictures

(Supervision in German-speaking countries is a very common method for maintaining high-quality job performance among professionals. As practiced among psychologists, it consists of a supervisor advising a fellow psychologist regarding an individual case or one's practice in general in order to enhance work quality or figure out a particular problem. It can be practiced either individually or in groups. The word might be variously translated as "professional consultation" or "coaching" or "continuing education". Translator's note.)

First I want to introduce a new form of group supervision for psychotherapists which developed out of our work in painting therapy and has withstood the test of time. Pictures painted by a client or patient are placed, one per supervisory session, in the middle of the supervision group, and from them all members of the group draw their own resonance images. These are then discussed in the group and thereafter applied to the patients' pictures and their situations in the therapeutic process as well as in their present lives. What happens here is the production of many counter-transferences to the patient which the painting triggers in the group of therapists. These are what the group notices and discusses. Such counter-transferences can give the patient's own therapist important hints and be a great enrichment to the further therapy.

The following procedure has proven useful: The therapist seeking supervision in this session chooses a patient's picture and brings it to the group of fellow therapists. The ideal group size is between 5 and 8 people. At the beginning of the supervision session the therapist informs the group only about the patient's age and gender. Then the therapist presents his/her basic questions about the picture which hopefully the other therapist to the group will answer. In other words, for what reason or need they want to bring this particular painting of their patient to the supervision and what they expect from the supervision group.

The steps within the supervision group are then the following:

- In turn all members of the group lay a sheet of tracing paper over the patient's picture and roughly copy the structures of the picture that strike them individually, using a pencil or wax crayon.

- Next, the members of the group individually paint their own pictures upon their tracing paper based on this structure. We understand each of these images as the group member's resonance to the patient's picture. A group member may want to trace part of the structure using the same color as the patient, or later fill the image out with the patient's color composition on their tracing paper copy of the painting, if the coloration was especially characteristic of the patient's painting and it particularly spoke to the observer. Understandably, we are especially close to a painter's emotions and feelings when we primarily notice the colors they use.

- Next follows the phase of evaluating the resulting therapists' pictures in view of the patient's picture upon which they are all based. The patient's original is laid in the middle and the therapists' *counter-transference paintings* laid around it. Each group member participates. They report how it went with them while painting the resonance image, and which emotions, feelings, interior images, and symbols came up. At first the therapist who brought the patient's picture only listens, but then subsequently formulates a verbal answer to the question, "What do these resonance images of my colleagues provoke in me?" In addition the therapist reports more about the patient and the therapeutic process.

- A discussion ensues in which the resonance experiences of the group, and accordingly their counter-transferences, are compared with that which the therapist brings in. The group's counter-transference is

based upon the patient's painting and reflected in the therapists' cop-
ies thereof and the presenting therapist's counter-transference upon
the mutual encounter with the actual patient within the therapeutic
process.

- It is of utmost importance that the original questions regarding this
  patient, which had been posed to the supervision group by the presenting therapist at the beginning of the session, be addressed first
  by the presenting therapist, then by each group member, and lastly
  by the presenting therapist with the group. Out of such cooperation
  between the supervision group and the presenting therapists over
  those patient pictures that were chosen, the presenting therapists can
  reflect on their own counter-transference and gather valuable insights
  conducive to the further treatment of their patients.

Example from a Supervision Session: The Picture of the Severely Cut-up Tree

As an example of such supervision work focused upon the painting
of a patient, I offer a drawing that was presented for discussion at such
a supervision session. Let us imagine the painting of a 55-year-old man.
It is a tree so severely pruned that it consists almost solely of the trunk.

Near the beginning of his therapy, when still relatively little information concerning the anamnesis was available, the painter himself at
first said of this painting only, "The tree is completely trimmed back.
I don't know whether it is still able to survive." As he said these words,
one sensed that the man knew well that the tree could be a symbol
of himself, his tree of life, symbolizing the situation in which he now
found himself. His life situation felt to him completely impaired in all
that had grown up until then. Among the therapists who were looking
at it, the painting immediately released a strong counter-transference,
above all a strong sympathy. What could have hit this man in the course
of his life inflicting whatever is now being symbolized by this being-cut-
back? Which storms must have swept over him? Which swings of the
ax must have struck him? What life possibilities must the individually
felled limbs have held for him? To which saws must his crown (that is,

his self-confidence) have been sacrificed, and with it perhaps his sense of dignity, his feeling of self-worth and his self-efficacy too?

Sympathy was the first strong reaction within the whole group, but thereafter anxiety also came up. There was concern about which life possibilities were even still open to him, given the severity of the pruning. There was uncertainty about whether therapy was at all possible, whether and where therapy could still find a foothold, whether therapy was still indicated, or whether therapy would only perhaps mean a last frustration for this man – for him and also for his possible therapist. And yet the patient himself really wanted to try this attempt at therapy, as he had made manifest to the presenting therapist: otherwise this picture would absolutely not exist. Add to that the fact that at 55-years-old he was in a life phase in which it would be high time for a last attempt at therapy – exactly at this time in the life of a man that has been completely cut apart. The form of this tree picture gives the impression that it is crying out to be seen and noticed. The presenting therapist, who felt stumped, fearful, and emotionally concerned by this impression, had already taken on the case. With her patient's permission she brought his picture to the supervision group. Her questions to the group were: What chance is there at all for this therapy? And where are possible resources and developmental possibilities to be found which one can build upon?

Now this painting of the cut back tree was laid before the supervision group for all the participants to look at, first only with the information that it was painted by a 55-year-old male. Then each member received a sheet of tracing paper, as described above, which could be laid over the original picture, and the members were instructed to draw the outlines of the patient's drawing, in this case that of a drastically pruned tree, so that, detached from and independent of the original, they could then draw their own pictures in which their countertransference would potentially reflect itself.

Using this method to reveal the countertransference of an entire group of supervised male and female therapists upon one patient's picture is shown to have its advantages, because it makes possible both traced and colored counter-transferences. First and foremost it is an expression of resonance and empathy. The resonance expresses itself in the participant's own picture in both a structural manner and in terms of color (an emotional manner), but also in a symbolic manner. By making the countertransference conscious, the individual group members become able to distinguish it from themselves, thereby avoiding a merely emotional spillover from the patient's picture. In this way a conscious therapeutic impulse for intervention with the patient can be stimulated by the countertransference.

Using some examples from the supervision group I would like to illustrate the resonance, by describing the way in which some of the resonance images to the 55-year-old man's drawing of the severely cut tree, were painted.

One younger therapist picture focused primarily the countertransference feeling that a monstrous radicalness of "being cut" desires to be expressed in this picture, a radicalness of the perception that one is deprived of all possibilities. The tree appeared like a skeleton in her picture, divested of any other material, the picture of an unfortunate life. However, she picked up on the desire to be seen which emanates from the radicalness of the patient's picture. She also picked up on a quietly emerging hope for this patient, who has at least mustered the courage to portray his radical being-cut-back in this impressive form. We see this in her own picture where she has a tiny new sprout shooting up from the root of the old tree, standing in contrast to it and perhaps also symbolizing her countertransference.

Another therapist from the supervision group, a somewhat elderly doctor, tried arduously in her picture to prop the cut off limbs onto the structure, realized herself however, that the idea actually wouldn't go, since already as she was painting them her branches kept breaking off again. That is how it would also be in a therapy, she thought, if some tried propping something up on this radically naked structure. Only a new start could work.

A third participant drew herself into the picture simply standing next to the tree and just grieving. She portrayed herself deeply bowed before that which for her was no longer only cut back, but also cut down – the tree stump bedecked with gaping wounds. Of all the pictures, this one most strongly took on the empathetic feeling of grief, that emotional sadness, which the patient himself may have discovered by painting his picture of a life cut down. From this countertransference, however, a weight-bearing emotional bridge to the patient could possibly be build, as long as the therapist's grief is not experienced as overwhelming her, but rather, has become conscious by painting it. Then, via this bridge she as can bring empathy to and receive it from the patient. With this picture we must take into account that the therapist had painted during her own grieving over a recently lost loved one an echo of her own grief upon the patient's picture.

A fourth participant of the supervision group tried to emphasize in his picture the roots of this tree, which apparently remained safe. He tried through thorough fresh watering to enable the amputated tree to put forth new shoots. In his countertransference while contemplating the picture, his attention was focused upon what was hidden under the earth, upon what was only suggested here, a root system apparently still thought-to-be-alive. This root system could at the same time be a symbol for the patient's unconscious, upon which his unconscious had answered with the picture of the tree. The supervision group later thought that this countertransference could lead to a therapeutic intervention which could spur the patient in the future and above all get him to heed his unconscious as it expresses itself in dreams and fantasies. From there completely surprising germs of new life could spring up. In a watered and revitalized unconscious restorative and healing impulses to new growth could be hidden.

The supervision group was most surprised by the thought of a fifth participant who opened up a new perspective for everyone. The patient's picture was for her in the countertransference clearly the picture of a pruned willow tree – a willow tree that had offered up its branches to be used by others, perhaps to the point of self-sacrifice. The therapist explained that one cuts willows knowing that the more one prunes them, the more vigorously they will sprout the following year. This therapist had painted her own tree unmistakably as a willow tree in spring. Out of its cut marks, mighty young branches are sprouting out, colored in youthful green.

That the patient's drastically cut tree could be some variety like the willow, which after a radical pruning and even thanks to the pruning is able to sprout again, and that such varieties of trees actually exist, made a new perspective possible for the supervision group thanks to the picture of this fifth participant. This therapist's empathy in her countertransference caused her to experience the patient as completely unprotected and, because he dared to draw himself, a courageous figure. This corresponds exactly with the fantasy that the tree could sprout even more vigorously next year the more it would be cut. Such a hopeful countertransference that the patient's nature could essentially be like a willow tree, which emboldened him to draw such a harsh picture of a lacerated tree would be translated into a therapeutic impulse something like "despite all the painful pruning, a therapy with him would have many chances at success".

As a therapist I can create my own supervisory perspective using this method. I transfer the graphic outlines and color composition of my patient's picture onto a sheet of tracing paper in order to draw my own picture from it. My picture makes graphically visible the way I spontaneously experience the situation of the patient. By the contemplation of my own picture my countertransference can become conscious to me in its emotionality as expressed in the coloring, and in its rationality as made visible and figuratively symbolized in the contours. As a countertransference-made-conscious it can be distinguished from an unconscious over-pouring of my patient's contents.

The supervisory perspective was given by my own echo image based upon the original picture of the patient. The perspective formed itself out of the countertransference, out of my empathy and resonance with the patient's picture. From this perspective, an empathetic intervention can be introduced into the therapeutic process. For that, let us look at a second example from the supervision.

Example from the Supervision: The Picture of the Witch

As one therapist brought her patient's picture of a witch to the supervision group, a picture that the therapist herself said was supposed to be of her, most group members became right away interested in how such a picture came about in the therapeutic process. What had caused the patient to see the therapist as a witch? Therefore, they concentrated mainly on the color impressions of their own pictures. The therapist briefly explained that because of her long vacation, during which the patient painfully suffered her absence, she should appear in her pictures as a witch. In the picture the witch is dressed in flaming red, that in some places however blend into tender violet and then into dignified, solemn crimson. I wondered what the individual therapists would primarily notice from this robe and this violet and take up in their own pictures.

How this red worked upon the five participants of the supervision group and was transferred onto their tracing paper alone demonstrates already the whole scale of possible counter-transferences here. A portion of the group experienced the red of this robe as highly aggressive, as the aggression which had been built up here against the treating therapist. The first group member's picture included not only aggression, but also a witch painted here as powerfully erect. This therapist expressed that her point here was an uprightness, which the presenting therapist noticed in herself to no longer show just the usual motherly softness toward the demands of the patient, but rather to present a justified boundary in relation to the patient's notion that the therapist might not be allowed to enjoy a vacation of several weeks. Out of rage at the therapist's vacation, whose presence she needed without interruption, the patient's wrathful projection of a witch came into being and was projected onto the therapist. Upon closer inspection, however, already in the patient's original picture, a self-critical element is discernible in that she ultimately did allow and also conceded to the therapist such a rebuff of her pretentiousness. One would possibly even be able to communicate this to her as an intervention during the discussion of her picture.

In the second participant's picture, the rights of this therapist came to the fore. The focus became the right to have one's own life and to defend it against the excessive demands of patients. The witch in this picture is still in fire-red, aggressive robes but has mutated herself inadvertently into a slim, young woman who looks like the patient. This participant somehow painted not the therapist but the patient. To him she looks like a witch burning with rage. This countertransference was an unconscious clue that it is indeed the patient and not the therapist who burned with rage and reacted so enviously.

The pictures of these first two group members were sparked solely by the fiery variant of red in the witch's robe. It is a color that expresses emotional wrath and anger, and readiness for aggression. These two therapists completely overlooked the other variants of red in this robe. But there was in the original picture of the patient also a crimson variant that ascribes to the witch dignity and a deepened feeling tending in the direction of wisdom. That is what the other three members of that supervision group positively reacted to. So each of them painted pictures in where the witch-like character of the original figure was exchanged in favor of a dignified reserve in their figures, in favor of a wise woman in a robe whose crimson even lightly slips into violet – into violet where the heat and hotness of red is subdued and tempered through the distance of a blue element. To the therapist wearing these robes is attributed more of a well-balanced bearing and discretion. In addition, violet is a nuanced color that can express the ability to transform and be transformed, while the crimson toning points toward wisdom. Here the hotness of the original picture is abrogated, directly in its coloring. This is an incentive to compensate for the over-reaction of the patient.

The fourth and the fifth participants depicted in their drawings the witch-like side again as a part of the patient herself. The fourth therapist transformed the red of the robes into a magician's lavender, making clear that the patient possessed similar traits, like a trickster capable of transformation and compensation. Some of these magical possibilities have not appeared at all yet because of the adaptive behavior she has practiced until now. But thanks to the picture of the witch that she projects upon her therapist, they have now come to expression.

The fifth participant's painting was the strongest inducement to a therapeutic intervention with the patient. She also depicted the rage by painting the patient and not the therapist. But she doused the wrathful patient in a deep warm crimson red, which causes her to express a warm feeling. And indeed she did have a warm countertransference to her therapist whom, during the vacation she had really missed and longed for. At the same time, for this fifth participant the patient portrayed in her crimson robe was also granted her own dignity as a person who raises herself up and decides to be true to her feelings, not only of rage and disappointment, but also of new self-worth and new self-efficacy. During that vacation, which the patient was experiencing as way too long, she struggled with her therapist, which caused a new up-rightness to express itself. This is what the fifth participant of the supervision group felt, and expressed this in the way she painted the patient so full of life.

Example out of the Supervision: The Picture of the Black Tree

Whereas in the last picture it was mainly the color nuances in the red robe which triggered the countertransference impulses and inspired the participants of the supervision group to create their own corresponding drawings, so in this painting of a tree by a 63-year-old nurse, it is the stark color contrasts, mainly between black and red. The woman sought therapy because of a serious depression that began when she retired. We briefly discussed her picture (Image 1) at the beginning of this book.

The nurse's therapist placed the picture in the middle of the supervision group. It was the patient's first, done in the beginning phase of her therapy. She painted it rather sullenly and angrily after the anamnesis session, in which the therapist had asked her, despite her being overwhelmed with frustration, what she had ever thoroughly enjoyed doing in her life. She actually replied "painting"! But she thought it would be irrelevant, now, in the midst of a depression. In fact, just the opposite is true. Every creative act that ventures to oppose the crippling feeling of a depression, brings about an experience of again being able to make something, again be a creator and not only a victim of circumstances.

Indeed the first hour, such an idea was still strange for the patient. She too painted a tree, but entirely in black with many wild, rough limbs broken off in places and the wounds gaping. Hanging at a wide distant from each other in this black branch system, and only recognizable at closer inspection, are five red dots. They could be apples. The background of the picture was left white except for a little patch of blue in the upper left. The tree seems to stand in empty space, except at the position where the trunk would come out of the earth, a little patch of green surrounds it.

The excess of black is what worked on the group members most, and in addition the bizarre branches. The five red spots were variously understood. The first participant to comment in the supervision group sensed the black as primarily an expression of grief. He had recently lost a loved one himself, and expressed in his picture that this 63-year-old patient also bore the weight of a fresh grief. He painted a black weeping willow standing directly over a grave. The five red dots become tender flowers on the grave for him, which somebody has lovingly planted. They stand in the middle of a tiny bit of green and at least a patch of blue sky is visible above. For him it was mainly deep emotional sadness that came out of the patient's black tree and filled him with his own related grief.

The second participant, in contrast, took the black, the heavy tree fork and the dark tangle of branches more as a background for the red dots. To him they appeared to glow brightly, so he made that clear and enlarged them. He experienced them as this person's remaining vitality that would once again intensify itself as she sought therapy. He also stretched that little patch of blue that had been visible only in the original picture's upper left, all the way across the paper above the entire tree until it reached into the "future corner" in his own painting. He placed the tree under a future perspective indicating that the sky is clear. He also placed the tree in a field of solid green – the contrast color to red. This reveals his countertransference, which was triggered by the red contrast points, saying to him that the black only appears to be overpowering. The so-called color quality contrast was working for him, namely that red with its radiant energy and frequency always seeks to outshine a larger amount of black.

For the third participant the three red points in his own picture were fruits. He imagined that this beat-up tree of life had still born them, and he painted them not only as red points, but also as large, round, ripe, glowing red apples. He also decked the entire ground of his painting with green grass and strewed it with even more red apples as a sign that the tree could actually produce a bountiful harvest in this life. He was approaching 60 himself, and naturally was also expressing his own feeling about life as well as the hope that his life had born fruit. His picture brings us close to a therapeutic intervention: Encourage the patient to review her life and ask what her life harvest could possibly be.

This could then be used against the current depression, which also has to do with her retirement.

The fourth participant let the blue patch of sky of the patient's picture become an entire background in her own picture, so that the black tree now stands before a strong and intensive sky. By doing this she revealed that she was touched by the patient's spiritual possibilities and brought her own religious hope to the counter-transference. It is a hope that a currently darkened tree of life tree can still be surrounded by the spiritual. The red spots became softer with her and remind one of apple blossoms. The tree became capable of blooming again, according to her picture.

The picture of the fifth participant in the end emphasized the "in spite of it all" that the patient's picture expresses primarily by contrasting red and black. Her counter-transference was conditioned by the "in spite of it all" which stands against whatever is momentarily dark in life. She insisted that there has to be an "in spite of it all" in this picture's overwhelmingly dark and black atmosphere. And she saw it depicted in the powerful five red dots. So she emphasized the red orbs and this contrast in her own picture. She experienced a strong emotion in the presence of the patient's picture in which great energy and power are hidden. This idea naturally reveals her emotion and power, which she knows how to wield in her own life, and which at the moment was also somewhat darkened. With her own picture she set the balance between black and red such that they are almost equally strong, whereby red, as already said, needs very little space in order to outshine black in radiance. Red as a color and as a radiance is energetically much stronger than black. This is how the participant perceived the attitude of vitality against depression in the patient. The participant gives the whole composition, painted almost abstractly, both a green foundation and a blue roof across the upper edge of the picture.

In the reflection round at the end, the presenting therapist gave the participants of the supervision group more information about the case. It was impressive to see how near the fifth participant had come in her own countertransference to the original emotion of the patient. This revealed itself as the therapist reported that the points really were five red apples. The nurse who painted the picture had once received them as a thank-you, after several weeks working in intensive care, from someone whom she had nursed back to health. Back then, she took it, humble as she was, as a symbolically fitting thanks for her life's work in nursing. This farewell gift of the five red apples came moreover from a particularly difficult patient whom, among all the other more resigned patients she always found likeable – precisely because of her power and her courage to resist the monotony of daily routine in the clinic.

In the ensuing discussion, and in comparing the countertransference pictures of the group of therapists with the patient's original painting, it became clear that in the countertransference of the group and their pictures, the black-red contrast had played a primary role. Red worked as a counterweight to the patient' depression, as expressed above all in the red of the apples, but also in the supportive green of the earth and the blue of the sky. These perceptions and creations in the resonance paintings of the group members gave the patient's therapist encouraging motivation to talk about the resources hidden in the wild apple tree picture and to make the patient conscious of them.

The Special Potential of Supervision in Groups

In conclusion it can be said that this method of supervision in which those supervised take note of their counter-transference to the patient in a self-drawn picture, recommends itself especially for use in a group, and proves itself especially fruitful there.

Naturally, the possibility to make myself aware of my counter-transference to a patient's picture exists for me as an individual therapist outside of a group too. But then it is only my own personal counter-transference, which naturally does not include all aspects. At first I can only perceive my personal counter-transference, which is colored by the context of my personal life history. Therefore, when I observe the patient, there is a necessary one-sidedness in my perception. But in a group of peers, all members can contribute their counter-transference, their emotions, their life history contexts and the resonances of their unconscious to their self-painted pictures. The group notices a plethora of counter-transference factors to the pictures of the patients, from the emotional coloring to structural and content considerations. The psychic condition of the patient who painted the original picture can, in the presence of the counter-transference pictures of the group, be mirrored from very many angles, indeed from sides that have so far remained hidden from the therapist. Therapeutic interventions can thereby be found and considered, which should then be applied in the therapeutic process in progress.

It is the archetype of the group that knows and shapes any group's levels of emotion and its unconscious generally. Groups build a certain unity and wholeness which enable them to more thoroughly make associations and experience emotions when perceiving a patient's picture. Out of this, the supervision group can derive a wealth of possible interventions to help the patient's development and unlock his or her inner resources.

Bibliography

English language references and citations are provided where available.

Anderten, Karin: *Traumbild Wasser*. Olten / Freiburg im Breisgau 1986.

Bach, Susan: *Life Paints Its Own Span: On the Significance of Spontaneous Paintings by Severely Ill Children*. Einsiedeln 1991.

− *Spontaneous Pictures of Leukemic Children as an Expression of the Total Personality, Mind, and Body*. Basel 1975.

− "Spontanes Malen schwerkranker Patienten: Ein Beitrag zur psychosomatischen Medizin" in *Acta Psychosomatica* 8, 1966.

− "Spontanes Malen und Zeichnen im neurochirurgischen Bereich: Ein Beitrag zur Früh- und Differentialdiagnose" in *Schweizerisches Archiv für Neurologie, Neurochirurgie und Psychiatrie* 87/I, 1961.

Bachmann, Helen I: *Malen als Lebensspur: Die Entwicklung kreativer bildlicher Darstellung–Ein Vergleich mit den frühkindlichen Loslösungs- und Individuationsprozessen*. Stuttgart 1985.

Bader, Alfred; **Navratil, Leo**: *Zwischen Wahn und Wirklichkeit*. Luzern 1976. An English review of the German language publication is available in *Art Journal*, Volume 38 issue 3 p 222.

Barnes, Mary; **Berke, Joseph**: *Two Accounts of a Journey Through Madness*. San Diego 1972.

Battegay, Raymond: *Der Mensch in der Gruppe*. Bd. I–III. Göttingen 1967ff. An English language review of the German language text is found in *The British Journal of Psychiatry*, Volume 115, Issue 527, October 1969, p. 1216.

Baumgardt, Ursula: *Kinderzeichnungen – Spiegel der Seele*. Zürich 1985.

Benedetti, Gaetano: "Psychopathologie und Kunst" in **Condrau, Gion** (Editor): *Die Psychologie des 20. Jahrhunderts*. Bd. XV. Zürich 1979.

– *Psychotherapie als existentielle Herausforderung. Göttingen* 1992. Available in French: *La Psychothérapie Des Psychoses Comme Défi Existentiel.* Translated by Patrick Faugeras. Erès,Toulouse 2002.

– "Die Symbolik des schizophrenen Patienten und das Verstehen des Therapeuten" in **Hartwig, Helmut; Menzen, Karl-Heinz** (Editors): *Kunst-Therapie.* Berlin 1984.

– *Todeslandschaften der Seele.* Göttingen 1983. Available in Italian: *Alienazione e personazione nella psicoterapia della malattia mentale.* Roma 2015.

– "Über die Kreativität der schizophren Leidenden" in *Psychologie Heute,* Heft 6. 1981.

Benedetti, Gaetano / Peciccia, Maurizio: "Die Funktion des Bildes in der gestaltenden Psychotherapie bei Psychosepatienten" in **Petzold, Hilarion; Orth, Ilse** (Editors): *Die neuen Kreativitätstherapien: Handbuch der Kunsttherapie.* Bd. I. Paderborn 1990.

Beuys, Joseph: "Kunst ist ja Therapie" in **Petzold, Hilarion; Orth, Ilse** (Editors*): Die neuen Kreativitätstherapien: Handbuch der Kunsttherapie.* Bd. I. Paderborn 1990.

Biniek, Eberhard: *Psychotherapie mit gestalterischen Mitteln.* Darmstadt 1982.

Bloch, Ernst: *The Principle of Hope.* (Volume 1 of Studies in Contemporary German Social Thought), MIT Press, Cambridge Massachusetts, revised 1959, translated 1986.

Blomeyer, Rudolf: "Kinderzeichnungen im Erstinterview in ihrer unbewußten Bezogenheit auf den Untersucher" in *Analytische Psychologie* 3, 1978.

Briendl, Linda: *Bilder als Sprache der Seele: Sich selbst entdecken durch Malen und Gestalten.* 2. Aufl. Ostfildern 2013.

– "Die Wiederbeheimatung in der Welt der Gefühle" in **Emrich, Hinderk; Riedel, Ingrid** (Editors): *Im Farbenkreis der Emotionen.* (Festschrift in honor of Verena Kast's 60th Birthday). Würzburg 2003.

Brutsche, Paul: *Die psychologische Bedeutung der Perspektive in Analysanden-Zeichnungen.* (Diploma thesis for the C.G. Jung Institute Zürich) 1975.

Clauser, Günter: "Gestaltungstherapie" in *Praxis der Psychotherapie* 5, 1960.

Czerny, Michael: *Gruppendynamik und Gestaltungstherapie* im Verständnis der analytischen Psychologie. Stuttgart 1983.

Dalley, Tessa *(Editor):* Art as Therapy: An Introduction to the Use of Art as a Therapeutic Technique. London / New York 1985.

Damasio, Antonio R: *The Feeling of What Happens: Body, Emotion and the Making of Consciousness.* Vintage, Berkshire 2000.

– *Self Comes to Mind: Constructing the Conscious Brain.* Pantheon, 2010.

Daniel, Rosmarie: *Archetypische Signaturen im unbewußten Malprozeß.* Fellbach 1993.

Dorst, Brigitte: "'Alles wirkliche Leben ist Begegnung' (M. Buber). Selbsterfahrungsgruppen als Orte der Begegnung und Individuation" in *Wege zum Menschen* 56, 2004.

– *Der Archetyp der Gruppe: Gruppen als Erfahrungsräume der Individuation.* (Diploma thesis for the C.G. Jung Institut Zürich) 1990.

D — "Der Archetyp der Gruppe: Gruppen als Erfahrungsräume der Individuation und Ko-Individuation" in *Analytische Psychologie* 181, 3/2015.

— "'Das Geheimnis des Lebens ist zwischen Zweien verborgen' (C.G. Jung). Der therapeutische Eros und die heilende Kraft der Liebe" in **Dorst, Brigitte; Neuen, Christiane; Teichert, Wolfgang** (Editors): *Liebe – die transformierende Kraft in Beziehungen und Gesellschaft.* Ostfildern 2014.

— *Therapeutisches Arbeiten mit Symbolen: Wege in die innere Bilderwelt,* 2nd Edition. Stuttgart 2015.

Dorst, Brigitte / Vogel, Ralph T. (Editors): *Aktive Imagination: Schöpferisch leben aus inneren Bildern.* Stuttgart 2014.

Edwards, Betty: *Drawing on the Right Side of the Brain: A Course in Enhancing Creativity and Artistic Confidence.* 4th edition, Souvenir Press 2013. Also: *Garantiert Zeichnen lernen: Das Geheimnis der rechten Hirnhemisphäre und die Befreiung unserer schöpferischen Gestaltungskräfte.* Reinbek bei Hamburg 1985.

Eschenbach, Ursula: "Sinn-Bilder eines Reifungsprozesses weiblicher Identität" in **Pflüger, Peter Michael** (Editor): *Die Suche nach Sinn heute.* Olten / Freiburg im Breisgau 1989.

Eschenbach, Ursula (Editor): *Das Symbol im therapeutischen Prozeß bei Kindern und Jugendlichen* (Therapeutische Konzepte der Analytischen Psychologie C.G. Jung). Stuttgart 1978. (*Psyche – Zeitschrift für Psychoanalyse,* 34(8):756-757).

Foulkes, Siegmund Heinrich: "Dynamische Prozesse in der gruppenanalytischen Situation" in **Heigl-Evers, Annelise** (Editor): *Psychoanalyse und Gruppe.* Göttingen 1971.

— *Therapeutic Group Analysis.* Routledge, London 2019.

Frankl, Victor Emil; Gebsattel, Victor E von; Schultz, Johannes Heinrich (Editors): *Handbuch der Neurosenlehre und Psychotherapie.* Vols I-IV. Munich 1959. (An English language review of the book is found in *The Journal of American Psychology,* Volume 118, issue 4, October 1961.)

Franzke, Erich: *Der Mensch und sein Gestaltungserleben.* Bern 1977.

— "Zur Indikation gestalterischer Verfahren in der Analytischen Psychotherapie" in *Zeitschrift für psychosomatische Medizin und Psychoanalyse* 18, 1972.

Furth, Gregg M: *The Secret World of Drawings: Healing through Art.* Boston 1988.

— "The Use of Drawings Made at Significant Times in One's Life" in **Kübler-Ross, Elisabeth**: *Living with Death and Dying.* New York 1997.

Gabriel, Holgrid: "Die Behandlung früher Störungen mit kunsttherapeutischen Mitteln aus der Sicht von C.G. Jung" in *Integrative Therapie* 2-3, 1987; See also: **Petzold, Hilarion / Orth, Ilse** (Editors): *Die neuen Kreativitätstherapien: Handbuch der Kunsttherapie.* Vol. 1. Paderborn 1990.

Giera-Krapp, Margitta: *Ein Beitrag zur Therapie der frühen Störungen.* (Diploma thesis for the C.G. Jung Institute Zürich) 1985.

Goethe, Johann Wolfgang von: *Goethe's Theory of Colours*, translated by Charles Lock Eastlake. Cambridge, Massachusetts 1970.

Gruber, Harald / Reichelt, Stefan (Editors): *Kunsttherapie in der Palliativmedizin*. Berlin 2016.

Haerlin, Peter: *Wie von selbst: Vom Leistungszwang zur Mühelosigkeit*. Weinheim, Berlin 1986.

Hampe, Ruth: "Ikonische Symbolisierungsprozesse im kunsttherapeutischen Bereich" in Petzold, Hilarion / Orth, Ilse (Editors): *Die neuen Kreativitätstherapien: Handbuch der Kunsttherapie* Vol. 1. Paderborn 1990.

Hartwig, Helmut; Menzen, Karl-Heinz (Editors): *Kunst-Therapie*. Berlin 1984.

Heigl-Evers, Annelise (Editor): *Psychoanalyse und Gruppe*. Göttingen 1971.

Henzler, Christa: "Aktive Imagination und Malen" in Dorst, Brigitte / Vogel, Ralph T. (Editors): *Aktive Imagination: Schöpferisch leben aus inneren Bildern*. Stuttgart 2014.

- *Aspekte der Mal-Therapie unter besonderer Berücksichtigung des tiefenpsychologischen Interpretationsansatzes*. (Diploma thesis for the Department of Social Sciences Universität-Gesamthochschule). Kassel 1985.

- "Malen gegen den Tod: Die Funktion des Malens bei der Durchschreitung von Trauerphasen" in Emrich, Hinderk; Riedel, Ingrid (Editors): *Im Farbenkreis der Emotionen*. (Festschrift in honor of Verena Kast's 60th Birthday). Würzburg 2003.

Henzler, Christa; Riedel, Ingrid: *Malen um zu überleben: Ein kreativer Weg durch die Trauer*. Stuttgart 2003.

Herrera, Hayden: *Frida: A Biography of Frida Kahlo*. New York 1983.

Heyer, Gustav Richard: "Künstlerische Verfahren" in Frankl, Victor Emil; Gebsattel, Victor E von; Schultz, Johannes Heinrich (Editors): *Handbuch der Neurosenlehre und Psychotherapie*. Vols I-IV. Munich 1959.

Hillman, James: *The Dream and the Underworld*. New York 1989.

- *Suicide and the Soul*. 2nd edition. Spring Publications Inc, Woodstock Connecticut 1997.

Hofstätter, Peter R: *Gruppendynamik*. Hamburg 1957.

Itten, Johannes: *Kunst der Farbe*. Ravensburg 1962.

Jacobi, Jolande: *Vom Bilderreich der Seele: Wege und Umwege zu sich selbst*. Olten/Freiburg im Breisgau 1969. Also available as Italian translation: *Dal regno delle immagini dell'anima percorsi diretti e vie traverse per giungere a se stessi*. Translated by Murrau, Marina Pia;, Editioni Magi. Roma 2003.

Jaffé, Aniela: *Memories, Dreams, Reflections by C.G. Jung*, Pantheon, New York, 1962.

- "Symbolism in the Visual Arts", in Jung, Carl Gustav; Henderson, Joseph L; von Franz, Marie-Louise, Jaffé, Aniela, Jacobi, Jolande: *Man and His Symbols*. London 1990.

Jung, Carl Gustav; *C.G. Jung Letters, 1906-1950*. Edited by Aniela Jaffé and Gerhard Adler. Princeton University Press, 1972.

Jung, Carl Gustav: *The Collected Works of C.G. Jung (CW)*, translated by R.F.C. Hull, Princeton: Bollingen series XX, 2nd Edition:

– General Aspects of the Dream Psychology, in *The Structure and Dynamics of the Psyche*, CW 8. § 443–529.

– The Spirit of Mercury, *in Alchemical Studies*, CW 13. § 239–303.

– *Mysterium Coniunctioni*, CW 14. sections I–III.

– *Psychology and Alchemy*, CW 12. See also: Rascher edition (German): 2nd, revised edition [Psychological treatises, vol. 5]. Zürich 1952.

– *Psychological Types*, CW 6, § 915–987.

– Psychotherapy Today, in *The Practice of Psychotherapy*, CW 16, § 212–229.

– The Transcendent Function, in *Symbols of Transformation*, CW 5, §§ 131–193.

– On the Relation of Analytical Psychology to Poetry, in: *Spirit in Man, Art and Literature*, CW 15, § 97–132.

– Concerning Mandala Symbolism, in *The Archetypes and the Collective Unconscious*, *CW 9.1*, § 627–712.

– The Aims of Psychotherapy, in *The Practice of Psychotherapy*, *CW 16*, § 66–113.

– A Study in the Process of Individuation, in *The Archetypes and the Collective Unconscious*, *CW 9.1* § 525–626.

– On the Psychology of the Trickster Figure, in *The Archetypes and the Collective Unconscious*, *CW 9.1* § 456 – 488.

– "Nietzsche's Zarathustra" (Notes from the seminar given in 1934-1939), 2nd volume edited by J. L. Jarrett. Princeton, NJ 1989.

– *The Red Book: Liber Novus*. Edited and introduced by **Sonu Shamdasani**. Preface by **Ulrich Hoerni**. Translated by Mark Kyburz, John Peck, Sonu Shamdasani. W.W. Norton & Company, Philemon Series, 1st Edition 2009.

– *The Black Books 1913-1932*: Notebooks of Transformation. Edited by **Sonu Shamdasani**. Translated by Martin Liebscher, John Peck, Sonu Shamdasani. W.W. Norton & Company, Philemon Series, New York & London 2020.

– *Modern Man in Search of a Soul*. Martino Fine Books, Eastford 2017 (reprint of 1933 US edition).

Jung, Carl Gustav; **Wilhelm, Richard**: *The Secret of the Golden Flower: A Chinese Book of Life*. Translated by Richard Wilhem and commentary by Carl Gustav Jung. London 1984.

Jung, Carl Gustav; **Henderson, Joseph L**; **von Franz, Marie-Louise**, **Jaffé, Aniela**, **Jacobi, Jolande**: *Man and His Symbols*. London 1990.

Kast, Verena: "Die Bedeutung der Symbole im therapeutischen Prozeß" in **Barz, Helmut / Kast, Verena / Nager, Frank**: *Heilung und Wandlung: C.G. Jung und die Medizin*. Zürich/München 1986.

– *The Dynamics of Symbols: Fundamentals of Jungian Psychotherapy.* Translated by Susan A. Schwarz. Fromm International Publishing Corporation, New York 1992.

– *Imagination as Space of Freedom: Dialogue between the Ego and the Unconscious.* Fromm International Publishing Corporation, New York 1993.

– *Kreativität in der Psychologie von C.G. Jung.* (Dissertation at the University of Zürich), 1974.

– *Folktales as Therapy.* Fromm International Publishing Corporation, New York 1995.

– *Nature of Loving: Patterns of Human Relationship.* Translated by Boris Matthews. Asheville2013.

– *Die Tiefenpsychologie nach C.G. Jung.* 2. Aufl., Ostfildern 2015.

– *Träume: Die geheimnisvolle Sprache des Unbewussten.* 7th Edition, Ostfildern 2015. Also available in Italian edition: *Sogni: la lingua misteriosa dell'inconscio.* Red Edizioni, Milan 2014.

– *A Time to Mourn: Growing through the Grief Process.* Daimon Verlag, Einsiedeln 1988.

– "Umschlagspunkte in der Analyse" in *Zeitschrift für Analytische Psychologie* 20/3, 1989.

Klee, Paul: *The Thinking Eye (The Notebooks of Paul Klee, 1961).* San Francisco 2013.

Klein, Melanie: "Early Anxiety-Situations and their Effect on the Development of the Child in The Psycho-Analysis of Children" (1932) in *The Writings of Melanie Klein,* Volume 2. Hogarth Press, 1975.

Kraft, Hartmund *(Editor)*: *Psychoanalyse, Kunst und Kreativität heute.* Köln 1984.

Kramer, Edith: "Art and Craft" in **Ulman, Elinor; Dochinger, Penny** (Editors): *Art Therapy and Practice.* New York 1975.

Kramer, Edith: *Art as Therapy with Children.* Chicago 1993.

Krapp, Manfred: *Die Gestaltungstherapie als Beitrag zur Psychotherapie der Psychosen.* (Diploma thesis for the C.G. Jung Institute Zürich) 1986. **Kutter, Peter** (Editor): *Methoden und Theorien der Gruppenpsychotherapie.* Stuttgart 1985.

Landau, Erika: *Kreatives Erleben.* München 1984. Also in Spanish: *El Vivir creativo : teoría y práctica de la creatividad.* Barcelona 2002.

– *Psychologie der Kreativität.* München 1969.

Leuner, Hanscarl: *Lehrbuch des Katathymen Bilderlebens.* Bern 1985.

Levick, Myra: "Art in Psychotherapy" in **Masserman, Jules** (Editor*)*: *Current Psychiatric Therapies.* New York 1975.

Mahler, Margaret S: "Symbiose und Individuation" in *Psyche* 29, 1975.

Meares, Ainslee*: The Door of Serenity: A Study in the Therapeutic Use of Symbolic Painting.* London 1958.

Menzen, Karl-Heinz: "Tendenzen der Kunsttherapie" in *Fragmente* 20/21, 1986. (Series of publications on psychoanalysis from Kassel University of Applied Sciences).

Menzen, Karl-Heinz; Hartwig, Helmut (Editors): *Kunst-Therapie*. Berlin 1984.

Miller, Alice: *Bilder einer Kindheit*. Frankfurt am Main 1985.

Milner, Marion: *The Hands of the Living God*. New York 1969.

— *On not Being able to Paint*. Routledge 2010.

— *Zeichnen und Malen ohne Scheu*. Köln 1988.

Naumburg, Margaret: *Dynamically Oriented Art Therapy*. New York 1966.

— *Schizophrenic Art: Its Meaning in Psychotherapy*. New York 1950.

Navratil, Leo: "Individuelle Kunst-Psychotherapie" in *Der Nervenarzt*, 1979 Nov; 50(11): 709-14.

Neumann, Erich: *The Great Mother: An Analysis of the Archetype* (1955). Princeton Classics edition, 2015.

— *Art and the Creative Unconscious: Four Essays*. Routledge, Abingdon 1959.

— *History and Origins of Consciousness* (1954). Princeton Classics edition, 2014.

— *Zur Psychologie des Weiblichen*. München 1975.

Oesterreicher-Mollwo, Marianne: *Herder-Lexikon Symbole*. Freiburg im Breisgau 1993. Also available in French edition: *Petit Dictionnaire des Symboles*. 1992.

Petersen, Peter (Editor): *Ansätze kunsttherapeutischer Forschung*. Berlin/Heidelberg 1990.

Petzold, Hilarion / Orth, Ilse (Editors): *Die neuen Kreativitätstherapien: Handbuch der Kunsttherapie*. Vol. 1. Paderborn 1990.

Pohlen, Manfred: "Psychoanalytische Behandlungsformen in Gruppen" in *Gruppenpsychotherapie und Gruppendynamik* 20, 1984.

Preuss, Hans G: *Analytische Gruppenpsychotherapie*. Reinbek bei Hamburg 1972.

Prinzhorn, Hans: *Bildnerei der Geisteskranken*. Berlin 1983.

Pütz, Rosa Maria: *Kunsttherapie – eine Alternative zur Regeneration des Menschen, Vol 1: Die Maltherapie*. Bielefeld 1981.

Refsnes-Kniazzeh, Carolyn: "Art Therapy" *in* **Arieti, Silvano** (Editor): *American Handbook of Psychiatry*. New York 1981.

Reichelt, Stefan: *Kindertherapie nach sexueller Mißhandlung: Malen als Heilmethode*. Stuttgart 1994.

— *Prozessorientiertes Malen als traumatherapeutische Intervention*. Regensburg 2008.

Reiter, Alfons: *Bildnerischer Ausdruck als methodischer, diagnostischer und therapeutischer Zugang zur Depression* (Habilitation treatise for the University of Salzburg) 1985.

Riedel, Ingrid: *Bilder in Religion, Kunst, und Psychotherapie: Wege zur Interpretation*. Stuttgart 1989. (Reworked and newly formatted under the title *Bilder in Psychotherapie, Kunst und Religion: Ein Schlüssel zur Interpretation*. Stuttgart 2005).

— *Demeters Suche: Mütter und Töchter*. Zürich 1986.

– *Farben in Religion, Gesellschaft, Kunst und Psychotherapie.* Stuttgart 1983 (Eighteenth printing completely reworked, expanded, and reformatted in 2008).

– *Formen: Kreis, Kreuz, Dreieck, Quadrat, Spirale.* Stuttgart 1985 (Fifth printing completely reworked, expanded and reformatted under the title *Formen: Tiefenpsychologische Deutung von Kreis, Kreuz, Dreieck, Quadrat, Spirale und Mandala.* Stuttgart 2006).

– *Marc Chagalls Grüner Christus: Ein ganzheitliches Gottesbild – Wiederentdeckung der weiblichen Aspekte Gottes.* (a depth-psychological interpretation of the Fraumünster windows in Zürich). 4th Edition, Olten / Freiburg im Breisgau 1991.

– *Die weise Frau: Der Archetyp der alten Weisen in Märchen, Traum und Religionsgeschichte.* Ergänzte Neuausgabe. Ostfildern 2016. (1st edition under the title: *Die weise Frau in uralt-neuen Erfahrungen: Der Archetyp der alten Weisen im Märchen und seinem religionsgeschichtlichen Hintergrund.* Olten 1989).

Riedel, Ingrid; Henzler, Christa: *Malen in der Gruppe: Modelle für die therapeutische Arbeit mit Symbolen.* Stuttgart 2008.

Riemann, Fritz: *Grundformen der Angst.* 41st printing, Munich, 2013.

Rosenberg, Alfons: *Einführung in das Symbolverständnis: Ursymbole und ihre Wandlungen.* Freiburg in Breisgau 1984.

Rubin, Judith Aron (Editor): *Approaches to Art Therapy: Theory and Technique.* New York 1987.

Sachs, Nelly: *Fahrt ins Staublose: Die Gedichte der Nelly Sachs.* Frankfurt am Main 1961, p. 308. The translated poem *is "Journey into a Dustless Realm".*

Schottenloher, Gertraud: *Kunst- und Gestaltungstherapie: Eine praktische Einführung.* München 1983. **Schottenloher, Gertraud**: *Das therapeutische Potential spontanen bilderischen Gestaltens unter besonderer Berücksichtigung körpertherapeutischer Methoden.* (Dissertation for the University of Zürich) 1989.

– "Das Unbewußte des Therapeuten als Mitgestalter der kunsttherapeutischen Beziehung" in **Petersen, Peter** (Editor): *Ansätze kunsttherapeutischer Forschung.* Berlin/ Heidelberg 1990.

Schottenloher, Gertraud; Tomalin, Elisabeth: "Der psychodynamische Aspekt gestaltungstherapeutischer Gruppenarbeit" in **Petzold, Hilarion / Orth, Ilse** (Editors): *Die neuen Kreativitätstherapien: Handbuch der Kunsttherapie.* Vol. 1. Paderborn 1990.

Schrode, Helena: "Die Gestaltungstherapie als Therapie mit bildnerischen Mitteln auf tiefenpsychologischer Grundlage" in *Praxis der Psychotherapie und Psychosomatik* 28, 1983.

– "Die Gestaltungstherapie-Gruppe als Ergänzung der stationären analytischen Langzeiteinzeltherapie" in *Gruppenpsychotherapie und Gruppendynamik* 17, 1981.

Schulz-Klein, Helmut: "Symbolisierung von Übertragungs- und Gegenübertragungsprozessen: Ausschnitte aus einer analytischen Psychotherapie eines Mädchens in der Frühadoleszenz" in **Eschenbach, Ursula** (Editor): *Das Symbol im therapeutischen Prozeß bei Kindern und Jugendlichen (Therapeutische Konzepte der Analytischen Psychologie C.G. Jung).* Stuttgart 1978.

Seifert, Theodor: "Die Gruppentherapie im Rahmen der Analytischen Psychologie" in *Zeitschrift für Analytische Psychologie* 5.1, 1974; see also: **Kutter, Peter** (Editor): *Methoden und Theorien der Gruppenpsychotherapie.* Stuttgart 1985.

– *Weltentstehung – die Kraft von tausend Feuern.* Zürich 1986.

Smerling, Walter von; Weiss, Evelyn (Editors): *Der andere Blick: Heilungswirkungen der Kunst heute.* Köln 1986.

Stahel, Nelly: *Das Erkennen seelischer Störungen aus der Zeichnung.* Zürich 1977.

Stern, Arno: *L'Expression.* Neuchâtel 1973.

Strubel, Robert: "Selbstwerdung und Gruppen-Selbst" in *Zeitschrift für Analytische Psychologie* 12.2, 1981.

Tschudi, L: *Regression, Depression und Suizidalität im bildnerischen Ausdruck eines Schizophrenen.* (Diploma thesis for C.G. Jung InstituteZürich) 1982.

Tüpker, Rosemarie: "Wissenschaftlichkeit in kunsttherapeutischer Forschung" in *Musiktherapeutische Umschau* 11, 1990.

Ulman, Elinor; Dochinger, Penny (Editors): *Art Therapy and Practice.* New York 1975.

Wadeson, Harriet: *Art Psychotherapy.* New York 1980.

Wellendorf, Elisabeth: "Ästhetische Produktivität und Therapie" in **Hartwig, Helmut; Menzen, Karl-Heinz** (Editors): *Kunst-Therapie.* Berlin 1984.

Wellendorf Elisabeth: "Individuation und individuelle Gestaltung" in **Petersen, Peter** (Editor): *Ansätze kunsttherapeutischer Forschung.* Berlin/Heidelberg 1990.

– "Die inneren Bilder des Therapeuten und ihre Bedeutung für die Therapie – Synchrones Geschehen in der Psychotherapie" in **Petersen, Peter** (Editor): *Ansätze kunsttherapeutischer Forschung.* Berlin/Heidelberg 1990.

Winnicott, Donald Woods: "Das Konzept der Kreativität" in **Petzold, Hilarion / Orth, Ilse** (Editors): *Die neuen Kreativitätstherapien: Handbuch der Kunsttherapie* Vol. 1. Paderborn 1990.

– *Therapeutic Consultations in Child Psychiatry.* London 1971.

– *Playing and Reality.* London 1971.

Wöller, Hildegunder: "Die Weisheit und ihre Verwirklichung durch die Frau" in **Pflüger, Peter Michael** (Editor): *Wendepunkte Frau-Erde-Gott.* Olten/Freiburg im Breisgau 1988.

Eva Wertenschlag-Birkhäuser

Windows on Eternity

The Paintings of Peter Birkhäuser

With an Essay by Marie-Louise von Franz

200 pages, with 53 color plates

ISBN 978-3-85630-715-8

Many of the dream images painted by Swiss artist Peter Birkhäuser (1911-76) portray the big problems of our time, as experienced one individual: our divisiveness, possession by unconscious factors, suffering from the loss of religious values, the "unknown God" knocking at the door and wanting to enter, our inability to understand evil, the world of the feminine yearning for redemption, and so on.

Because the paintings of Birkhäuser come from the deep wells of dreams and give them authentic form, they are mirrors of healing processes in the soul. Marie-Louise von Franz said of Birkhäuser's work: "His paintings are not depictions of his own problems, but rather seek to reveal what is taking place in the depths of the collective unconscious in all of the people of our time. Because of this, they are not easy to decipher: they are simply there, and wish to be experienced".

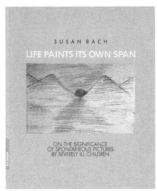

Susan Bach

Life paints its own Span

Part I (Text): 208 pages, Part II (Pictures): 56 pages, with over 200 color illustrations, ISBN 978-3-85630-516-1

The pioneering work, *Life Paints Its Own Span*, with over 200 color reproductions, is a comprehensive exposition of Susan Bach's original approach to the physical and psychospiritual evaluation of spontaneous paintings and drawings by severely ill patients. At the same time, this work is a moving record of Susan Bach's own journey of discovery.

English Titles from Daimon

Ruth Ammann - *The Enchantment of Gardens*
Susan R. Bach - *Life Paints its Own Span*
Diana Baynes Jansen - *Jung's Apprentice: A Biography of Helton Godwin Baynes*
John Beebe (Ed.) - *Terror, Violence and the Impulse to Destroy*
E.A. Bennet - *Meetings with Jung*
W.H. Bleek / L.C. Lloyd (Ed.) - *Specimens of Bushman Folklore*
Tess Castleman - *Threads, Knots, Tapestries*
- *Sacred Dream Circles*
Renate Daniel - *Taking the Fear out of the Night*
- *The Self: Quest for Meaning in a Changing World*
- *Psyche and Soma*
Eranos Yearbook 69 - *Eranos Reborn*
Eranos Yearbook 70 - *Love on a Fragile Thread*
Eranos Yearbook 71 - *Beyond Masters*
Eranos Yearbook 72 - *Soul between Enchantment and Disenchantment*
Eranos Yearbook 73 - *The World and its Shadow*
Eranos Yearbook 74 - *The Age of Immediacy at the Test of Meaning*
Michael Escamilla - *Bleuler, Jung, and the Schizophrenias*
Heinrich Karl Fierz - *Jungian Psychiatry*
John Fraim - *Battle of Symbols*
Liliane Frey-Rohn - *Friedrich Nietzsche, A Psychological Approach*
Marion Gallbach - *Learning from Dreams*
Ralph Goldstein (Ed.) - *Images, Meanings & Connections: Essays in Memory of Susan Bach*
Yael Haft - *Hands: Archetypal Chirology*
Fred Gustafson - *The Black Madonna of Einsiedeln*
Daniel Hell - *Soul-Hunger: The Feeling Human Being and the Life-Sciences*
Siegmund Hurwitz - *Lilith, the first Eve*
Aniela Jaffé - *The Myth of Meaning*
- *Was C.G. Jung a Mystic?*
- *From the Life and Work of C.G. Jung*
- *Death Dreams and Ghosts*
C.G. Jung - *The Solar Myths and Opicinus de Canistris*
Verena Kast - *A Time to Mourn*
- *Sisyphus*
Hayao Kawai - *Dreams, Myths and Fairy Tales in Japan*
James Kirsch - *The Reluctant Prophet*
Eva Langley-Dános - *Prison on Wheels: Ravensbrück to Burgau*
Rivkah Schärf Kluger - *The Gilgamesh Epic*
Yehezkel Kluger & - *RUTH in the Light of Mythology, Legend*
Nomi Kluger-Nash   *and Kabbalah*
Paul Kugler (Ed.) - *Jungian Perspectives on Clinical Supervision*
Paul Kugler - *The Alchemy of Discourse*
Rafael López-Pedraza - *Cultural Anxiety*
- *Hermes and his Children*
Alan McGlashan - *The Savage and Beautiful Country*
- *Gravity & Levity*
Gregory McNamee (Ed.) - *The Girl Who Made Stars: Bushman Folklore*
- *The North Wind and the Sun & Other Fables of Aesop*
Gitta Mallasz / Hanna Dallos - *Talking with Angels*
C.A. Meier - *Healing Dream and Ritual*
- *A Testament to the Wilderness*
- *Personality: The Individuation Process*
Haruki Murakami - *Haruki Murakami Goes to Meet Hayao Kawai*
Eva Pattis Zoja (Ed.) - *Sandplay Therapy*
Laurens van der Post - *The Rock Rabbit and the Rainbow*

English Titles from Daimon

Our books are available from your bookstore or from our distributors:

Baker & Taylor
30 Amberwood Parkway
Ashland OH 44805, USA
Phone: 419-281-5100
Fax: 419-281-0200
www.btpubservices.com

Gazelle Book Services Ltd.
White Cross Mills, High Town
Lancaster LA1 4XS, UK
Tel: +44 1524 528500
Email: sales@gazellebookservices.co.uk
www.gazellebookservices.co.uk

Daimon Verlag - Hauptstrasse 85 - CH-8840 Einsiedeln - Switzerland
Phone: (41)(55) 412 2266 Email: info@daimon.ch
For detailed book descriptions visit our website: **www.daimon.ch**

Printed in Great Britain
by Amazon

86860005R00210